IN THE DESERT

OLD ALGIERS.

IN THE DESERT

THE HINTERLAND OF ALGIERS

BY

L. MARCH PHILLIPPS
AUTHOR OF "WITH RIMINGTON"

WITH ILLUSTRATIONS

DARF PUBLISHERS LIMITED
LONDON
1985

First published 1909
New impression 1985

ISBN 978 1 85077 072 5

TO

MY FRIEND

HUGH HOARE

IN MEMORY OF OUR

DESERT TRAVELS

IN 1899

Preface to the First Edition

THE form this book has taken needs perhaps a word of explanation. Descriptions of Arab art and poetry may seem out of place among travelling notes; but it has always seemed to me that the Arab is so much a child of the desert, and all he has ever done is so impregnated with the character of his own curious and peculiar birthplace, that to understand him in any particular it is always necessary to realise the desert first. Whether you consider Arab architecture, or Arab religion, or Arab poetry, or Arab philosophy, it seems that a description of the desert forms the indispensable preface to them all. Accordingly I think that, if I can succeed in giving the reader a true impression of desert scenery, he will not object to tracing the effects of that scenery in desert poetry and art. In short, I have hoped that the reader's interest would follow my own. It was the desert that aroused my own curiosity in Arab life and art, and seemed the clue to so much of Arab history, and perhaps this, to some extent, may be the case with other people.

Some of the matter in this book has appeared

viii PREFACE TO THE FIRST EDITION

already in two articles in the *Edinburgh Review* and in a few shorter ones in the *Speaker*. I thank the editors of those publications for their kindness in allowing me to use this material again; and Mr. John Murray for permission to reproduce four plans from Fergusson's "History of Architecture."

NOTE TO NEW EDITION

IN the present edition I have made some slight alterations and corrections, and have added a few final pages which might give, I thought, a summary of the Arab influence, as far as I understood it. From some kind expressions which have reached me from travellers, I am not without hope that the book, in its present form, may prove useful to visitors to Algeria.

Contents

CHAPTER I

ARAB INSTABILITY 1

Old and new Algiers—The gap betwixt past and present—The Arab town a reflection of Arab character—Incoherence of Arab history—Incidents of the death of Okba—His energy and lack of system—Similar traits in Arab civilisation—Fancifulness in all the Arab did—His show and splendour—Lack of a solid foundation—His history and romance—His personal heroism—Algiers the Arab's chance—What he made of it—Piracy, its extent—Fall of the town—Justification of French interference.

CHAPTER II

FRENCH DISCIPLINE 19

The *cafés* of Algiers—Cosmopolitan character of the people—Moor and Arab—Arab dependence on the desert—His virtues desert virtues—The Jew in Algeria—His place in society—His political importance—French sociability—Its influence in colonisation—France's peaceable intentions—Pacific penetration—The slowness of French colonisation—Striking likeness between Algeria and Cape Colony—French and English methods—The French excel in collective work, the English in individual initiative—French instinct for organisation—The Latin race in Africa—Part played by the Government—French progress.

CONTENTS

CHAPTER III

THE FRENCH OCCUPATION 45

    African scenery, its clearness and regularity—Divisions of Algeria—Line of the French advance—A distracted colonial policy—The anti-colonial party—Indifference of the French people—France makes up her mind—Interest awakened in colonisation—Increase of immigration—Character of Arab warfare—The North African problem—Impossibility of dividing state from state—The pacification of any part of the country involves the pacification of the whole—France forced to advance—The Arab the leading African race—Gives its own character to the politics of the country.

CHAPTER IV

THE FRENCH IN THE SAHARA 59

    Early exploration of the desert—The French make a beginning—Unlucky ending to many of their expeditions—De Brazza and the Congo—Advance from the south and west—The idea of a united Colonial Empire—The convention of 1890—Monteil's expedition—Fernand Foureau—The Touareg tribes oppose the French advance—Occupation of the desert—Consistency of the French scheme—French rights in North Africa.

CHAPTER V

BISKRA 72

    A desert port—The Atlas mountains—"The door of the desert"—El Kantara—Importance of Biskra—French officers—Part played by the army—The oasis—Irrigation—Arab isolation—His individual charm—His sentimentality—Arab manners—His chivalrous impulses—Arab horse-dealers—We fit out our caravan—What to take and what to leave behind—We leave Biskra.

CONTENTS

CHAPTER VI

IN THE DESERT 94

Some first impressions—Absence of detail—Sense of space—Its natural features—The feeling of isolation—Invigorating effect of great light—Bedouin gipsies—The attraction of the desert—Influence of primitive scenery—Escape from custom and routine—Burton on the desert—The senses sharpened and stimulated—Power of noticing things.

CHAPTER VII

THE ARAB AND THE DESERT 104

Excitement of the desert—Its stimulus of the nerves, not of the mind—Corresponding excitability in Arab temperament and character—Their campaigns—Non-intellectual nature of desert scenery—Its deadness—Effects on the Arab—Lack of coherence in Arab character—Destructiveness of the desert—Its object to blot out all life and all form—Similar aim of all Arab activity—His history a history of destruction.

CHAPTER VIII

WHERE THE "ARGO" SAILED 115

Ahmeda's horse and horsemanship—The Shott Melrir—The old river system—The drying-up of the desert—Arab metaphors—The tradition of the sea—Greek corroboration—Yarns of the Argonauts—Modern science contemptuous—Evidence of the inland sea—Arab and Greek tradition confirmed.

CHAPTER IX

WELL-SINKING IN THE DESERT 127

The underground water supply—Importance of the artesian process—Arab legends about water—Their notions of well-boring

—Their fight with the desert—Invasion of their oases—" Dying " of their wells—Arab engineers—Their failure—The French intervene—Their success—Gratitude of the Arabs—Renovation of oases—Apparent happiness and content—The rising of 1870—Re-establishment of order—What the French have done in the Oued Rir.

CHAPTER X

TUGGURT 151

Arab love of display—Entering the town—A visit to the Marabout—Arab silence—An Arab *café*—Oriental colour—Colour emotional and belonging to the East—Form intellectual and belonging to the West—Incompatibility of the two ideals—Oriental colour an expression of Oriental life and character—St. Mark's the great artistic example—Its colour-effect obtained by banishing structural forms.

CHAPTER XI

THE OUED SOUF AND ITS OASES . . . 162

The region of dunes—Aspect of the scenery—Difficulty of judging size and distance—The several kinds of oases—The hope of well-sinking—The "cup" oases—Our stay in an Arab village—The Souf dates—The census of palm-trees—The date harvest—The cares of desert husbandry—The source of desert life—The attack of the sand.

CHAPTER XII

A HAVEN OF REFUGE 175

The desert in a rage—A rough ride—Arrival at Nefta—Fertility of the oasis—Composure of camels—Death of one of our camels—Their adaptability to the desert—Their beauty amidst this scenery—Our camp in the oasis—A night scene—Sensuousness of Oriental scenery—A scrap of poetry.

CONTENTS

CHAPTER XIII

SCENES BY THE WAY 184

The evening camp—Birds—A moonlight start—Cold nights—Instincts wakened by desert scenery—Sunrise—The sound of it—A desert landscape—Arab poetry—Its insistence on shade and water—Arab society—The spring grazings—Their poetic treatment—A scene in Devonshire—Tendency of the imagination to recall such scenes in the desert—The mirage—The desert's sense of humour.

CHAPTER XIV

ARAB POETRY 200

Its portraiture of Arab life and character—Its genuineness and vigour—The type it describes—The death of Rabíáh—The traits it dwells on—Limitations of the type—Arab love-poetry—Its contrast with modern—Lack of depth in the Arab—The type common among Moslems—The Afghan—The Turk—The Albanian—The Moslem stage in civilisation.

CHAPTER XV

MOHAMMEDANISM 220

The desert religion an incentive and a bond—The Arab as propagandist—The sects of Islam—Conservatism of the orthodox faith—The Shíites—Their efforts to infuse emotional depths and warmth into the religion—Fruitlessness of the attempt—What backs up the orthodox party—The influence of the desert—The standard of life it maintains—Mecca the Mohammedan Rome.

CHAPTER XVI

KAIRWÁN 233

Approach to the town—An ideal bathe—Arab roads—Aspect of Kairwán—Loneliness and desolation of its surroundings—The beginnings of the city—Choice of a site—Early miracles—Warlike character of the town—Its luxury and culture—Fanaticism of the town—Early visits and reports—Violation of the sanctuary—French occupation—A broken spell.

CHAPTER XVII

ARAB ARCHITECTURE 245

The romance of the Arabs—Quality of their architecture—The early mosques—Difference between Moorish and Arab architecture—The Great Mosque—Fine effect of the whole—Slovenliness of detail—Indistinct arches—Arab and Gothic architecture compared—The Arab lack of purpose—Quality of his masonry—Decorative design—Corresponding mannerisms in life—Arab crowds and streets compared to English—Fickleness of the desert.

CHAPTER XVIII

THE MOSLEM SPHERE OF INFLUENCE . . . 270

Arab society, its nebulous and incoherent character—Arab thought, its lack of depth and solidity—Immobility of Arab civilisation—The same true of all Moslem races—The orthodox faith responsible for this—Parallel between Islam and Christianity—Influence of Christianity on Western thought and society—Moslem liberalism anxious to attain the same results—It adopts principles similar to the Christian—The Wahhabi reaction—The Babis—Prospects of Moslem liberalism—Real strength of Islam in the orthodox party—The life of the desert the source of its strength.

APPENDIX 289

List of Illustrations

OLD ALGIERS	*Frontispiece*	
EL KANTARA	*Facing p.*	76
THE LAST TUFT OF PALMS	,,	98
A BEDOUIN CAMP	,,	100
A DEAD LANDSCAPE	,,	110
SKETCH MAP SHOWING THE FLOW OF THE GREAT NORTH SAHARAN RIVERS TOWARDS THE SHOTTS	*Page*	119
THE IMMEMORIAL SHADOOF	*Facing p.*	138
A RIVER OASIS	,,	166
IN AN ARAB VILLAGE	,,	170
CAMP IN AN OASIS	,,	178
THE ATTRACTION OF MECCA	,,	228
PLAN OF GREAT MOSQUE OF KAIRWÁN	*Page*	249

LIST OF ILLUSTRATIONS

CORNER OF THE GREAT MOSQUE . .	*Facing p.* 250
PLAN OF MOSQUE OF AMRU . . .	*Page* 252
THE INDEFINITE ARAB ARCH . .	*Facing p.* 252
PLAN OF MOSQUE OF SULTAN BARKOOK .	*Page* 255
PLAN OF MOSQUE OF SULTAN HASSAN . .	,, 257
GOTHIC SURENESS OF PURPOSE . .	*Facing p.* 258
ARAB LACK OF PURPOSE . . .	,, 262
STREET ARCHITECTURE IN KAIRWÁN . .	,, 266
ARAB DECORATIVE DESIGN .	,, 268

IN THE DESERT

CHAPTER I

ARAB INSTABILITY

Old and new Algiers—The gap betwixt past and present—The Arab town a reflection of Arab character—Incoherence of Arab history—Incidents of the death of Okba—His energy and lack of system—Similar traits in Arab civilisation—Fancifulness in all the Arab did—His show and splendour—Lack of a solid foundation—His history and romance—His personal heroism—Algiers the Arab's chance—What he made of it—Piracy, its extent—Fall of the town—Justification of French interference.

TWO hills look at each other by the bay of Algiers. One is crusted over with white and yellow houses, sunbleached, roofless, and so close packed, and probed by passages and tunnels so narrow and intricate, that they look like a piece of honeycomb, or bit of old ivory carved into illegible design by the ingenuity of some Indian artist. Figures in white gowns pass in and out of the mouths of passages, or flit like white moths across the open space by the sea. The white domes of a mosque swell up at its base; the walls of an antique fortress crumble at its summit.

The other is laid out in beautiful gardens, with rose-covered villas at frequent intervals, a comfortable club, and many luxurious hotels. Paths run under shady avenues, and groves of pines and blossoming shrubs vary the view and scent the air. Smart carriages and electric trams roll up and down the smooth roads, and men and women in summer clothes, with straw hats on and parasols up, saunter under the trees or pause to admire the view over the sea far below.

Of these two hills, the first is the old Arab town, the second the modern French suburb. Here among the villas and hotels presides modern civilisation with all its comforts and conveniences. Yonder in the Arab city still survives the semi-barbaric orientalism of the Moorish dominions.

How many centuries would you guess must separate the two hills? Certainly not less than five or six. Now let your eyes drop to the space between, and you will see what really separates them. This space is occupied by the quays and shipping, the shops and streets and warehouses of the French port. The steamers hoot and whistle, the drays thunder, the great cranes swing their bales out and in, the hum of industry and commerce fills the air. The whole scene throbs and echoes to the pulse of modern progress, and across it, with a fixed and curious attention, the two hills, Arab and French, stare at each other as across a gulf there is no spanning.

This, not five centuries, is what divides them. Indeed, it is a curiosity of Algiers that its barbaric past, which already seems so remote, treads so closely on the heels of the civilised present. All this structure of European luxury and prosperity has been built up within living memory. Old men must creep about

ARAB INSTABILITY

these alleys still whose cradle-slumbers were disturbed by the guns that ended the adventures of Old Algiers.

Taking one morning the tram that runs down the French hill, the hill of Mustapha Supérieur, as it is called, to the town below, I found myself sitting next to an aged Moor, with beady black eyes and parchment skin, the countless wrinkles in which seemed traced with the point of a needle. His memory, it struck me, might conceivably go back to the days before Algiers closed for ever her career of mischief. The Exmouth bombardment took place in 1816, and the release of 1,200 Christian slaves followed it. But this was not the end. Algiers was used to these interruptions. The damage done by the British was repaired, a new fleet built, and the buccaneering business was carried on down to the time of the blockade which ended in the fall of the town in 1830. So that the man whose memory could go back a stretch of about three-quarters of a century might recall something of that extinct industry, and, as a child, might actually have seen the corsair fleets ruffling the waters of the bay on their outward and homeward voyages.

Perhaps, I amused myself with speculating, the old Moor in the corner, who looked ninety if a day, might have been equal to such a retrospect. We turned a corner and the bay lay beneath us. A Messageries mail boat was slowly pulsing seaward, attended by the usual retinue of small craft that tossed in her wake or clung to her skirts as though loth to let her go. The dark eyes of the old man dwelt on the scene with imperturbable composure. Just opposite him sat an English girl, tennis-racquet in hand, to whom, I suppose, he was merely one of those local curiosities which had outgrown the interest of novelty and were no longer worth the snap-shot of a kodak, but who, to him, was the representative of a race his fathers had bought and sold like pigs in the slave-market below. I would have given much to have been able for a moment to look at the view through his eyes and clothe it in his memories and associations.

When I walk among the shrubberies and hotel gardens of Mustapha Supérieur I find it difficult to believe in the Arab town at all. I know it is built of solid plaster and brick; but I should not be much surprised, so incongruous does it look, to see it melt away like a cloud at sunset, and vanish out of the picture. On the other hand, when I lose myself in its dim passages, it is the hill of modern progress that seems unreal, and I am ready to expect when I come out that that will have disappeared, and the hotels, and hooting steamers, and girls with tennis-racquets be all vanished like a dream.

To pass into this crumbling mass of masonry is to pass into all the intricacies of Arab life. Winding, tortuous alleys meander aimlessly in all directions, drilled along their bases with deep holes, out of which protrude piles of merchandise, richly coloured, making deep blots of purple and crimson in the shadowed way. At the mouths of their burrows the owners squat, conning the passers-by with an air of serious indifference. Overhead the zigzag cliffs of white walls, latticed with faded shutters, rise irregularly, and tottering towards each other for support, block out all but a crooked chink of blue above, and shroud the dim creeks beneath in an unnaturally cold twilight.

And through the gloom mysterious figures move

ARAB INSTABILITY

with noiseless footsteps, in white flowing garments, with twisted turbans or veiled faces, who, as you tell yourself, are leading a life just as real and matter-of-fact as your own, with the usual everyday duties and worries, but whom no effort of your imagination can make to seem other than curious and fantastic, and outside the natural order of things, and who look at you with eyes in which all you can read is the depth of the abyss that lies between you. Like all Oriental towns, Old Algiers leaves on the memory an impression of a haunt of animals or insects rather than of men, a mass of crumbling masonry, honeycombed, corroded, and eaten through and into, as by ants or bees, in a network of minute passages and tunnels.

I have exactly the same feeling when I stand or wander in this picturesque labyrinth as when I turn the pages of an Arab history. There are the same striking individual figures and incidents, the same brilliant glimpses and vivid little scenes; and behind and around all there is the same inextricable confusion, the same lack of all coherence and definite plan. The details of Arab history, however full of romantic and exciting adventures, are to the Western mind inevitably tedious. Of what causes are these events the effects? of what effects are they the causes? are questions which repeatedly recur while you study the thrilling but inconsequent narrative. One receives an impression as of the wrong side of a tapestry. The brilliant colours are there in every stitch, but they are woven into no intelligible design.

This incoherence is the Arab's mark in history. It is worth dwelling on a moment, for it is this which led to the downfall of Algiers, which introduced the French into the country, and which lies at the root of the whole question of a North African settlement.

It seems scarcely to matter what incident we turn to as an illustration of the characteristic, for the Arab is so much of a piece that his least acts betray him; but I will take the following one:—

The most revered of names in North Africa is Okba ibn Nefi, the soldier-saint of Islam, whose tomb is in the desert near Biskra. Okba carried on the conquest of the country begun by Abdallah. Whatever the Arab does he does in a hurry, and Okba's furious advance was only stopped by the Atlantic Ocean. His remarks on reaching this unexpected obstacle have been recorded by Gibbon. "He spurred his horse into the waves, and, raising his eyes to heaven, exclaimed with the tones of a fanatic, 'Great God, if my course were not stopped by that sea I would still go on to the unknown kingdoms of the West, preaching the unity of Thy holy name and putting to the sword the rebellious nations who worship any other God than Thee.'" This is the temper that underlies all Arab achievement, and it is a temper more adapted to rapid conquest than stable settlement. While Okba was occupied with the Atlantic and a vague idea of riding to America, the conquests he had won were already slipping from him. The Arabs in their advance were innocent of an established base or lines of communication. They had no plan of campaign, and were far too intent on what was in front to have any thought to spare for what had been left behind. When Okba recalled his attention to what was happening round him, he found that the Berber tribes, dispersed rather than conquered by his impetuous advance, had risen in his rear, and hopelessly surrounded him.

ARAB INSTABILITY

The last act is signalised by one of those chivalrous touches so common in Arab chronicles. A chief who had tried to raise a mutiny in the army was a prisoner in the Arab camp. With his own hands Okba released him, and advised him to fly while there was time. His answer was that he would die by his rival's side. "Embracing as friends and martyrs, they unsheathed their scymetars, broke their scabbards, and maintained an obstinate combat, till they fell by each other's side on the last of their slaughtered countrymen."

How characteristic all that is! The enthusiasm, heroism, fancifulness of it; the show of conquest, the swift march, the mighty appearance of vigour and energy; and under it all no substantial basis, no plan, no permanence, no stability : these are traits common to Arab civilisation. An Arab renaissance as early as the eighth century had revived something of classic knowledge. The poetry and philosophy of Greece were studied, and the taste for learning was cultivated with the enthusiasm which the Arabs infused into all their undertakings. Every one knows the fascinating account of these things in the pages of Gibbon. How the tide of progress flowed from Samarcand and Bokhara to Fez and Cordova. How a visir consecrated 200,000 pieces of gold to the foundation of a college. How the transport of a doctor's books required four hundred camels. How a single library in Spain contained 600,000 volumes, while seventy public libraries were open in Andalusia alone. How the Arabian schools of Spain and Italy were resorted to by scholars from every country in Europe.

The palaces and gardens of Zehra, near Cordova, testified to the magnificence of the Ommiades. Twenty-five years and over three million sterling were spent on the work. Architects from Constantinople superintended the building. "The Hall of Audience was encrusted with gold and pearls, and a great basin in the centre was surrounded with the curious and costly figures of birds and quadrupeds. In a lofty pavilion of the gardens one of these basins and fountains—so delightful in a sultry climate—was replenished, not with water, but with the purest quicksilver. The seraglio of Abdalrahman, his wives, concubines, and black eunuchs, amounted to 6,300 persons; and he was attended to the field by a guard of 1,200 horse, whose belts and scymetars were studded with gold."

Here was a state of luxury and learning which contrasted strongly enough with the barbarism of the age. But under all this show where was the substantial basis? How much of all this was real? Arab architecture, in so far as it was Arab, and not built for them by the Greeks, was a concoction of whim and fantasy. In those nervous hands every strong and simple feature was distorted into endless complications, and, as always happens, lost in stability what it gained in eccentricity. Their learning was of the same character. Though they disputed interminably on the rival merits of the Greek philosophers, they were content to receive all their knowledge of them through indifferent translations. When the real revival of learning came, and a genuine Renaissance set in, the six or seven centuries of Arab civilisation were simply ignored and passed over. There was nothing, or almost nothing, of any value in all that fanciful structure; nothing that could be used as permanent building material.

An incurable fancifulness infected the whole of it.

ARAB INSTABILITY

The Arab mind seems to turn by a sort of instinct to the occult, the mystical, the fantastic. It is always sighing for new worlds to conquer before it has made good the ground it stands on. It has the curious gift of turning everything it touches from substance to shadow. Astronomy changes into astrology, and the main business of the science becomes the casting of horoscopes. The study of medicine changes into the composition of philtres and talismans and the reciting of incantations. Chemistry changes into a search for the secret of the transmutation of metals and the elixir of immortal health. In short, the tendency always was to shift the appeal from the intellect and reason to the fancy and imagination; and their zeal, instead of being devoted to laying firm foundations, evaporated in vague aspirations after the unintelligible or the unobtainable. Okba's cry, " O God, I would still go on to unknown kingdoms," seems the spirit of all their undertakings; and underneath them all there is the same deficiency that brought Okba himself to ruin, the want of a coherent plan, tested and made good at every step of its development.[1]

And the consequence is that not only has the Arab left us little or nothing, but his whole history seems already more legendary than real. Other civilisations abide our question. Not the Greek and Roman only, but the remote Assyrian and Egyptian are definite and real in comparison with the Arabian. This seems of another texture. It is such stuff as dreams are made of. Sober historians hardly know how to handle a tissue of circumstances which falls to pieces in their hands, and cold narrative seems out of place in dealing

[1] See Appendix, Note A.

with such romantic situations. Even the style of a Gibbon, woven out of solid circumstance and panoplied in fact, feels the contagion of a warmer sentiment, and glows and flushes, half wondering at itself, as it recounts the wild deeds of romance and valour, of incredible cruelty and incredible chivalry, which in their inextricable confusion do duty for Arab history.

Ballads and romances are the proper Arab histories. The Arab has nothing to give us of intellectual, nothing that can help us in the work of civilisation we have in hand ourselves, of which coherence, continuity, that stable and sure method of building which enables each generation in turn to take up the work where its predecessor laid it down, is the main characteristic. His is an emotional value. He is a sensation, not an idea. You may say of him what Matthew Arnold said of Byron—

> "He taught us little, but our soul
> Has felt him like the thunder roll."

Arab history is alone in this, that the personal events in it seem of more importance than the general ones. The battles and sieges of Okba's campaigns are like empty explosions that strike the ear without a meaning. But Okba himself, riding into the waves, chiding the Atlantic, turning to meet death against a host of foes, is still a figure that counts.

So it is to this day. The bloody rebellion that in Algeria followed the withdrawal of the French garrison in 1871, and flickered along the margin of the desert and up and down the length of the Atlas with the uncertain movement of all Arab actions, is already

ARAB INSTABILITY

almost forgotten. But El Mokrani lives. El Mokrani was a chief who had accepted an office under the French Government, and been the friend and comrade of French officers. Patriot though he was, he conceived himself bound by those obligations and those ties of friendship to take no advantage of the moment when France was struggling with an overpowering enemy. Deliberately he let that opportunity pass, and only when peace with Germany was declared did he issue a formal defiance, and after an interval of forty-eight hours lead his men against the invaders. The end came at Souflat. Seeing defeat inevitable, Mokrani dismounted from his horse and led his last charge on foot. He was shot through the forehead.

Such are the kind of incidents that the worth of Arab history resides in. Splendid deeds are scattered thickly all through it. And between all these deeds there is a curious family likeness. They are all of them lonely acts, not sociable ones. Their aim, I mean, was not to benefit mankind, or help a cause, or an idea, but simply to vindicate what, as an ideal of personal conduct, was lofty and becoming. For such an ideal the Arab has always been ready to lay down his life; but he lays it down for himself, not for others.

If you would realise what all this led to, what a civilisation that had no coherence and a heroism that was only personal resulted in finally, the answer lies round us in Algiers. The strange history of the place is already almost unrealisable, and is made the more so because of the quaint, picturesque, and fantastic aspect of the place. It is difficult to associate so bright and curious a scene with its own past. The first view I had of it was through the tiny disk of a cabin porthole. A northerly storm had chased us southward, and I had turned in in wet and mist. When I woke we were coming in on a following sea, but the wind had chopped about and blew off shore with a freshness and fragrance which, since I came to know them, I have attributed to the pine-woods of these hills and the flowers of these gardens. The long steamer lifted and sank with the varied cadence that makes being " rocked in the cradle of the deep " so much the pleasantest kind of rocking there is. I heard the waves peel off the iron side and flop back into the trough. Then I lifted myself on my elbow and looked out. The sun was rising, and its first beams rested full on the tall, cone-shaped, lemon-coloured hill of houses. Between us and it stretched a sea of the deepest blue, broken into dark ridges, with white splinters of foam breaking from their crests. The contrast between this powerful foreground, dark and strong and vigorous, added to the ghostly brilliance of the pale hill that rose beyond. One thought of Turner and his ivory white. The light on *The Fighting Téméraire* is the light on Old Algiers.

How much else was visible I have already forgotten. I have a vague recollection of the infinitely remote peaks of the Atlas, showing a white tooth or two through the haze, and of the darker hill in the foreground near the town. But what held all my attention was the wan pyramid of clustered buildings, rising like a spectre out of the dark blue of the sea.

A saint or anchorite of old might have dreamed a dream like this of the Celestial City. It looked too bright for earthly taint to rest on, or common men to live in; and yet it is doubtful whether, if you were

ARAB INSTABILITY

to search the world over, you could find a spot with a bloodier and darker past.

The chance denied the Arabs elsewhere was given them here. They were turned out of the East by the Turks, and out of the West by the Goths; but here, and in the other North African states, they had the chance of working out their system to an end. The insignificant Turkish garrison certainly offered no obstacle, especially after the Moorish emigration from Spain, to Arab national aspirations if they had possessed any. Nor could a better opening for national development be offered. A central position, a fertile soil, a delicious climate, and a long seaboard were among the advantages provided.

At the end of nine centuries of Arab occupation the outcome of these advantages was a pirate state with its hand against every man and every man's hand against it. A state which had become so intolerable a nuisance that it was found necessary at last to stamp it out of existence, in the interests of society, as you might stamp upon an adder in the public highway.

That has been the outcome of the Arab civilisation as far as Algiers is concerned. And if one looked elsewhere, east or west, to Tunis and Tripoli, or to Morocco, we should find the same result. A red-hot state of zeal enables Arabs to act together for a little time, and carry on the same movement; but as soon as it cools the lack of any real cohesion shows itself at once, and society drops to pieces of its own accord.

It is this dropping to pieces that the history of Algiers illustrates. In the strong, lawless Turk the fickle but equally lawless Arab found a leader after his own heart. The two seemed made for each other. Their operations extended over many seas and many coasts. Besides being the terror of the Mediterranean they were the terror of the English Channel. "Those roguish pirates," writes in 1644 Edmund Rossingham to Lord Conway, "which lie upon the western coast have taken from the shore about Penzance near St. Michael's Mount sixty men, women, and children." Five years later the at that time prosperous port of Baltimore, in Ireland, was sacked and 237 captives carried off to slavery. The place has never recovered its prosperity, but probably few people realise that its decline has been due to a Saracen foray.

About the same time we hear of a petition from the shipowners of Exeter, Plymouth, Dartmouth, Barnstaple, and other towns, representing that the pirates had become so numerous that English ships dared not put to sea. Sailors refused to man them, and even fishermen were afraid to go out fishing. On the common everyday acts of piracy committed it would be endless to enlarge. An idea of the familiarity of the pest may be gained from a resolution passed in Parliament to the effect that fines levied on members who were late for prayers should be distributed among the poor women "*who daily attend the House,*" whose husbands were captives in Algiers.

The usual way of dealing with the evil was by ransom. As late as 1810 Sir Arthur Paget, of the frigate *Thetis*, bought off a couple of English slaves for a gold snuffbox set in diamonds, valued at £500; and the Ironmongers' Company at the same time paid £465 for the liberation of thirteen others. It is hardly too much to say that the pirates, by the

ARAB INSTABILITY

energy and tenacity they threw into their business, had made lawlessness lawful, and established a sort of right to violate right. The recognition of this privilege is testified to by the regular tribute paid by the national governments to Algiers, to secure their merchantmen from pillage—a tax as extraordinary, surely, as any mentioned in history. The American tribute was paid down to the year of the battle of Waterloo.

Algiers was the thorn in the side of European civilisation. Gradually, as the nations settled down and society arranged itself, there came into being that method of modern progress, of which, as I said before, the main characteristic is its strict coherence and power of carrying on a purpose from generation to generation. Of course, when Arab anarchy perceived this system of order emerging, it flung itself at its throat with all its might. For a while, too, it held its own. Its fleets were in the Channel. It exacted recognition and a tribute. But order grew. International ideas of responsibility and equity began to establish themselves. Slowly anarchy was driven back as the definite scheme more and more emerged. Like those weeds which take root in the interstices of masonry, Algiers had fed on the dissensions of nations. It was the closing-up of European society which was fatal to her.

Curiously enough, when one remembers the excesses of violence that had marked her course, it was a blow with *a fan*, of all weapons, which was the signal for her downfall. But the old Bey who allowed himself this trifling indulgence had mistaken the times he lived in. It was safer to shoot a consul from a gun in the seventeenth century than to raise a fan against one in the nineteenth. The city's hour had struck. A fleet and army answered the insult, and three years later the French guns were singing the requiem of Algiers.

Walking among these alleys, or standing under the bleached walls of the old fort overlooking the Arab town and the blue bay beneath, that history passes before one like a panorama. What a mess they have made of it all! one is tempted to exclaim, thinking of the opportunities wasted and the chances thrown away. What an extraordinary difference between the beginnings of Arab conquest and this helpless, hopeless disintegration and falling to pieces of society in Algiers! And yet even in the first flush of their enthusiasm we see that secret spirit of incoherence working in all their designs like a solvent; a spirit which forms part of the Arab character, which was fated to haunt him all through his history, and finally to crumble all his work away. Had Okba marched more warily, with an eye on his lines of communication, he would not have been cut off in his hour of triumph. Had the Arab scholars and scientists been content to build up their civilisation by degrees, basing it on reason and solid fact, instead of dissipating it in transcendental fancies, they would no doubt have achieved something which would not have been swept out of existence as a housemaid sweeps a cobweb from a wall. Had the solid qualities of slowness and sureness, which are the basis of social and national existence, been inherent in Arab character, Europe would not have been treated to such a spectacle as the decline and fall of Algiers.

ARAB INSTABILITY

There is a particular interest here in Algiers in noting this haunting deficiency in the Arab character and civilisation, for it is on this that the French claim to the right of interference is really based. Two principles confront each other in North Africa to-day: the principle of anarchy which is going out, and the principle of order which is coming in. What European civilisation stands for, before all, is just that coherence and continuity which the Arab is destitute of, and for want of which he has been brought to such melancholy shipwreck. It is because these things are absolutely essential to any kind of advance, or social stability even, and because France can supply, and has the best right to supply them, that she is justified in intervening.

I confess I do not see myself how in this matter the line can logically be drawn between any of these North African states. They are all out of the same egg. All are inhabited by the same race and wedded to the same lawlessness. It seems to me that if the French were justified in interfering with Algiers, they were justified in interfering with Tunis, and will be justified in interfering with Morocco. All these states, left to themselves, make any system of law and order impossible, not only within their own borders, but also in their neighbourhood. The Bedouin and Touareg nomads are the pirates of the Sahara. They deal with the Sudan caravan trade just as the Algerine fleet dealt with the commerce of Europe. Lawlessness knows no frontiers, and it is difficult to see how any settlement of the country can take place, until the nation whose interests are paramount in this part of the world assumes responsible control. What the claims of other nations may be to influence France's action is, of course, another matter. But so far as the main question of interference is concerned, that is not a question of France *versus* Algeria, or France *versus* Tunisia, or France *versus* Morocco, but of order *versus* anarchy in North Africa.

As I correct these pages (June 21, 1905) the interference of Germany seems to have introduced a new complication. What the upshot is to be it is impossible to say. My own impression is that the course of events will not be greatly changed. Germany's politics are, I imagine, more European than North African. On the other hand, France's interests and responsibilities in North Africa are so far-reaching and deep-rooted that, guided with patience and tact, it seems as if their ultimate development was assured.

NOTE, JULY, 1902.

Four years have passed. Germany has retired. The Moors have added, and are daily adding, fresh proofs of their instability. The French policy remains what it was, the one solid factor in the situation.

CHAPTER II

FRENCH DISCIPLINE

The *cafés* of Algiers—Cosmopolitan character of the people—Moor and Arab—Arab dependence on the desert—His virtues desert virtues—The Jew in Algeria—His place in society—His political importance—French sociability—Its influence in colonisation—France's peaceable intentions—Pacific penetration—The slowness of French colonisation—Striking likeness between Algeria and Cape Colony—French and English methods—The French excel in collective work, the English in individual initiative—French instinct for organisation—The Latin race in Africa—Part played by the Government—French progress.

THE Café de Bordeaux stands at the corner where the Boulevard de la République and the Place du Gouvernement join. There are many other *cafés* in the near neighbourhood—the Café de l'Oasis, the Café de la Bourse, the Café d'Apollon, the Grand Café d'Alger, the Café Continental, the Café Gruber, the Café Glacier, and others. I mention only the chief. My recollection of this part of the town, facing the Quay and the bay with the dark palms of the Jardin d'Essai in front, lifting their arching fronds of leaves against the sky, and making networks of flickering shadows on the white dust of the roads, is that it consists mainly of crowds of little iron tables with little iron chairs set round them.

The atmosphere of these *cafés* is the *ne plus ultra* of catholicism. All races, all classes, all colours, avail themselves of the hospitality of these acres of chairs and tables. Here gathers a group of young Moors, who are the town-bred Arabs, and worth a moment's attention. They have taken to trade and shopkeeping, and spend their time in distilling scent and making embroidery, and smoking cigarettes in the dim twilight of their shops. The fire of the desert is extinct in them. They are often handsome in a disagreeable effeminate way, with pale smooth faces, velvety dark eyes, and soft, rather fawning manners. They are dressed very gay in silk-embroidered jackets and waistcoats and big linen trousers. An indescribable sense of unhealthiness and decadence attaches to them.

Compare them with the Arabs of whom a few are scattered in the crowd. Under the hood of the latter's burnous looks out a face darkened and polished by the sun, seamed with countless wrinkles, with eyes whose piercing and restless glances, darting from group to group, bespeak, under his restrained demeanour, the prompt and wary character of the man. In a fashionable photographer's window in Piccadilly there are generally to be seen several large portraits of English generals and soldiers, with the carefully-prepared rice-powder complexion which has become a photographic tradition. The difference between those egg-like faces in the gilt frames, with all their life-work, furrowed into cheek and forehead, smoothed away, and a mask of pink-and-white porcelain substituted—the difference between these and the originals, as you remember them, scorched and tanned under their helmets in real life, is the difference between Moor and Arab. You can trace a resemblance, it is true ; but all that gives expressiveness and vigour to the Arab's face, and stands for the racial significance of the type, is gone from the Moor's ; and in the same way, too, the slack and languid movements and step of the Moor, compared with the Arab's alertness and the evident strength of his lean but sinewy limbs, shows what a physical deterioration has taken place.

So fares it with the Arab when he forsakes desert life for cities. On no other race does such a change work so fatally, for there is no other race whose virtues and fine qualities belong so inextricably to the conditions he was grown under. Other conditions, up and down the world, are more or less similar, and people bred in one place are effective in most others. But the Arab is not transferable. He has started forth from the desert imbued with a set of vices and virtues all his own, which make him as much an anomaly among men as his home is an anomaly in scenery. The children of hill and wood and valley and plain—of the mixed scenery generally, who are all much of a muchness—stare in astonishment when the child of the desert comes among them, and mentally ejaculate, " What the devil have we here ? "

Cut the Arab off from the desert and you doom him. His energy always abates as he retires from that source. The fearful desert *élan* droops in the damp and cold of the north. Indeed, his whole career was checked ultimately not so much by hostile races as by hostile conditions of soil and climate. His conquests were regulated by the thermometer. Gibbon says somewhere that if it had not been for Charles Martel we might all be living in England now under an Arab dynasty. But that shows that Gibbon had failed to take into account the Arab's dependence on a special physical environment, and his inevitable deterioration when separated from it. A country with a climate like England's has nothing whatever to fear from Arab enterprise.

In everything we shall find it the same. In their poetry, in their architecture, in their military prowess and achievements, in their own courage and dignity and sense of honour, there is an invariable and generally very rapid falling off so soon as the Arab and the desert are divorced. Here in Algiers, in the person of these young Moors, mostly descended from the Spanish Moors, you may see some of these effects. The Arab burst into Spain ; the Moor crept out. All the striking and virile qualities in the Arab are desert qualities. His fantastic chivalry and generosity, his intense susceptibility to what is honourable and seemly, combined with an equal indifference to what is right and wrong, are qualities which show in his bearing, which you may admire and which certainly add to his picturesqueness, but they are, nevertheless, not exactly the qualities that go to make a useful citizen and a peaceable member of society. It is a pity that it should be so, but it seems, nevertheless, to be the case, that if you subtract from the Arab's character everything that stands between him and citizenship you subtract from it everything that was worth having.

Another prominent item in an Algerian crowd is the Jew. He is something of a factor in the settlement of Algeria, and will, they say, be more of a factor still in

FRENCH DISCIPLINE

the settlement of Morocco. His importance consists in the fact that he is a sort of middleman between the French and the natives ; that he mingles easily with the native population on the one hand, and is naturally pledged by self-interest to the French Government on the other.

Under the old Moslem rule a Jew's life in Algiers was certainly not a happy one. Death and torture were forthcoming at the smallest provocation, and insult and contumely at no provocation at all. A "city" man once told me that between the money-making Jew and the money-making Gentile there was the difference which always distinguishes the professional from the amateur. He was thinking of that earnestness of purpose which works on patiently and mechanically in the face of all obstacles and rebuffs. Certainly the quality was never more strongly illustrated than in the history of Algiers. Weak and hated, rich and unprotected, what lot could they expect among a people with whom plunder was an instinct? Hens among hawks might have led such a life. An instinct that they were layers of golden eggs hindered their total extermination, but persecution often ran the issue fine. Other people have suffered martyrdom for country or for faith, but only the Jews have suffered it for money.

However, the coming of the French brought a change. In 1871 the Jews obtained the rights of citizenship, and their gratitude to the French Government was naturally lively. They are said to have shown it in the enthusiasm with which their conscripts joined the ranks of the army. No section of the community had profited by the French invasion as they had. For them it meant a change in the conditions of life which can only be compared to coming into harbour after a raging sea. The calm has been disturbed once or twice since by anti-Jewish riots and demonstrations which were in themselves an indirect testimony to the excellent use the race has made of its opportunities and its rapid rise in wealth and influence. Under French rule the number of Jews has increased by leaps and bounds. In all matters of trade and business with the native races they have an enormous advantage over Europeans, in that their own mixed origin and more or less Oriental breeding places them on terms of something like confidence and equality with those races. On the other hand, they fully appreciate the opportunities of European trade, and the advantage of a strong and orderly form of European government. In short, the Jews have a marvellous power of adapting themselves to all the conditions that foster their own special line of business, and are such thorough cosmopolitans that the gulf which usually separates East from West seems in their case to have no existence. It is the fact that this gulf exists which more or less paralyses French and European enterprise when it comes in contact with Oriental races. And it is their being able to bridge the gulf that gives the Jews their unique position in North Africa, and accounts in a great measure for their rapid growth in numbers and importance.

Moreover Jewish action promises to be much more important in the future than it has yet been. In Morocco the number of the Jews is said to amount to the gigantic total of 200,000. The bulk of these are scattered among the trading towns on or near

FRENCH DISCIPLINE

the coast. A very large share of the trade in European goods, especially of the retail trade, has fallen into their hands. They have managed to recommend to the suspicious Berber and Arab tribes a great many things, useful or otherwise, which, failing their explanation and soothing assurances, would have roused hostile prejudices. The growth of their trade has extended their influence, which, among the Berbers, is now said to be very considerable. Of course this influence is exerted in favour of France, for the Moroccan Jews are keenly alive to the advantage which their Algerian neighbours have gained from French rule, and are fully aware of the immense opportunities which a large extension of European trade in Morocco would confer on a people who hold as they do the position of middleman.

The importance of the Jew in North Africa, then, is easy to see. His commercial importance will amount to a good deal. In the traffic between European and Oriental, the Jew in a sense is the natural broker, and he may be trusted to make full use of his chances. But his political importance is also very great, and for the time being eclipses the other, since it has a more immediate bearing on the circumstances of the day. If the Moroccan newspapers are to be believed, the Jews are the most indefatigable and most powerful agents of the French cause that exist in the country. Just as they paved the way by slow degrees for European trade, administering it first in homeopathic doses, so now they are paving the way very gradually and tentatively for French political influence. They are, indeed, looked upon by some people as a kind of advance guard of the French occupation, and it is maintained that they have by degrees introduced into Morocco a general sentiment which, though it would take instant offence at any high-handed action, is not really unfavourable to a gradual propagation of European ideas.

All this is remarkable testimony to the value of the Jew as a political agent. There may possibly be another side to the business of which we may hear when the country has become settled. One writer says that it is difficult to see how France can repay such services. That, I imagine, is a matter which the Jews will see to for themselves.

Besides Jews and Moors there are Maltese, Turks, Spaniards, Berbers, several different breeds of negroes from the Sudan and various other odds and ends of more or less equivocal generation, not classed under separate headings, in the crowd that fluctuates up and down in front of our *café* or gathers and settles at its tables. There reigns, as I have said, a spirit of absolute catholicity. French officers and citizens and visitors mingle freely with Moors, Arabs, and Jews. The groups are intermixed. The talk is easy and general. An old beggar comes along, gets a sou and a drink of water, and hobbles on his way. A negro carrying a bundle stops for a light for his cigarette, and a French officer hands the man his own cigarette for the purpose quite as a matter of course. There is a total absence of constraint, of a feeling of exclusiveness and superiority in any section. All garbs, types, languages, and classes seem intermingled in a common sociability which recognises no distinction of caste or calling.

It was particularly to observe this phenomenon

FRENCH DISCIPLINE

that I brought the reader to the Café Bordeaux. For I find, on looking back at the time spent here, that it is this wonderfully easy social intercourse, so characteristic in every way of the French genius, that strikes me as the most significant trait in the life of Algiers.

People who have visited Paris in spring know the change that comes over its streets at that season. They remember the crowds of white-napkined tables that overflow and spread across the side-walks and out under the trees in ever-growing borders and parterres. Street annuals, Lamb would have called them,

> "That come before the swallow dares and take
> The winds of March with beauty."

They transform the scene. And more than that, they transform the Parisian, and from that hour he begins to live his own life again. The biting east may blow, but it will not prevent a few of the old *habitués* from creeping back to sit, blue with cold, in their accustomed seats and pass a few words of gossip or greeting with the neighbours. That first glass of hot coffee and snatch of talk mark the turn of the year for the Parisian. When he gets home he says to his wife, "I stopped at the Café des Voisins to-day." And she cries, "Aha! go along! it begins, then!" And both laugh and nod at each other. So ingrained in the Frenchman is that sociable instinct which we are sometimes inclined to put down to mere manner.

And it is a hardy instinct and works under all circumstances. However small and remote the settlement, if there is a Frenchman in it to organise its society the *café* flourishes. The guests include all the respectable male population, French and native. The commanding officer of the little garrison is a kind of honorary president. When he takes his sword off and hitches it to the wall it is a sign that he relapses into that easy sociability which, after all, is the Frenchman's native element. He loves these moments. The probability is that he is a keen soldier; but after all he is a Frenchman before he is a soldier, and the *café* is dearer to him even than the barracks.

Up and down the French colonies there are thousands of these little agencies busy, mixing and fusing and kneading together in some slight degree the human paste that comes under their influence; patching up, as you may say, with tiny stitches the rents made by sword and bullet in days gone by. They are symbolic of much in the French character. "Pacific penetration" in a Frenchman's mouth is no mere phrase. The Commandant Godron, after long service in Algeria, used to maintain that the Sahara frontier should be extended day by day as the gardens and oases invaded the desert. "We must bombard the country with cabbages and crops," he used to say; and every one who has followed the history of the French army in Algeria will acknowledge that that, too, was no mere phrase.

If one listens to-day to the plans laid and theories suggested for the extension of French influence in Morocco, one is struck by the genuinely peaceable intention that runs through them all. There have been things done in Morocco lately that seemed to

FRENCH DISCIPLINE

countenance decisive interference. Disturbances, raids, and acts of brigandage that almost invited such interference. Yet, judging from the tone of the French press, such a policy finds no backers. The schemes which do appeal to the French imagination, and which are eagerly discussed, are such as those brought forward from time to time for the conquest of the country by doctors and schoolmasters. A hospital is to be opened at Tangier. Later on another is to be started at Fez. Step by step the number is to grow, following a preconceived plan which will result in their regular distribution over certain portions of territory. The treatment of out-patients and the supply at cheap prices of the simpler kinds of medicine are features of the scheme. The schools are to be branch institutions, linked to the hospitals. The schoolmasters and mistresses are to be familiar with the Arab language and customs, and the entire movement is to be inspired by the desire to win the confidence of the native tribes.

Such schemes, no doubt, lend themselves to eloquent discussion, and often look better in print than they work out in practice. Nevertheless, they help us to realise the temper in which France is approaching this latest colonial problem of hers. The *Dépêche Coloniale*, which certainly represents the most intelligent ideas in France in colonial affairs, has of late years published the views of many influential and experienced men on France's policy in Morocco. And what every one must be struck by in these views is the entire absence of anything in the least arrogant, or dictatorial, or militant in them. I have quoted one suggestion by way of a sample, but they are all much alike in character. They are all occupied with the idea how and at what points to tack on French influence to native life; how to allay suspicion and distrust and lead the native imagination into an easy and natural recognition of certain benefits that Western civilisation may perhaps be able to bestow upon them.

The truth is we in England are apt to make too much of the French military excitability. That mood of theirs is altogether abnormal. The consciousness nations have of each other is generally confined to the moments when they have something to fear from each other. Once in twenty years or so French excitability makes us conscious of her as a nation. The danger passes and we relapse into unconsciousness again for another twenty years. But we carry into and through those twenty years the image of France as she appeared at the moment when she mattered to us. We have seen the mountain in eruption, and think it is always thus. We know nothing of its benigner moods, of its green nooks and pleasant valleys, its cottages smothered in vines, its pastoral farms that nestle in its slopes. After all, it is not what a man is in moments of rare excitement, but what he is in the tenour of his daily life that matters. France's daily life is influenced much less than we think by an excitable vanity, and much more than we think by that strong human instinct, which, making an ideal as it does of the social life, instinctively adopts towards all it comes in contact with such an attitude as makes social life possible.

This is the instinct that the pacific penetration theory is founded on; and the more closely one watches French life wherever it is lived, and especially the more closely one watches it in the colonies where it is brought into contact with divers races and nationalities, the more one will note the solidity of the basis. The Bordeaux, the Apollon, the Continental, and the rest of them, stretching their tables right across the town front, give us glimpses of this influence at work. When the claims of school and hospital to act as civilising agents are pressed, it is time some one stood up for the *café*.

If an Englishman were asked in what scenes or plans the British influence over native races is best displayed, he would think of the justice and firmness of our rule, and would instance probably our courts of justice or government offices. If a Frenchman were asked the same question as to French influence, he would think of the social catholicism of the French people, and would focus its general character and action for us in the Café Bordeaux.

Whether this universal sociability of the French tends to the rapid opening up of the country and settlement of colonists on the soil is, of course, another matter. It probably has rather the opposite effect. People who colonise in the spirit of the *café* must needs colonise deliberately. A Frenchman landed on a new coast would plant a tree and place a table and sit down to wait for other Frenchmen. When there were plenty of them they would perhaps set off to explore the interior, which, by the way, would probably by that time have been annexed by an Englishman. Coming as they would not in single spies but in battalions they would not travel too far in a day, nor scramble up and down precipices, nor wander off by themselves to explore alone. Not that they would be in the least afraid of doing any of these things, but because, if they did them, they would have to forego each other's society and conversation.

It is important, I think, to notice this distinction. There have never been a more daring and pertinaceous lot of explorers than the French have proved themselves during the last thirty years in North-West Africa. Scores have risked their lives in that time among the treacherous tribes of the central Sahara. Many have lost them. Their work has been of enormous importance in the expansion of the French colonial empire, for it has inspired and directed every new move and every fresh acquisition of territory. Never had any government a more zealous and devoted intelligence department, and it might seem absurd in face of their performances to accuse the French of any lack of personal initiative.

The fact is, if there is any adequate motive for his doing these things, no one is more ready to do them than the Frenchman. To take part in the colonial movement, to be a pawn in that great game which France is playing in North Africa, is to him a motive sufficient. The coherence and logic of the game, the sequence of the moves, appeal to every Frenchman. He thoroughly appreciates his country's play, and is keenly ready to cut in at the game himself. But when you speak to him of exploring as a matter of private pleasure, of adventure for its own sake, of the delights of lonely and perilous sport, of the joy of tracking a buffalo in a swamp, or being mauled by a tiger in a jungle, or even of the possibilities of prospecting for diamonds or gold—why, then you speak to inattentive ears. *Ça ne vaut pas la peine*, would be his simple

FRENCH DISCIPLINE

comment on such undertakings. They would involve for him a sacrifice incommensurate with the object to be attained—the sacrifice of that sociability which is what, for him, makes life worth living.

So the work of colonisation and the settlement of the country proceeds slowly in French hands. It proceeds smoothly and comfortably and steadily, but owing to this intense sociability of theirs and their passion for moving *en masse*, it certainly proceeds very slowly.

We and the French are the only Powers whose colonisation in Africa is vital to-day; that is, whose colonies would endure if the protection of the mother country were withdrawn. France has made her entrance from the extreme north, England from the extreme south. The vast bulk of Africa lies almost evenly balanced on the equator, and between the opposite ends there are close resemblances. Cape Town lies in latitude 34·20 South; Algiers in 36·47 North. The former has a rainfall of twenty-four inches and a mean temperature of sixty-two degrees; the latter's rainfall is twenty-nine inches, and temperature sixty-six degrees. Algiers is, therefore, slightly warmer and damper than Cape Town, but the difference is inconsiderable.

There is the same likeness in the physical features of the two countries. What is called the Tell district in the north—that is, the fertile strip of land along the coast—is balanced by a similar margin of fertility in the south. The fruit gardens of Natal are reproduced along the shore of the Mediterranean, and when I was staying in the Mitidjeh valley in Algeria, with its deep black soil and loaded vines, I could fancy myself strolling among the famous Constantia vineyards of the colony.

Inland the mountains rise at about the same distance, the Drakensberg in the south answering to the Atlas in the north; while, inland of these again, the veld and the Sahara correspond at least in their general aspect and sense of barrenness. Here you have two rival systems of colonisation pitted against each other on equal terms. In each you hear the same problems discussed: How to pacify the country, how to irrigate those barren inland tracts, how to establish settlers from home on the land, how to push on the Cape to Cairo railway which is to unite the British possessions, or the trans-Saharan which is to unite the French. Has such a spectacle ever been seen before as that of two great colonial empires spreading and extending from opposite ends of the same enormous continent with equal swiftness and equal energy?

At the same time the methods adopted by each country, and the spirit in which they go about the work of colonisation, are very different; and if we turn back up the road that climbs the wooded hill of Mustapha Supérieur, and sit on the low wall overlooking the town and bay, we shall get an idea, perhaps, of what the difference consists in.

Below us, north and south, two long piers extend into the sea, like outstretched arms, to embrace a steadily-increasing commerce. Beside the shore stretch the long quays and ample warehouses of the port. Then come the Boulevard de la République, the squares, gardens, public buildings, statues, fountains, hotels, theatres, the long arcades, and roomy, tree-shaded streets of the Algerian capital.

FRENCH DISCIPLINE

There is a good deal of dignity and discipline in all this. The regularity and breadth in the thoroughfares and the uniformity in the buildings convert whole streets into single architectural features. Dirt and squalor and confusion do not exist; in short, the intention of the inhabitants is evident—to endow themselves with a dignified, convenient, and well-arranged capital.

It is impossible to deny an attractive flavour to the life of such a place. Behind us the electric trams run smoothly down the hill, carrying prosperous-looking occupants to business or pleasure in the town below. On the slopes, among dark evergreens and trees, comfortable villas stand in their well-ordered gardens. Most of them are built in Moorish style, with deep verandahs, fantastic arcades, and ogive windows. Their snowy architecture gleams, like marble sculpture, through glossy leaves and evergreens. The gardens glow with a profusion of flowers; arches and verandahs are half smothered under a surprising display of roses, and the great bougainvillea creeper bursts in purple surf on frequent walls and balconies.

And all this—this disciplined and well-thought-out arrangement of the town and careful utilisation of the hilly ground commanding the sea breeze and view—is not only very pleasant and rather imposing in itself, but it is also distinctively French. Cape Town and Algiers are as like in their sites as two towns could well be; Cape Town having an advantage, indeed, for there is but one Table Mountain in the world. But between the towns themselves what a contrast! Cape Town is all at sixes and sevens. Its streets are inconvenient and ill-arranged. Its architecture is a jumble of hovels and palaces. The town has grown on the hand-to-mouth principle, big buildings, one by one as they are needed, replacing mean ones. At every step it has to fight it own past, and the incoherent style in which it started life will probably always prevent its attaining to much in the way of dignity and convenience. Nothing is more difficult than to evolve order out of chaos in matters of bricks and mortar, when once the chaos has laid good hold. We know that in London.

These things are not unimportant, surely. A fine capital attracts citizens, encourages settlement, and gives a certain stability to colonial life. It reacts on industry and agriculture. Markets are established, commerce stimulated, trade knocks at the door. A certain prestige and dignity attach to a young colony from the possession of a worthy capital. Strangers think more of it, and it thinks more of itself. The presence or absence of these effects is what makes the difference between Algiers and Cape Town.

You must look elsewhere than in towns for English efficiency. The indomitable Anglo-Saxon penetrates far into the interior. He exploits the country, civilises the natives, and employs the survivors. His Government watches him from afar in nervous perplexity, repudiates his action, and with an ill grace appropriates the fruits of his energy. The whole British Empire bears the impress of our individual initiative. Nevertheless it is a quality which has its *per contras*. It gave us India, but it gave us the East India Company, the Rajahs, and the Mutiny. It gave us Rhodesia, but it gave us the Chartered Company and the Matabele rebellion. It gave us Mr. Rhodes, but Mr. Rhodes gave us the Jameson raid. At the same time it is this individual initiative that lends to our colonising the vigour that has always characterised it.

This quality of individual initiative, with its advantages and drawbacks, the French have not got; but in their capacity for collective action they have something that in part at least makes up for it.

The instant he comes within range, so to speak, of the *collective* principle, the efficiency of the French colonist reveals itself. Here he has all the boldness and the big ideas that the Englishman develops in the backwoods and jungles. I have instanced Algiers, and I might go on to instance such lesser towns as Sfax, Monastir, Gabes, and others, some of which are the merest sketches. Though only the first touches are visible on the bare canvas, these are already the decisive strokes of the artist who foresees a picture. Streets, boulevards, gardens, quays, and harbours are already indicated. All is rudimentary, yet a certain greatness is foreshadowed. Scorched with desert sun, and blurred with desert sand, these embryo cities are nourished on a high tradition. You can trace in them the largeness of frame that shows the young of a fine species.

The whole French scheme is of a piece. Their colonial empire is laid down just as their towns are laid down, with the same coherence and regard for discipline and order. They have explored the interior, extended their conquests, advanced their frontiers, with the same sense of method. Colonists, on the same principle, are imported in counted batches, settled in villages duly prepared and arranged for them, provided with all necessaries, such as roads and water, and periodically visited, advised, and superintended by Government officers.

A singular instance of this love of arranging and predisposing is attracting some attention at the present moment. A little while ago a book was published on the advisability of the French leaving Asia and confining themselves to the development of Africa. "Lachons l'Asie, Prenons l'Afrique" was the title of it. It was, according to the writer, in Africa that a future lay for the Latins. This was as obviously the sphere for the old race as America was the sphere for the new. When the Gallic imagination gets started on a theme of this kind it runs briskly on, and M. Reclus had no difficulty in composing an eloquent work on the subject. If it had not a great success, this was due apparently to the "Lachons l'Asie" not to the "prenons l'Afrique" part of it.

The idea of a Latin race, resuscitated and vigorous, overspreading the great southern continent caught on. Indeed, the advice is not wholly new. A score of years ago the division of North Africa marked out was Morocco for Spain, Algeria for France, and Tunisia for Italy. Of these, France has been the only Latin nation capable of taking up her liabilities. Italy has been hampered by the tremendous strain involved in keeping up appearances as a great Power, and Spain has been for long almost bereft of national vitality. France, accordingly, has already appropriated the portion reserved for Italy, and is now about to appropriate the portion reserved for Spain.

Apart, however, from the national aspect of these transfers, there is their democratic aspect. Spain, as a nation, is not able to undertake any responsibility as to the control of Morocco, but that does not prevent Spaniards from crossing in large numbers into the country. Italy, as a nation, has lost the chance of securing Tunisia, but that does not prevent a steady stream of emigrants from the south of Italy and Sicily settling in the new colony. So that the fact that France ostensibly governs, or soon will govern, the whole of this part of Africa· has had no effect on the Latin movement, and each of the three Latin nations is steadily pouring in a stream of colonists into that part of the African coast lying opposite its own shores.

What M. Reclus calls, then, the building up of a great Latin race in Africa seems to many people already begun. M. de Pouvourville, a member of the International Colonial Institute, contributed an article on the subject to the *Nouvelle Revue* of September 15, 1904. The intermixture and gradual fusion of these strains of Latin blood on African soil and the formation of a new race of the old stock, but braced and invigorated by a hardy life in a new country, are to M. de Pouvourville events of surpassing interest and significance. Nor is that to be wondered at. It is a movement of great interest, and a movement well worth calling attention to, and judging from the effects that a colonial life is already having on the character of the inhabitants of Algeria and Tunisia, it may be fraught with far-reaching consequences to the Latin race.

But what is interesting to note in the discussion on this matter which is going forward is the attitude of the French towards their Government. It does not need saying that if such a mixture of races were taking place in any colonies of ours—if English and

Boers were mingling in South Africa, or English and French in Canada—we might be very glad, and we might congratulate ourselves, but it would never occur to us that it was a matter for the Government to interfere in. We should just as soon expect the Government to attempt to influence the succession of the seasons, or the rise and fall of the tide.

With the French, on the contrary, the first question is—how is the Government to get control of the movement? They do not consider it safe, they do not feel that it is in a way to bear fruit, until the Government has taken charge of it. Here is a work of tremendous responsibility, says M. de Pouvourville, for the Government. The Government must watch over the evolution of this new race and inoculate it with all the qualities that are to fit it for its magnificent destiny. Here are "vast conceptions," indeed, which may, as he says, "employ unceasingly all the thoughts and efforts of our statesmen."

Something, it seems, is already being attempted. The French and Algerian Governments are looking into the matter. An inquiry is going to be opened with the object of arranging immigration and concessions to colonists. The fusion into single communities of hitherto separated groups will, it is hinted, be a main object. M. de Pouvourville ends his article by remarking that up to now this phenomenon of the birth and development of a new people has gone on unconsciously, under the impulse merely "of hazard and chance circumstances"; now, however, the Government must take charge of operations and establish them on a logical and rational basis.

It is easy to smile at such a notion of colonising,

FRENCH DISCIPLINE

but any one who from our point of vantage looks down over Algiers, or allows his thoughts to dwell for a moment on the vast scheme of expansion which has given France control of practically the whole of the great North-Western protuberance of Africa, must know that the smile does not end the matter. The most interesting thing of all about French colonising is, not that it differs at all points and pursues diametrically opposite methods from ours, but that it succeeds. About this there is no doubt whatever. Whatever tests we apply—whether we take the rise in population, the steady flow of immigration into the country, the increase of births over deaths among colonials, the yearly progress of its wealth and its trade, the cultivation and irrigation of a constantly-increasing area of its soil; or whether we look further afield, and watch the handling of the whole group of French colonies in North Africa, their steady enlargement and simultaneous advance towards the unity of a single empire—the result is the same. All the evidence points one way. There is no gainsaying it. The effectiveness of the collective system in French hands is written across half a continent. It is a sight that may well make an Englishman stare. Nowhere through all these great new countries is there a trace of individual initiative save in subordination to Government control. Not only is the whole colonising movement and the settlement of immigrants on the land supervised and arranged by Government with a minute and scrupulous attention, but all the work of exploration in the uttermost parts of the Sahara is under the same careful direction. I imagine, if you went to an English official at the Colonial Office and asked him what exploration was going on in British Central Africa, he would say, "The Lord knows! Why do you come to me about it?" If, on the other hand, we went to a similar official in France, he would have his finger on the map in a moment. "Here," he would say, "in the Adrar Hills I have a party under Captain A. prospecting for gold. Here in the Gourara Valley, Lieutenant B. is cutting a road. On the south side of the Tademait Plateau, Major C. is making a map of the watercourses. Among the oases of Tidikelt, Colonel D. is sinking artesian wells. Professors Y. and Z. are classifying the fauna and flora of the environs of Lake Chad"; and so our official would take us from one end of the Sahara to the other, and in every valley and river-course and on every frontier line he would have his busy agents gathering intelligence or carrying out his plans. Here, in this office is the nerve-centre of the whole system, the box-seat to which all the reins converge.

And it succeeds? Amazingly! It is ridden by officials and it goes admirably. It is swathed from top to bottom in red tape and it overflows with strength and vitality. And the reason it succeeds so well is because Government control, being the greatest possible convenience, or rather, an absolute necessity, for a people who wish to do things *en masse*, the French people not only acquiesce in it, but act in sympathy with it and vigorously second all its attempts at intelligent organisation. While our colonists and pioneers *cut* our Government, the French are hand in glove with theirs. Just as the energy and enterprise of a people who move in ones is to be looked for in the individual, so the energy and

FRENCH DISCIPLINE

enterprise of a people who move in masses is to be sought in its Government; and, in effect, the Government which has created the French colonial empires of North-West Africa and Indo-China is a vastly different affair from the Government which our pioneers have periodically to goad into a reluctant acknowledgment of the results of their personal initiative.

There is no need to determine which system of colonising yields the better results. All that is important is that we should realise that the French *have* a system, and a system which, as they work it, works well. Their methods, like their manners, are the outcome of something profound and genuine in themselves. French colonisation proceeds in a very amicable and conciliatory spirit; it also proceeds with a good deal of method and coherence; and it also proceeds, so far as the settlement of the country is concerned, with an ineradicable deliberation. And all these three characteristics it owes to the strength of the social instinct in the Frenchman.

There are many beautiful things to be seen in and about Algiers. Many things that it is tempting to linger over. Her roses alone, those masses of yellow that cluster on every wall and load every verandah, are worthy of a chapter to themselves. I came back here in late spring, when the place was deserted and the hotels all shut up, and walked among these gardens, the only person in them. The roses were full-blown and falling and the ground was carpeted and paths strewn with their blossoms. Every moment a tuft of petals broke and fell as I walked under the trellised pergolas. Never have I seen decay so lovely. Air and earth were yellow with rose-leaves. It was like walking in an autumn wood of Marshal Niels.

But still, among all the impressions I have of the place, the two that strike me as most characteristic are those belonging to the two hills I spoke of to begin with, one carrying the jumbled, crumbling mass of the old Arab town, the other the orderly gardens and villas of the French suburb. The ideas these hills stand for, of incoherence and method, are the ideas that are fighting it out to-day in North Africa; and, having done our best to realise them, we may travel on now towards the Sahara, where lies the last refuge of the Arab principle and the final test of the French.

CHAPTER III

THE FRENCH OCCUPATION

African scenery, its clearness and regularity—Divisions of Algeria—Line of the French advance—A distracted colonial policy—The anti-colonial party—Indifference of the French people—France makes up her mind—Interest awakened in colonisation—Increase of immigration—Character of Arab warfare—The North African problem—Impossibility of dividing state from state—The pacification of any part of the country involves the pacification of the whole—France forced to advance—The Arab the leading African race—Gives its own character to the politics of the country.

IT seems a constant endeavour of Nature in Africa to work with as few forms and on as simple a plan as possible. In South Africa every one will remember how curiously monotonous was the effect of the vast flats sparsely sprinkled with pointed kopjes, sometimes in groups, sometimes in strings, sometimes isolated, but always of the same shape, always built on the same model, though perhaps now ruined and defaced. The plain and the pyramid are Nature's only two motives in South Africa. On these two notes she strums contentedly for a thousand miles.

In the Nile valley there is the same pre-Raphaelite simplicity of arrangement. There is the single river, the single narrow, flat valley, shut in each side by the long, interminable range of yellow hill. Valley and river here take the place of kopje and plain, but they are insisted on with the same childlike fixity of purpose. Where but in primitive Africa could you imagine a whole country composed of one valley and watered by one river?

Long ago, when Nature first started work, when she first said the words "plain" and "hill" and "valley" and "river," these things, as we see them in Africa still, were the ideas she had in her head. She no longer sees in her own mind now as clearly as she did in those days. She has grown perplexed and divided in her aims. Hills and plains have lost their old exactness and become confused together. Valleys, too, and rivers are but the broken fragments of the original idea. Nature's hand has lost its sureness. It is difficult often to know now what name to put to her designs.

Only in Africa are we able to see how simply and tremendously effective these great fundamental principles of her architecture could be. Their clearness and conscientious precision appeal to the love we all have for what is definite and unmistakable. Their very clearness impresses one with a feeling—quite mistaken, of course—of the extreme antiquity of African scenery. Just as one is accustomed to recognise the earliest forms of archaic art by the rigidity of the drawing and the repetition of a few formulæ in fold and gesture, so here the same characteristics, the same rigidity and precise repetitions, seem to vouch for the same antiquity. These hills and valleys you instinctively feel were the first of their kind. They belong to the early era of a limited and accurate

THE FRENCH OCCUPATION

reiteration, while Nature was still at her pothooks, and before her hand had acquired its subsequent fluent illegibility.

Algeria, though European in many ways, shows to some extent this gift of distinct articulation. The country is divided, east and west, by the Atlas ranges. Between the northernmost range and the sea is a margin, averaging a hundred miles wide, fruitful for the most part, in some places exuberantly so, broken with short spurs of hills running from the main range to the sea. This margin of fertility lying along the coast is called the Tell. South of this lie the High Plateaux. The Atlas mountains, rising in Tunisia, diverge as they travel west in two main ridges, like the opening blades of a pair of scissors, and between and among these main ridges lie wide-bottomed valleys or upland plains, suspended, as it were, like lofty hammocks, between the peaks which rise above them. These uplands are quite distinct in every particular from the rich and flowing Tell. They produce plentiful crops of corn and barley and maize, but they have a desolate and bleak appearance, and with their dull colouring, and stony peaks in the distance, and absence of trees are extremely like the Karroo district in South Africa. The climate, too, is very different to the sunny warmth of the coast-line. The mountains attract cloud and rain, the wind whistles through the rocky gorges and across the desolate flats, and the air is often wet and chill, bitterly so in winter. South of the Atlas, again, there is a still more sudden and startling descent, and we come to the third of the Algerian divisions, namely, the Sahara.

The reader now has the articulation of the country

in his mind—the Tell, the High Plateaux, and the Sahara. The first a fertile coast-line, the second wheat-growing flats hoisted four thousand feet in air by the Atlas peaks, the third an interminable expanse of sand and stone, with which we shall by and by make a closer acquaintance.

And now, as, leaving Algiers, our train drags its low, rolling cloud of dust eastward to Constantine before striking south to penetrate the rocky barrier between shore and Sahara, let us cast a glance backward at the history of French occupation up to the present, in order that we may understand the stage it has reached and the prospect that lies before it. Naturally French progress is from north to south. We follow, therefore, the lines of its advance as we travel towards the desert, only that we cover in hours a distance which it took the French armies as many years to accomplish.

It was a long time before the French took any interest in the development of their new territory in North Africa. Algeria continued for years to be thought and spoken of as if it were at the Antipodes, instead of almost within sight of Marseilles. Its beautiful scenery, its delicious climate, its rich and fertile soil attracted little attention. The invasion of the country had been imposed on France against her own will. It was only when the anachronism of a pirate state, subsisting by the plunder of its neighbours, in the midst of Europe and in the nineteenth century, had become too glaring to be longer tolerated, and when, moreover, it had been made evident that if France did not move in the matter England would, that the French expedition was at

THE FRENCH OCCUPATION 49

last despatched. Once embarked on the enterprise there was no drawing back. The capture, or at least the retention, of Algiers necessitated the conquest of Algeria, since it is absolutely impossible among a people so fierce and warlike as the Arab tribes to hold one portion of the country without holding it all. The attempt to do so has been made again and again, and always with the same results: frontier troubles, armed forays, plunder and murder, a rising of the tribesmen, a massacre, and the invader is forced to resume an advance which should never have been interrupted.

Thus, after a long interval the renewal of colonial expansion was forced upon France in a manner there was no evading. It is curious to remember, in these days of universal land hunger, how reluctantly and by what slow degrees she was induced to appropriate the fertile province lying at her very door, which for centuries had seemed to be crying out for annexation.

The succession of languid campaigns that followed failed to arouse any kind of national interest in the colonial policy of the Government. Indeed, a definite colonial policy did not at that time exist. The presence of enemies induced battle. The Arabs broke themselves by degrees against the military strength of France. But France herself showed no wish to extend and regulate her conquests. Throughout the first half of Louis Philippe's reign the French Chamber was hostile to a definite occupation. The political economists were against it. For long it was uncertain whether the Government would be content with holding one or two of the coast towns, or would seriously undertake the conquest of the country.

An expedient, which was again and again attempted, and which showed the entire misconception under which France laboured as to the part she was called to play in the new territory, was that of governing through native chiefs, and making use of these as instruments of her own authority and influence. Mustapha Ben Omar and others in the beylik of Titeri were thus employed. A more important intermediary was the celebrated Abd-el-Kader, for fifteen years the open enemy or doubtful friend of France. Iusuf and Achmed, in the province of Constantine, were others. Even the Bey of Tunis was called in to act as middleman between the French Government and the native tribes.

The whole structure of Arab society was, however, too loosely put together to admit of being influenced by means like these. It was disorderly in its elements. Stability was lacking not only in the authority of the chiefs to whom France appealed, but in the lives and characters of the people. Indeed, for France to seek stability from them was to require that at their hands which it was her own special business to confer; the need of which was, and is, the main justification for her own presence in North Africa.

Nevertheless this vacillating policy was persisted in for years. In 1834, M. Dupin, procureur-général, in a speech in the Chamber, declared that the whole idea of colonisation was absurd. No one wanted to colonise, there was no territory to bestow on colonists, and no way of safeguarding their future. "The thing to do," he insisted, "was to reduce expenditure to the lowest possible limit, and hasten in every way the moment that would free France from a burden which

THE FRENCH OCCUPATION 51

she could not and would not support much longer." Three years later, M. Thiers, not usually lacking in energy, declared that, " If we could secure a few leagues of land round Oran, Algiers, and Bone, I, for my part, should be satisfied. I am no friend of a general occupation." What was still more remarkable, Marshal Bugeaud, one of the most successful of the French commanders in Algeria, was at this time so opposed to a policy of conquest, and so persuaded that the country would never be worth the blood and money spent on it, that he could not conceal his opinion from the troops he was actually leading. "Unfortunately," wrote a subordinate in 1836, just after the brilliant campaign of Tlemcen, "he professes these opinions all day, to every one, and at the top of his voice, which, though he may not be aware of it, is rather discouraging to the army."

When such were the convictions of the leaders in Parliament and in the field, it was no wonder that the resulting operations should be of a desultory nature. Luckily, perhaps, for the future of French colonisation, the restless excitability of the tribes goaded it perpetually to unwilling efforts. It was not, however, until after repeated experience of Arab unreliability that France, convinced, on the one hand, of the danger of abandoning the country altogether, was convinced, on the other, of the disagreeable necessity of governing it for herself. In 1838 Kolea and Blidah were garrisoned, Medea and Miliana were occupied in 1840, Biskra and Delleys fell in 1844. The Moroccans were defeated in the same year, and three years later, Abd-el-Kader, rebel, deputy-governor, and independent chief, surrendered himself prisoner. In 1852 Laghouat was taken. The expedition against the Khabilis followed in 1856–57, and it was only after the successful issue of this campaign that the conquest of Algeria, north of the desert, could be said to be complete. It had taken twenty-seven years.

Marshal Bugeaud himself defined the cause of the dilatory nature of the French invasion when, in answer to certain critics, he pointed out that the whole enterprise had been undertaken without a definite end in view, and with a total lack of earnestness and conviction. It had been often said that the country [was conquered when it was not conquered at all. He was told that he ought to do with 21,000 men. He asked for 45,000 as a minimum. The French held several towns, but were little the further advanced for that. "But," he added significantly, "when France *makes up her mind* to conquer the country—when she makes up her mind seriously, I mean—she will, no doubt, achieve her object."

Meantime the colonisation of the country partook of the same character as its conquest. During these early years the French Government, so far from encouraging immigration, set itself deliberately to check it. At the end of 1832 an order appeared which provided that, "to prevent a too numerous and plentiful immigration, and to safeguard individuals from destitution in consequence of their having inconsiderately transferred themselves to a new country without possessing any assured means of livelihood, the French Government, besides the measures it has already taken to prevent spontaneous immigration into Algeria, has thought fit to put a stop altogether to ingress into the country until further orders, except for those who

THE FRENCH OCCUPATION 53

can prove that they have ample means of subsistence."

Nor was this a temporary precaution. For thirty years the same opposition was offered. During all this time the Government acts the part of an exceedingly fussy master of ceremonies, who, instead of throwing open the doors and letting the public scramble for their seats, admits them one by one and conducts each one personally to his place. Now and then at long intervals the door was opened for a moment, a required number was admitted, and it was promptly shut again. Five years after the taking of Algiers the number of European colonists of all countries only amounted to 11,221. During the next ten years the number rose to 95,531. After this again the usual disabilities were imposed. No one was allowed admittance who had not employment assured beforehand. When in 1853 the Swiss desired to found a colony at Setif, the French Government stipulated that each member must possess capital to the amount of 3,000 francs. The result was that in the ten years following 1845 the average yearly immigration was reduced to a little over a half of what it had been in the previous ten years. "The salient characteristic of Algerian colonisation," says M. Leroy Beaulieu, "was the systematic, almost constant, opposition of the home Government to any considerable immigration during a period of thirty years." And he adds, "This hostility to the idea of immigration was a settled policy which for years influenced the Government in its conduct of Algerian affairs. A study was made how to limit the number of immigrants, and the task was not a difficult one. New arrivals were required to possess an amount of capital rare for such classes. Simple workmen had to show 400 francs, and people who went out with the idea of investing in land were obliged to own a fortune of 1,500 or even 3,000 francs."

We are not to suppose, however, that during these years the Government was suppressing a movement of any vigour on the part of the people. The task of controlling immigration was, as M. Leroy Beaulieu says, "not a difficult one." It required no exertion to shut the door, and a good deal of persuasion to induce any one to take advantage of its opening. In 1857, 80,000 free passages were granted to colonists, of whom 70,000 promptly returned to France. It is really the indifference on the part of the French people which explains both the vacillation and the fussiness of the Government and the lack of energy in the campaign. Conquest and colonisation alike were waiting for France to "make up her mind" on the Algerian question.

A glance at the census returns shows about when she made it up. Taking periods of five years we find that from 1861 to 1866 the population rose by 890. From 1866 to 1872 (no census was possible in 1871) it rose 7,482. From 1872 to 1876 it rose 26,764, and during the next five years from 1876 to 1881 it rose 39,043, the increase being entirely due to immigration, for the deaths in those days exceeded the births in the colony itself. The remarkable point in these figures is the tide of immigration that set in after 1872, and which has been steadily maintained ever since. The ten years previous to 1872 brought in about 17,000 immigrants into Algeria, the nine years following brought 65,000.

THE FRENCH OCCUPATION 55

It is from about 1872, from the time, that is, when she received a blow, which, so far from prostrating her, seems to have had the effect of stimulating her vitality, that we are to date this renaissance of French colonising. Down to this time the weak trait in her colonisation, its lack of personal initiative, has been the ruling characteristic. The scheme has been backed up by no real interest on the part of the people. But French colonisation has other characteristics besides this weakening, negative one of lack of personal initiative. A people who move *en masse* may be slow to move, but when they do move they move with effect. The strength of the French system consists in its instinct for organisation and method. This from 1872 on is the factor that comes into play. Backed up by the tardily-awakened interest of the nation, it set itself to carve out, rapidly, daringly, and systematically, the French colonial empire as it exists to-day.

There can scarcely be, I imagine, a contrast in history more dramatic than that between France's colonial policy before and after the year of her awakening. The characteristics of the two seem to be irreconcilable. The earlier policy is typical of a people who, if not on the decline, had used up their expansive energy and reached the slack water of their flood; the latter is the policy of a nation still young in enterprise and physical vigour. It is difficult to believe that the Power which in the later period we find everywhere advancing her frontiers with such boldness, whose explorers and pioneers are scattered through the Sahara and the Sudan, whose territories have spread from the Congo in the south, from the Senegal in the west, from Algeria and Tunisia in the north, until they have included almost the whole of this vast protuberance of the north-west in a single colonial empire, can be the same Power which so lately shrank from assuming control over a country almost in sight of her own shores.

A remarkable feature, from the Arab point of view, about all these campaigns and native risings is the violent, sudden, inexplicable bursts of passion that rise and die down and rise again. The war spirit darts hither and thither with a sort of electric agility that takes no account of divisions or frontiers. The contagion of an indefinable excitement seems the only motive. There is no foreseeing its course or duration. Let a chief or a district rise in revolt, and you may have that chief and district only to deal with, or you may have the whole province and neighbouring states as well. Nothing is more difficult to follow than the rapid changes and fluctuations in the Arab resistance. On Monday the country seems settling into peace, on Tuesday it is up in arms from the Gulf of Gabes to the Atlantic Ocean. Such is the case still among the Saharan tribes, whether belonging to the hinterland of Morocco or of Algeria, who, while they acknowledge no law and no sovereign, are capable of sinking personal quarrels to make common cause against a common enemy. The ties of blood and religion, which, under all their distractions, bind the tribes of North Africa together, may at any time unite them in frantic opposition to a European and Christian Power.

It is this fluidity of the North African races that gives its peculiar character to the whole question of the settlement of the country. It makes the question *one;* a problem of which no part is separable from the

THE FRENCH OCCUPATION 57

rest. It lays down the condition, that any Power which engages in the pacification of any part of North-West Africa must be prepared to pacify the whole of it.

It was long before France grasped this fundamental condition of the problem she had tackled. Only when she entered seriously on the question of the settlement of the Sahara, where, of course, this fluidity of the tribes is much more pronounced, and where frontiers have no existence, did the full significance of it begin to dawn upon her. The steps she thereupon took to bring the whole of this enormous territory under her sway have seemed to some people to reveal an altogether excessive thirst for dominion. But an imperious necessity urged her forward; the same necessity which from the moment of her taking Algiers had pushed her step by step along the road of conquest.

No one will rightly understand the North African problem as it exists to-day who fails to realise the primary condition that it is a problem which must be treated as a whole. Arab blood and the Moslem faith are two forces which acknowledge no restraints and no boundaries, and it would be as reasonable to expect a prairie fire in full blast to respect the invisible boundary-line of your property as to suppose that the Arab tribes, in one of the periodical fits of excitement to which they are subject, will pay the slightest regard to treaties or frontiers.

In North Africa it is the Arab race that leads. That race is in a small minority. It probably does not number more than fifteen or twenty per cent. of the native population. Nevertheless it forms the dominant caste. Though the Berbers outnumber the Arabs by three or four to one, and are themselves a fine and hardy mountain people, yet they submitted to receive the Arab language and the Arab religion from their invaders. To this day the natives of Algeria are usually referred to in daily talk or writing as " Arabs." The truth is that the Arab is the driving power in North African politics. Other races may supply the physical energy, but it is the Arab temperament and the Arab religion which supply the nervous energy. It is these which inspire and direct; and more especially it is these which give their character of universality to the questions which agitate North Africa. The Arab is a wanderer. His religion is a call to action. In those two conditions you have the politics of the country.

CHAPTER IV

THE FRENCH IN THE SAHARA

Early exploration of the desert—The French make a beginning—Unlucky ending to many of their expeditions—De Brazza and the Congo—Advance from the south and west—The idea of a united Colonial Empire—The convention of 1890—Monteil's expedition—Fernand Foureau—The Touareg tribes oppose the French advance—Occupation of the desert—Consistency of the French scheme—French rights in North Africa.

THE great African feature that comes into prominence with the sudden awakening of French energy in colonial matters is the Sahara. Hitherto this had been a *terra incognita*. There now appeared a succession of explorers who set about the investigation of the desert in the characteristic French way. The English explore for love of adventure, the Germans for love of abstract science, the French for the attainment of practical ends. From 1780 to 1850 practically all the desert explorers are English. Lucas, Ledyard, Ritchie, Lyon, Wenham, Oudeney, Clapperton are the names we meet with, few of whom returned to tell the tale of their adventures. Following them we come to certain famous Germans, Barth, Rohlfs, and Nachtigal, who carried on the work down to about 1870, and established our knowledge of the Sahara on something approaching a scientific basis. Then at last come the French. Hitherto the only French explorer of note has been Henri Duveyrier, whose great journey dates from 1859. The French occupation was then beginning to confirm its hold. In 1854 the victory of Meggarine, and the submission of Tuggurt and the tribes of the Oued Rir, introduced France to the desert. The work of sinking wells to revive certain of the decaying oases, which was immediately undertaken, and which met with conspicuous success, suggested a wider occupation. It was not, however, till after 1870 that the exploration of the interior began to be systematically carried out, and there commenced a series of attempts to explore the oases of the mid-desert occupied by the dangerous tribes of the Touareg confederation. In 1873-74 Soleillet reached Insalah. In 1874 Dourneaux-Dupérré and Joubert were assassinated near Ghadames, which town was reached by Victor Largeau in 1875. The attempts of Largeau and Louis Say to penetrate southward were frustrated by the Touareg in 1877, and in the following year Erwin von Bary was assassinated by the same tribes. In 1878, the Government having recognised the difficulty of carrying on the work of exploration in the face of the hostile tribes that held the central desert, an armed expedition was organised under the command of the ill-fated Colonel Flatters. It started in 1880, but was far too weak for its purpose, and appears to have been somewhat recklessly led. It was ambushed and cut up by the Touareg, a few natives only escaping to carry the bad news to Algeria. The blow was followed by the massacre of the missionaries, Richard, Morat, and Pouplard; by the

THE FRENCH IN THE SAHARA 61

assassination of Lieutenant Palet in 1886, and of Camille Douls in 1889.

If many of these expeditions had an unfortunate ending, their multiplication in the face of difficulties shows at least the interest which was beginning to concentrate round the North African problem. The annexation of Tunisia in 1881 revealed the progressive nature of the French occupation. A similar spirit was developing along the southern borders of the future colonial empire. The name of Savargnan de Brazza is identified with the creation of the French Congo State. His expedition occupied the years between 1875 and 1878, and between 1879 and 1883. De Brazza was an ardent believer in that system of "pacific penetration" which, though chiefly heard of lately in reference to Morocco, has really been a pretty constant feature of the French occupation, and he undoubtedly employed it with great effect on the tribes of the Congo. Mainly by treaties with the natives he extended the French protectorate from an undetermined coast-line to something like its present dimensions. His labours were rewarded at the Berlin Conference, when the conquests of his urbanity were duly included in the French colonial empire.

In all the hitherto isolated and disconnected colonies of the Gulf of Guinea, Dahomey, the Ivory Coast, French Guinea, and Senegambia, the same leaven was working. The year 1854, which saw the conquest of the Sahara begun in the north, saw the beginning in Senegambia of the governorship of General Faidherbe, commonly known as the founder of the French Sudan. The foundations then laid were extended by Brière de l'Isle, whose treaty of 1881 contained the recognition by the Sultan Ahmadou of the French Protectorate. The treaty in 1887 with the formidable Samory marked a further extension of French influence, and about the same time took place the expedition of Captain Binger from Bammako in the Upper Niger, by Sikasso, and down the Comoe into the Ivory Coast State, an expedition which gave a decisive stimulus to French influence by linking together the hinterlands of Senegambia and the Ivory Coast.

This junction effected, the occupation of the interior was swift and uninterrupted. In was continued by Archinard, Combes, Audéoud, Bonnier, Soffres, Destenave, Voulet, and other French soldiers, who, in a series of expeditions, swept the French frontiers northwards and eastwards till they occupied the whole bend of the Niger, and flowed round the English territory of Sokoto, to join, at Lake Tchad, with the Congo advancing from the south.

These events show what a spirit of movement and enterprise was animating all the French colonies from 1870 onwards. From all sides they were pushing forward a simultaneous advance; and though this advance was begun probably in the interest of each individual colony, it ended by and by in making them aware of each other's purpose and presence, and suggesting the idea of a united empire.

In 1890 the decisive event took place which showed that the thought of consolidation had flashed on the French mind. In that year the convention was signed between France and England which recognised France's claim to the whole of the Sahara between a line drawn from Say to Lake Tchad on the south, and Algeria and Tunisia on the north. The delimitations of frontiers

THE FRENCH IN THE SAHARA 63

were indefinite in this treaty, however, and they were not finally specified until the convention of 1899. In the interval of nine years France carried on her investigations with increased energy. To these years belong the greatest names among the explorers, Foureau and Monteil, besides a host of lesser ones. The idea of the Sahara had "caught on" in France, and was recognised as the proper field for patriotic enterprise, just as the south of Africa was so recognised by England.

Monteil was a captain of Marines. Two campaigns in Senegal had seasoned him to the African climate and instructed him in the character of African races. In scientific knowledge he was well equipped for the undertaking he meditated. He came to Paris and interviewed an under secretary, and was asked to make out an estimate. He required £3,500 to cover all expenses, ten rifles, and 3,000 cartridges. The under secretary accepted the offer with alacrity. If the worst came to the worst and the expedition were wiped out, as it probably would be, the loss of three or four thousand pounds and a captain of Marines was unlikely to make much stir in the world. Monteil was given *carte blanche* to conduct his own expedition in his own way, and decided to start from Senegal on the west instead of from the north. He left St. Louis with a little party of twelve men, soon to be reduced to eight, on October 9, 1890, and in the following December passed through the last French outpost, and plunged into the silence of the African Sudan. Months passed bringing no news of him to the outside world. When over a year had elapsed the destruction of the frail caravan was looked upon as certain, and people began to talk of Monteil in the past tense.

Then suddenly, in May, 1892, the black curtain that had shut him out lifted a little. Letters came to hand reporting the expedition up to Kano. Kano is in Sokoto, 300 miles west of Lake Tchad. The letters had come right across the great desert to Tripoli. The news was old, but it had the effect of stimulating French interest in the explorers. While Monteil had been discovering Africa, France, as M. de Vogüé says, had been discovering Monteil. The daring of the adventure, the long suspense, the word of news breaking the silence, struck the imagination of a people always alive to a dramatic situation. Six months later a small and very weary caravan emerged from the Sahara and shaped its course for Tripoli, which it reached on December 10, 1892. In the two years and two months since he had set out, Monteil had covered a distance of 5,000 miles. He had entered the desert quite unknown; he emerged from it the hero of the hour. The bewildered traveller was bombarded with congratulatory letters and telegrams from friends, admirers, and scientific societies. He laid the fruits of his journey, in the shape of much valuable information concerning the southern borderland between the desert and the Sudan, and the interior of the Sahara, before the French authorities, and immediately returned to Africa on a new mission. One practical result of his observations was the inclusion of Zinder, the important frontier town on the trans-Saharan caravan route, in the French sphere of influence.

It would take a volume to deal with all the explorations which have since been organised. One name, however, stands out above all competitors, not only as that of the man who will probably rank in

THE FRENCH IN THE SAHARA 65

history as the greatest of Saharan explorers, but as one who, from his breadth of view and grasp of all that the Sahara meant in the French scheme of colonisation, was less the instrument than the guide and inspiration of his country's policy.

Fernand Foureau was born in 1850, and began his African explorations at the age of twenty-seven. After several preliminary expeditions in the Northern Sahara, he turned his attention to what had come to be recognised as the chief danger of the desert and the chief obstacle to a complete exploration. The Touareg tribes of the Central Sahara, occupying positions from Ghadames and Ghat in the east to the great oases of Insalah and Twat on the west, formed a cordon across the desert south of Algeria, completely masking the southern frontiers of the colony. The oases and hills which formed their headquarters fed a cloud of wandering marauders who were scattered over the country wherever a scanty herbage offered sustenance for their goats and camels, or a caravan route promised the chance of blackmail or pillage.

In 1890 Foureau began a series of expeditions, the object of which was to explore the Touareg country, and from thence the route south by Air to Zinder and the Sudan, a route never yet traversed by a European in its entirety. Alone, except for a handful of natives, protected only by his own intimate knowledge of the Arab character and country, he made, between 1890 and 1899, no fewer than seven expeditions into a region which had proved a veritable death-trap to French explorers. He made many valuable discoveries, and brought home a fund of information on the country lying between the Algerian desert and the Touareg settlements; nevertheless, from each of these journeys he returned a disappointed man, in that the inveterate suspicion and hostility of the tribes had each time defeated his object of penetrating to the south.

Two conclusions, however, had by this time defined themselves clearly in his mind. The first was, that the Insalah position, standing midway between French Algeria and the French Sudan, was the key of the Sahara. And the second was, that the opposition of the Touareg would never be overcome by anything but armed force. For years he had tried to pick the lock; now he was resolved to force it. "You will never traverse the Touareg country," he writes in one of his reports, "with any kind of security except by depending on force and by establishing all along the route well-manned positions, the garrisons of which will police the road throughout. This you will have to do if you wish to open up communications between the Sudan and Algeria."

As for the Touareg themselves, Foureau, who certainly knew them far better than any living European, had little sympathy to spare for them. "Their life," he writes, "is a constant succession of ghazis (pillaging forays). Every tribe of them, except the Ifoghas, takes part in the business, which means for them a livelihood without the trouble of working. The consequence is, that the Sahara is in a constant state of turmoil and insecurity; murders, theft, pillage, and ambushes are of everyday occurrence. Not a quiet month ever passes in the desert, and it is quite certain that this state of things must stop all intercourse and commerce, as well as all hope of exploring the

THE FRENCH IN THE SAHARA 67

country." He then urges that France should undertake the work of pacification, and points out that the more peaceable tribes are agreed that there can be no settlement of the Saharan question until France makes up her mind to police the country.

Foureau's advice had great weight. Already the advanced positions of the Algerian army were pressing southward along the whole line of the desert. Up to 1890, El Oued, Tuggurt, Ouargla, Ghardaia, and Ain Sefra had been the outposts. In the years 1891 and 1892, a general move forward had been made of about 100 or 150 miles. El Golea was occupied in strength. Hassi Inifel and Fort MacMahon were garrisoned. At the same time a similar advance was taking place in the south. Between 1887 and 1890 French gunboats were exploring the Niger. In 1893 Segu and Massina were occupied by Colonel Archinard, and in 1895 Timbuktu, the great exchange and mart betwixt the Sahara and the Sudan, fell into the hands of France.

So between 1890 and 1900 it was coming to be realised that the Sahara might be made a means of communication rather than division. Distant colonies were beckoning to each other across the enormous gulf. Moreover it was found that the desert itself was not quite the utter void it had been supposed. Oases, in some parts, dotted its surface, and caravan routes, which in old days had carried a rich trade between the Sudan and the northern states, crossed it from north to south. Now trade had fallen off; caravans had to face the risk of being plundered and pillaged in the desert; the great market-towns on the borders of the Sahara which had collected the produce of the

Sudan and despatched it northward, or received and distributed the goods arriving from the north—these teeming cities had now sunk into squalid and miserable villages. In the desert itself the oases were falling into decay. The working inhabitants were being enslaved by the robber tribes. The wells were "dying," the sand was encroaching, security for life or property did not exist. The source of the mischief was the Touareg tribes. It was they who watched the routes, plundered caravans, murdered pioneers, and preyed on the trans-Saharan trade as the Algerian fleets had preyed on the Mediterranean merchantmen. And the chief strongholds of the great robber confederation were the mid-desert oases and groups of hills lying, like clusters of pirate-infested islands, off the distant coasts of Algeria.

The truth of the great explorer's definition of these Touareg strongholds as *la clef de nôtre occupation* had now become evident. The French Government yielded to his wishes, and in 1898 Foureau was accompanied on his eighth journey by a force of 310 men and two guns under Commandant Lamy.

The description of the hardships, sufferings, fights, the death of Lamy, and final triumph of the expedition must be sought in Foureau's own book. But the final stage in the long voyage is in a special degree noteworthy. By an extraordinary coincidence, or a more extraordinary feat of organisation, three expeditions, which had set out many months before from the three main bases and starting-points of the new colonial empire, all met in the neighbourhood of Lake Tchad, These had come from Algeria, from the Congo State, and from Senegal, and their final meeting in this remote

THE FRENCH IN THE SAHARA 69

region was naturally hailed as symbolical of the consolidation of French interests in North Africa, to which the successful passage of the Sahara by Foureau had put the finishing touch.

Lake Tchad is the nucleus to which all the French spheres of influence converge, and the movement of these three expeditions towards this spot and final junction there epitomises the whole scheme of French colonisation, and sums up for us its method and instinct for organisation. Every move in France's policy during the last fifteen or twenty years has been opportune. Every delimitation of a frontier has shown an accurate appreciation of the value of the territory at stake. The central Government has been informed by a body of pioneers, not only energetic and enterprising, but perfectly organised and disciplined, and all working together towards a common end. The breadth of handling, as an artist would call it, resulting from such a system is very remarkable. Here are no petty or contradictory aims; no moving forward and turning back again; no energy in one place and stagnation in another. The advance is general everywhere. The same thought rules north and west and south. The same object animates the explorer in the desert and the Government that backs him up. What has the result been? If we glance at a map of about 1880 we find merely a few coloured spots round the coast of North-West Africa to register the extent of European occupation. There is no marked predominance of one over the others, and nothing to indicate which of them is destined to spread and extend over the interior. But if we turn to a map of twenty years later what do we find? No great changes have taken place save in respect of one of the colours. This, from every point along the coast-line at which it was established, has extended inland until the advancing currents, meeting and mingling, have overflowed practically the whole of the north-west. It is the moment of their meeting that the conjunction of the three expeditions at Lake Tchad typifies; and it is in every way appropriate that the final triumph should have taken place under the personal auspices of the man who had so much to do with insuring it. The French occupation of the great central oases round Insalah which formed the Touareg stronghold, and on the capture of which Foureau had so strongly insisted, was not long deferred. The Flamand mission partially occupied the position in 1899, and was shortly followed by several columns which, after some sharp fighting, finally possessed themselves of these centres of anarchy,

Such in outline is the French "scheme"; and I have dwelt upon it with some care, because it seems to me impossible to take the right kind of interest in any one colony, or bit of a colony, in French North Africa, unless the general scheme of Empire in which that bit plays its part is first grasped. It is impossible to understand France's action in the Sahara unless the Sahara is considered in its relation to this scheme; and it is impossible to understand her attitude with regard to Morocco unless Morocco, also, is so considered. In the realisation of the French idea of an African Colonial Empire, the control of Morocco is, indeed, an essential factor. With Morocco independent, the idea becomes impracticable. To attempt the pacification of the Sahara and the re-establishment of the old trade routes, with the hinterland of Morocco offering a secure refuge

THE FRENCH IN THE SAHARA 71

and recruiting-ground for all the lawless and unruly elements of desert life, would be attempting a task foredoomed to failure. It is in its threat of constant interference with their own widely-laid plans for the settlement and development of all these regions that the French find their justification for the control of Morocco. The existence of a scheme such as theirs, a scheme which has proved its stability, and its capacity for dealing with the problems involved, confers certain rights and claims a certain recognition. We can all remember how keenly this was felt to be the case when the French attempted, in their occupation of Fashoda, an interference with a scheme of our own. It was our scheme that gave us our right in the Nile Valley. Similarly it is the French scheme that gives them their right in Morocco. There have been writers, and even some liberal critics of the Government, who have argued that in the agreement which led to the *entente* we should have held out for more advantageous terms. I cannot think that this view does justice to the French claims. Our agreement to French control in Morocco, though we may ask and receive something for it, as is the way of diplomacy, was in the main the frank recognition of a title which France, by many years of hard work and a sustained and coherent policy, had already made good.[1]

[1] See Appendix, Note B.

CHAPTER V

BISKRA

A desert port—The Atlas mountains—"The door of the desert" —El Kantara—Importance of Biskra—French officers— Part played by the army—The oasis—Irrigation—Arab isolation—His individual charm—His sentimentality—Arab manners—His chivalrous impulses—Arab horse-dealers— We fit out our caravan—What to take and what to leave behind—We leave Biskra.

BISKRA leaves on one the impression of a little town moored off shore by its rope-end of railway and floating by the margin of the desert. Cut the rope, and it might, you would think, float away upon the yellow waves of sand. North of it, but at no great distance, the cliffs of the Aurès lift themselves into the air. They are a branch of the great Atlas formation which bounds the desert on the north. Seen from the Sahara, itself about on the sea-level here, you get the full effect of their 7,000 feet of elevation. Built up of pale limestone, and destitute, apparently, of any trace of vegetation, they remind one of the battlements of some great border fortress guarding the marches of the north. The desert sand shifts and plays below, and beats in dry, scanty waves against their feet, and creeps in to every interstice and creek, with the soft fluidity

BISKRA

and patience of water lapping among cliffs; it meets here the effectual barrier to its advance.

I have seen these cliffs sometimes at evening, riding back from the palm-groves round Biskra, range shadowed by range, one in the light of the setting sun the colour of pale primroses, and the next to it, in shade, the colour of dark purple clematis. There is one giant of a hill—

> "The last that parleys with the setting sun,"

which the Arabs, from the pinky hue that rests upon it, call Tebel Hammar Kreddou, or the pink-cheeked mountain.

If you imagine yourself to be standing, sentinel-like, on the summit of the mountain wall, you would have a large bit of the Northern Sahara mapped out at your feet. Almost straight beneath you Biskra lies among its oases. The thickets of palm are fed by the Oued Biskra, itself collected from many lonely hillsides and gorges of the Atlas, to be poured forth here, a quite considerable stream, into the thirsty desert.

Besides the large groves round Biskra there are other lesser patches of green, diminishing to a speck or two in the southern distance, marking the places where wells have been sunk and a spring of life-giving water set flowing, and showing up in startling relief on the pale and sandy surface of the desert. South, east, and west the Sahara stretches to the distant horizon, apparently perfectly flat from this elevation, but broken really by stony ridges and plateaux, and more or less undulating. The transition from mountain scenery to plain is startling in its abruptness, and suggests the constantly-recurring idea of cliffs overlooking the sea.

This, according to some geologists, is what these cliffs once actually did. It has been suggested that Morocco, Algeria, and Tunisia, compacted as they are into a mountain system of their own, were once cut off by an ocean from the main continent, and formed a large peninsula attached to Europe by the isthmus of Gibraltar. The pleasing plausibility of the theory, though Schreiner discountenances it, is obvious. The three states together form a distinct excrescence in an otherwise monotonous coast-line, having something the effect of a small forage cap stuck on the huge bald head of Africa. This projection belongs in many ways more to the European than the African system. It is European in aspect, in its bold and broken variety of hills and valleys; it is European in its fertility, in its olive groves and vineyards, its chestnut and pine forests, and uplands waving with wheat; and it is European in climate, in the moderation of its heat and the comparative plenteousness of its rainfall. The towering precipice of the great Atlas cuts it off from the south, on which it seems to turn its back, while it faces in more gradual descent the Mediterranean and the company of northern nations of which it feels itself to be one.

Only when you have passed the Atlas, when the built house gives place to the camel-skin tent, the pines and olives to occasional palm-tufts, mountains and valleys to the naked plains of sand, and the settled population to wandering desert tribesmen, do you really feel yourself in Africa.

The transition, when it comes, is dramatic in its suddenness. The glare of the Sahara as, travelling south, you emerge out of the mountain passes, strikes you like the glare of some great furnace-mouth suddenly thrown open before you. For many hours the journey has been through a bewildering array of cliffs and peaks, gaunt and white, much like what the Alps might be if the Alps can be imagined picked of all flesh and reduced to a bare skeleton of rock. Our train has panted and puffed and bored its way through range after range, only to be confronted, on emerging from each, by another still more formidable in its wan and lifeless serenity. We have wakened echoes with our impudent whistle that seemed as if they had lain dormant since these cliffs were built. I had felt half amused, half abashed, at the contrast between this fussy child's toy of a train of ours, with its slapdash, up-to-date ways, and the imperturbable giants of hills whose sleep of ages we disturbed.

Through these precipices and defiles and turrets, wet with clinging mist, our train glides down quietly on its last descent. Now we are in a narrow gorge with white cliffs towering left and right and the white waters of the El Fedala tossing at the bottom. The presence of the Sahara is unguessed. We have had no hint of it. At the end of the gorge the cliff makes a turn to the right and bars the way. With its usual *savoir faire* the train dashes into a tunnel. An instant's darkness and you are shot out into the Sahara on the far side. You look back. There is the cliff like a prison wall, with the door you left it by. Foum es Sahara, the Door of the Desert, the Arabs call this gorge with their wonderful knack for hitting on the right name.

The exit is made the more lovely by the little oasis of El Kantara, whose palms await with impatience the stream of water we have just been following. Nothing can be imagined more exquisite than this thicket of dark-green feathery heads, in contrast with the rugged scenery we have just emerged from. They nestle in the most confiding manner under the very brow of the precipice. Some of the more adventurous even explore the beginnings of the defile, and enter for a few steps, like inquisitive children, into the, to them, forbidden precincts of the mountains.

Forty miles more and a few minor descents land us in Biskra. It is an important place, strategically and fashionably; a mixture, you might call it, of Brighton and Aldershot. It represents France's grip on the Northern Sahara, and is a place of holiday resort for tasters of desert air. The town is strongly garrisoned, and strengthened further by the great fort of St. Germain's. France's hold on the desert is tolerably secure nowadays, unless there should come one of those general conflagrations not altogether unknown to these fiery regions. Her positions and outposts extend in a far-flung net across the Sahara, and feel for foothold in the few oases that exist, to get in touch with the outposts of her colonies in the south. Nevertheless, of all this vast system, Biskra, the terminus of the railway, which feeds and supplies it, and links it to France and the outer world, is one of the main bases. The Western Railway, starting from Oran and ending, for the present, at Figuig, is another. The great Saharan net is pinned down and held along the north at Gabes, Biskra, Tuggurt, and Ain Sefra, and the outlying forts that extend to and include the central oases.

Besides this Biskra is a health resort of some fashion.

EL KANTARA.

BISKRA

The hot, pure, exhilarating desert air is an attraction in itself, and Biskra is the most accessible place to which people can resort for a taste of it. They take the air at Biskra as at watering-places they take the waters. It is a cure for most ills. Our little train brings its daily loads of passengers and dumps them down by the edge of the desert, and scuttles back for more. There are samples from all nations, but the predominating element is, of course, French.

Confronted with this great colonising problem of theirs, of which your first glimpse of the Sahara just hints the magnitude, I find myself scrutinising the French folk with a new interest and curiosity, wondering what they will make of their new country, and whether they are the sort of people to turn its opportunities to account. There is no doubt of their pleasure in their new possessions. Their glee at the sight of palms and sand and Arabs, their exclamations and hand-clapping, remind one of a child opening a new box of toys. It is a way so different from ours, and one has got so much to associate toughness and perseverance with a certain reserve, that the doubt at first suggests itself if these loquacious and vivacious creatures have the requisite gifts of character. Similarly, too, the French officer, with his dapper ways, carefully-trimmed moustache and finger-nails, affection for his dinner, and attentiveness to women, seems, it may be, at a first glance, scarcely the ideal man for frontier service.

And yet, curiously enough, it is just in this frontier life that these officers have most distinguished themselves. Whatever criticism the civil government may now and then come in for, there exists only one opinion as to the work done by the army. It has been used not only for fighting purposes, but for preliminary exploration and subsequent settlement. Many dapper gentlemen like these, so eager over trifles, so keen about soups and salads, have met their death unflinchingly in the great void to the south, questioning the desert's secrets and mapping out yard by yard the path where the flag would follow.

After the exploration the fighting. There are few more picturesque sights than a column of native police met in the desert, slinging along silently on their soft-footed camels; and few more rousing campaigning tales than the episodes of their mid-desert fights. Perhaps some day those dramatic incidents, those lonely reconnoitrings, those struggles round the ksours and in the narrow lanes between the mud huts of the village, the silent gathering of vengeful tribesmen, the night attack, the rocket calling to the companion squadron, the long straight rush to the rescue, the sandhills sparkling with rifle fire—perhaps incidents like these will some day be made real to us. But if they are, I suspect we shall owe the debt to fiction rather than history, and that a Pierre Loti will come nearer the truth about desert warfare than a Leroy Beaulieu.

The Saharan Spahis, Méharistes, or camel-riders, as they are called, have been recruited themselves from the desert tribes, having been at one time or other in arms against the enemy whom they afterwards joined. Their readiness to fight on either side has been but one of many indications of the general state of faction and chaos prevailing among the Saharan tribes, with whom licence has come to usurp the meaning of liberty.

BISKRA

Their fighting capacity, however, seems undoubted: "Amateurs friands de la poudre et de la lutte," one officer describes them. He praises their courage, endurance, and marvellous acuteness as scouts and guides. The capacity of this formidable cavalry has been put to its full use by French officers. The Arab and Berber tribes of the interior can still be dangerous enemies, and the struggles that have taken place among their strongholds in the central Sahara have been both frequent and fierce.

And after the fighting has come the settlement. Territory as it is subdued is first administered by military rule, and when finally pacified is taken over by the civil government. Thus for a while each extension of territory is governed and administered by the army which first reconnoitred and afterwards conquered it. Roads, bridges, irrigation works, the building of barrages, and the sinking of wells are among the active labours of the French army.

The importance and extent of the regions under its control are, however, daily declining. Since 1871 the government of the colony has been nominally a civil government. Since 1879 its chief has been a civilian. Nevertheless, the names of some of its earlier military Governors, of men like Bugeaud, Pélissier, Gueydon, Chanzy, are closely bound up with the history of the development of the country. The army's new sphere of influence is limited now to the outlying districts of the Sahara. In the southern colonies, too, the civil power is extending its dominion, and the military retiring inland to the hinterlands of the unpacified interior. This is, of course, a quite logical process, and it is only reasonable that each district should receive civil government as soon as it is ready for it. In fitting it, however, to receive civil government the army has played a great part, and in the triple work it has carried out of exploring, conquering, and administering, it has shown itself possessed of a flexibility and tact which makes it a first-rate colonising instrument.

Realising these various and laborious works accomplished, you are aware under the gesticulatory French manner of a tenacity of purpose and strength of character greater, perhaps, than you had suspected.

Queen of the Ziban, chief among the oases of the Zab district, is the proud title that Biskra bears. Paths lead into the depths of the oasis; those lovely paths strewn with fern-shaped shadows from the arching palm-leaves above. Silent Arabs pass up and down, and vistas open between the groves of green waving corn and clusters of native huts. Here and there round the outer verge groups of Bedouins sit among their low black tents, who have put in from the outer desert into this port of refuge to refit themselves for another voyage.

The oasis itself stretches for several miles. You can lose yourself in it for the day. Walking among these palms I used to fancy myself back in the low country of Ceylon. The fields of corn and barley, knee-high, green and waving, stretch in and out among the plantations exactly as the Ceylon paddy fields do; here, spreading into a smooth expanse of green, there narrowing to slender straits and estuaries between palm-covered islands; the pale green ground, level as a lake, fitting itself in bays and creeks to the darker edges of the palm-groves; the palms themselves crowding

BISKRA

in one place into a great throng of dusky, starry heads; in another stretching out in long array; or standing in detached clumps, a dozen or two together, with the emerald sea flowing round them and cutting them off from their fellows.

How many scenes can I not call to mind round about Kalutara exactly like this! The huts of dry wood beneath the slanting stems, the little brown children, naked or almost, playing in the dust, the limp, dejected dog that slinks growling out of sight at your approach, the women and girls carrying babies tied to their backs in linen garments, all combine to reproduce the idea of a Cingalese village.

In the same way, too, the water that nourishes these fields and groves is led, as through Ceylon rice-fields, by a network of tiny canals, some only a few inches broad, from patch to patch and tree to tree. The system of irrigation is quite a scientific achievement. The water, except a certain amount drawn from wells, all comes from a single stream, the same that has already begotten the El Kantara oasis, but now re-christened, after the manner of the Arabs, whose rivers never carry the same name any great distance, the Oued Biskra. Its waters are carefully distributed first in larger brooks, and then in threadlike channels. As each corn-patch and every separate palm-tree has to be watered, and, moreover, must receive its allotted amount, neither more nor less, at prescribed intervals, it will be seen that the distribution of the current involves a good deal of care and management and a certain amount of engineering skill. The tracing of veins on a leaf, springing from the mid-rib and ending in the maze of tiny veins no larger than the meshes of a spider's web that intersect the whole surface, gives an excellent idea of the irrigation of an oasis.

These twilit haunts, with their grave suggestion of a half-melancholy Orientalism, have now strange visitors. Gays groups of French ladies explore them with delight. There is always something quaint and incongruous in the meeting of East and West. Madame's skirt as she trails it in the soft dust, the veils and curls that envelop her head, the children in their high-heeled boots pirouetting in front, have a whimsical effect under these palms. They bring with them an odd, not unpleasant whiff of a life that here seems so remote and unreal, the far-off, tinkling life of boulevard and Parisian *café*.

More whimsical still, the occasional long-drawn "saay" of the American is heard in the grove, cutting the air as the cry of a jay cuts the silence of English summer woods. When East meets West it is usually the West that is at a disadvantage. But the American is an exception. From the vantage-ground of a brand-new civilisation he surveys the Orient with an imperturbability equal to its own.

Less complex and varied than Europeans, more primitive and of one piece, it is, no doubt, a comparatively easy business to get an insight into Arab character. What I was just now trying to prove from the Arab's history—that he has no coherence, no instinct for thinking and acting collectively—is exactly what you feel when you come face to face with him. The Englishman, the Frenchman, the American is sustained by the consciousness of a national civilisation. The weight of his race is behind him and you feel it in all he does and says. Whatever he may be in himself, he can say "We." The Arab can only say "I." He

BISKRA

is lonely, a solitary and fierce figure. And in his mien and manner, his composure and reserve, his instinctive haughtiness, his wariness and alertness, the isolation of the man speaks.

It is the clue to his temperament. Directly or indirectly most travellers have been struck by it. Most travellers bear witness to the strange contrast between the personal nobleness of the man and the collective failure of the race. I was turning over the pages lately of a book by Mr. Pruen, who was, some years ago now, attached to one of the mission stations of Central Africa. Engaged though he was in a perpetual controversy with the Arab slavers who carried off whole batches of his most promising converts at a time, he cannot help dwelling every now and then on their personal gifts of courage and courtesy. They were the terror of the country. No fixed and settled life was possible in their neighbourhood. Their visits were marked by ruin, and their paths could be traced by skeletons. We should expect one who had seen the burning villages, and watched the terrible march to the coast, to be unreservedly indignant against the authors of such mischief. But Mr. Pruen knows the Arab from the other point of view too. He knows him as an acquaintance and friend, and has had personal dealings with him; and the consequence is he is never able to proceed far with his denunciation without some particular recollection cropping up, and quite altering the tenour of his discourse. We start upon a tale of wholesale devastation to find ourselves in the next paragraph presented with some incident in which the high breeding and sense of honour of these human panthers is strikingly manifested. A pest he is, and a scourge, and a blight upon the country; but then, he is such a gentleman!

Part of what we do belongs to Society, part to ourselves. Society's share is governed by principle, our own share by sentiment and feeling. The Arab knows nothing of principle; he would not, I believe, admit as an abstract proposition that it is wrong to steal. It depends. It may be wrong to steal from you, yet not wrong to steal from another man; or it may be wrong to steal from you now and here, yet not wrong to do so under other circumstances. Not principle, but sentiment and feeling are what govern Arab conduct. In all matters of sentiment his instinct is sure. If you can appeal to him on any ground of hospitality or generosity; if you can touch his emotion in any way; if you can say that you trust him because your father knew his father, or because your child and his have the same coloured eyes, you have a hold on him. But it is always the personal claim, no abstract rule, which he recognises. Establish such a claim, visit him as a friend, break bread with him, claim the hospitality of his tent, and you may rely implicitly on the personal sentiment you have touched. Trust, on the other hand, to precept and law, and, as the Yankees say, you will "get left."

All this is terribly anti-social, but it has its charm. Their habit of judging by sentiment invests all intercourse with Arabs with an added interest and significance. Seeing how entirely your future relations with each other hang on the issue, it is natural that the Arab should enter on the acquaintanceship with all possible dignity and deliberation, and should express in his countenance and bearing his sense of the importance of the occasion. Under such circumstances the question of *manners* becomes a matter of the first moment. So accustomed is the Arab to study every tone and lineament for the faintest indication of a meaning, and so accustomed is he to convey his own sentiments by the same subtle means, that manner with him becomes charged with expression. He is an artist in manners. It is the one thing he is an artist in. The gravity of his bearing throws into relief each inflection of voice or look, just as a smooth background sets off the artist's touch. A stranger who might happen to be present at any meeting between Arabs would be struck first by their gravity and composure, and if he were a dull observer would note nothing beyond it. If he were acute, however, he would almost instantly perceive that the air was electric, and that currents of meaning were darting to and fro expressed in a language of manners which owed their significance to their imperturbability. The best description of the Arab manner I have come across is M. Clamageran's, who has defined it as "l'art de rendre des sentiments délicats par des moyens très simple," a sentence which it would be hard to beat, perhaps, as a definition of artistic expressiveness of any kind.

And then, too, people who judge thus, in this personal direct way, are saved from that terrible old mistake of estimating a man by his belongings and accessories. It used to be the boast of Arab poetry in its great days that it "never praised a man except for what was in him," and although that level was certainly not maintained by later poets, yet the habit of judging directly and without regard to surroundings has always been an instinct of the race. All those evidences of worldly prosperity and success, which turn the heart of the Anglo-Saxon to water, leave the Arab quite unmoved. Not that he does not value splendour, especially splendour in arms and horses: on the contrary, he values it highly. But he values it only as a setting. The kind of character he admires, masterful and intrepid, will naturally possess it. His own strong hand will have conquered it. Still, it is a consequence, not a cause. He is splendid because he is a fine fellow. He is not a fine fellow because he is splendid. In a word, the Arabs, like all Mohammedans, are free from the least taint of snobbishness.

There is a fascination in such a type. Memory brings me back man after man possessed of all the charm that Mr. Pruen felt so keenly and M. Clamageran so happily defined. It brings me back a certain sheyk, who was once my travelling companion on the Upper Nile—a tall, lean, keen-faced man, of a complexion almost black, with a glitter on it like the sun polish on desert stones, who walked among the fellaheen on the crowded deck like a chief among his slaves. With him I shared—for I was a steerage passenger myself in those days—the same narrow corner of the deck. He was strict in his religious duties, and at the appointed hours would spread his mat on the deck, and, turning in the supposed direction of Mecca, would kneel and rise and kneel again, bowing with his forehead to the ground in the imposing attitudes of Moslem prayer. Quick at detecting the least sign of consideration or respect, if we stopped talking or moved to make room, he would treasure up the courtesy, and, when his prayers were over, turn and acknowledge it with a grave gesture, and a smile that seemed no conventional

BISKRA

grimace, but expressed the intention of a deliberate friendliness. How can one help, with such recollections to look back to, sympathising to the full with Mr. Pruen's secret liking for the Arabs?

Our plan at Biskra was to conceal the purpose of our journey altogether, and without proclaiming our need of horses, which of course would have the effect of doubling the price of them, by an adroit question here and there and the exercise of a little patience and a little tact, to explore without alarming the market.

I smile now when I think of our innocent cunning. Before a word had been spoken, or a question asked, it was round the town that two rich young Englishmen were looking out for horses. Before ever we set foot in the bazaars our business was known to every soul in them as clearly as if we had placarded the walls with it. How and by what means acquired Heaven only knows, but news of us had somehow been diffused over the place, carried on the electric atmosphere, like the clang of a gong echoing east and west. Men looked up and recognised us.

Thenceforward we lived in a whirl. We could not set foot in the street but instantly parties of Arab horse-dealers would swoop upon us out of passages where they had been lying in ambush, or from behind clumps of palms, dragging their lean quadrupeds on strings behind them. We passed along the street like figures in Greek friezes, leading long processions of sacrificial victims. It was in vain we feigned indifference, turned away bored, chaffed them, protested we were at our journey's end. By some mystic instinct, from the instant we set foot among them they had scented a prey.

Orientals have this power of divination. It is their gift and must be reckoned with. It admits of no argument. The clumsy protests of the European are to them like the transparent acting of a child. They ignore it; unconsciously, with a faith in their own insight which is almost terrible, they address themselves to the knowledge of your real intentions which you hold in common. You feel the rebuke. To have your declaration that you are going back to Algiers by train to-morrow met by the quiet assurance that your interlocutor's brother has a pony to sell, well used to desert travel, is to feel your own nothingness. Arabs, like women, deal in intuition as common currency. We had of course, in the long run, to accept the corner in horses as a *fait accompli* and buy at sellers' prices.

But it was when we had acknowledged our intention and set to work dealing that the fun began. Biskra is dusty even for an Algerian town, and during the time of our stay there a yellowish pall hung above the place continually, raised by hoofs of galloping horses. An Arab's notion of showing off his horse is to charge down the street past you as hard as he can lay legs to the ground, uttering short shrieks and brandishing a long thin rifle over his head. Wherever we went we were pursued by these thundering cavaliers. Down they would charge, their dark features convulsed with excitement, their white burnouses blown out in the wind behind, and go whirling down the road in a cloud of dust and *débris*. It was an appeal to our imagination, designed to fire us with the idea of their steed as of something fleet and strong and terrible. Their contempt when we set about the cold-blooded process of prising open mouths and pinching legs was unutter-

BISKRA

able. What a lack of poetic instinct was here! What base-born giaours we must be to entertain a low curiosity about Mazeppa's legs and teeth! Had we the spirit of a louse we should leap upon his back, cast our purse at his owner's feet, and speed forth incontinently into the boundless desert. Indeed, as Mazeppa was usually a broken-down cripple, or a lanky, weedy foal, a cloud of dust often set him off to the best advantage.

A desert journey is the one of all others on which it is well to be loaded with no superfluities. Murray, I see, has the advice that you should take with you as much as may be portable of the paraphernalia of civilisation, including bedding, wine, provisions, and a carriage. Before following that advice it is worth reminding oneself that there is no surer sign of a simpleton in travel than is shown in the effort to carry about into other countries the things belonging to his own. The necessaries of life in one place are its lumber in another. The food, dress, customs, and habits of any particular country and climate are the *necessaries* of life in that place. You will not improve on them. On the contrary, the closer you adapt yourself to them the closer you draw to the genius and spirit of the country.

I can imagine no more pitiful spectacle than the sight of a European equipped as Murray advises and lugging beds and wine about the Sahara with him. Such a man has no right to be travelling at all. As long as these things represent the necessaries of life to him, let him stay in the life in which they are necessary. It is argued, "If I like to have these things, and think them worth the expense, why should

I not take them? I like my comforts, I choose to pay a heavy price for them, and there the matter ends." But that is exactly where it does not end. The cumbrousness and expense of these luxuries is their least evil. The real evil of them is that they obstruct observation by hampering you with a whole set of ideas which are nothing to the purpose. They are irrelevant, and that is bad; but they make their owner irrelevant too, and that is worse. It is next door to impossible to really enter into the life of any new country while one carries about with one the old symbols of one's own previous existence.

The right preparation for desert life consists not in what you take with you, but in what you leave behind. The desert stands for emancipation. It gives you the chance of laying aside for a little while all the accumulated trappings of an elaborate civilisation. The few things it is really necessary to take are soon enumerated. People who live much on horseback in a hot country never wear tight clothes. The Boers wear trousers, the Arabs a burnous. I think, if I were making the journey again, I should as a matter of comfort adopt the Arab dress, which for day or night is a perfect adaptation to the needs of the climate. Failing that, the best substitute is a suit of old flannels.

A grass mat spread on the sand is a sufficient mattress. This rolls up into a small space and is light and easy to carry. Your saddle turned upside-down makes a very comfortable pillow. One rug, an old one, is all the bedclothes you will need. A greatcoat should be taken for the early, before-dawn rides, when the air is sharp, and a small shelter tent is

BISKRA

useful in case of occasional sand or rain storms at night and to give a shade from the dazzling light of the moon. These, with a spare shirt or two, a few pairs of socks, a soft hat, Arab slippers, tooth-brush, hair-brush, soap, shaving-things, a small looking-glass, and a sponge, make up all your personal equipment. For the camp you will need several good water-skins, a saucepan and frying-pan, a kettle, matches, a gun and a few cartridges for knocking over an occasional partridge, and plenty of cigarettes. That, I think, is all, unless I include in the list that most important article of all, a friend; such a one as Bacon defines him, who halves griefs and doubles joys; whom you can share talk and jokes, and, above all, silence with. I wish the reader my own luck in the matter. This desert journey was but one of many pleasant memories that my friend and I had placed to a common account.

There is no need to bother about provisions, and especially avoid all the tinned meats and extracts, and condensed abominations, the only effect of which is to bring on great thirst without appeasing hunger. Buy at each village you come to enough food to last you to the next. A kid, a few pigeons or chickens, rice, bread, dates, and oranges can be obtained at any oasis village, and at each of these you will lay in a store sufficient to last you for the one, two, or three days from there to the next oasis. Of coffee I would make an exception. It is the drink of the desert. Take a liberal supply, with sugar, coffee-pot, and a cup or two, and pack these in a separate parcel where they are easily accessible. If you add to that parcel a handful of rusks, or a few dried dates, you will be independent of fate, and any chance delay, such as might occur from extra-violent sandstorms or an accident to one of your beasts, will not matter. Besides which, nothing is more delightful than to come to some dell or glade in dazzling mid-desert, where a few thorn-trees and grass tufts sprout, and call a halt and light a blaze, and fling yourself on the sand and enjoy a cup of coffee and a cigarette. These unforeseen impromptu picnics are among the most charming moments of desert life, and ought to be provided for.

All you want can be obtained at Biskra. Ponies cost about £10, camels about £4. It is best to buy these outright, as you will be able to sell them again without any difficulty when the trip is over, probably for little less than you gave for them. It is economy to buy good beasts, even at a rather higher figure, for not only are they pleasanter to ride and use, but they are more likely to fetch their price again. The French remount officers are always on the look-out for good and well-bred ponies for mounting their Spahis on. These are always saleable. Of our two ponies, one bought for £8, but not up to army form, fetched £4. The other, a rather smart little grey, for which we gave £12, we sold to the remount department at Kairwán for £15.

When at last our little caravan was complete and marshalled for departure it presented what I took to be an imposing appearance enough. First walked our three camels, laden with our tent, blankets, sleeping mats, water-skins, cooking utensils, and a few provisions, stealing along with noiseless footfall and gazing left and right with that expressionless expression of theirs which they seem to have inherited from

BISKRA

their desert home. Each is guided with a single string by its rider, perched aloft and swinging to the long stride. The most important personage in the cavalcade by far is Ahmeda, our guide. Arms to the Arab are what jewels are to a woman; and Ahmeda, besides being gorgeously arrayed in other respects, is slung about with all the matchlocks, pistols, and knives which he either possessed himself or had been able to borrow for the occasion. The inhabitants of all the hotels came out on to the verandahs to watch our start. It was evident they had all had enough of our horse-dealing, and were heartily pleased to see the last of us.

CHAPTER VI

IN THE DESERT

Some first impressions of the desert—Absence of detail—Sense of space—Its natural features—The feeling of isolation—Invigorating effect of great light—Bedouin gipsies—The attraction of the desert—Influence of primitive scenery—Escape from custom and routine—Burton on the desert—The senses sharpened and stimulated—Power of noticing things.

IF one could imagine a country like England entirely stripped of all verdure, its green pastures turned into sandy wastes, all trace of man's work gone too, houses and cottages, farmyards, the banks and hedges of fields—in short, if one could conceive the whole country reduced to dry, crumbling rock and sand and ourselves travelling through it, the impression we should have of it, I imagine, would be that it was almost quite flat, practically an endless plain.

Little inequalities count for a great deal with us because we are always studying detail. There is so much to look at close round us, such variety and such richness! The meadows and woods, the villages, the dark and shady hollows, the bubbling stream at our feet, the birds in the trees, the flowers in the hedges, the cottage garden or an orchard in blossom—these

IN THE DESERT

things one after the other draw our attention. Our eyes have no wish to stray far, nor can they. Hedges banks, and enclosures, or woods and bushes usually bound our view at a few hundred yards.

So our eyes, accustomed to observe the things close round us, take note of the most trifling irregularities. None is so small as not to be of great effect in our little foregrounds. The knoll that lifts the village church tower, though it be only fifty feet high, is a distinguished eminence. And the wooded hollow where the smoke of some snug manor house rises through clustering trees, or the hardly perceptible trough where a little brook or river runs, instantly in the same way become marked features. But take away the things that emphasise them, take away the manor house, and trees, and church tower, and brook, and they are marked features no longer. Let your valley and hollow and knoll be all mere monotonous sand and rock, and, as you ride by them, your wandering, roving glance will not even notice their existence.

So it is with the desert. If you think of it as a vast expanse of level landscape rolled out flat, it is only because nothing clothes its little ups and downs with interest and keeps you studying the lie of the land fifty yards round your feet. It is not flat really. Reefs, tablelands, and long ridges of rocks protrude from its surface. It is seamed with ravines, sometimes flanked by precipices, with dry watercourses cut in the rock between. It has its valleys, its mountains, and its plains. There are the makings here of much picturesque and varied scenery if they were properly worked up.

The immense spaciousness of the Sahara is due not

so much to its flatness, in fact, as to its deadness. "The vasty halls of death" is a line that recurs to me as I think of those solitudes. It is a landscape entirely of distances, of a released attention; and it brings no grist to your little mill in the shape of definite thoughts and interesting observations, though it does sharpen and quicken every faculty you possess. The Arabs have the habit of holding up their heads and looking at the horizon, and that is where the charm of desert scenery lies. Things at a great distance put on a mystery and attractiveness of their own. They mean nothing, but they suggest a lot, and perhaps the mere capacity for taking so huge a range and the dagger-like penetration of your glance in the pure air gives a secret pleasure and excitement to the distant view. Moreover, in that vast monotony the horizon line is the only strong one, and the eye has a natural inclination to run along it. Any conspicuous object breaking it will attract attention, and a far-off peak on the line of march will hold your gaze for hours.

Put it down to the deadness and monotony that throws attention away into the distance, or put it down to the unstained clearness of air which doubles your range of vision—it is due to both causes, no doubt—one is made conscious in the desert, in a degree I have never felt elsewhere, of the grandeur of the feeling of mere space. It is the idea of lateral expansion as opposed to the vertical expansion we admire so much in Alpine scenery; the idea, in architecture, of the old basilicas as opposed to the Gothic minster. And, it seems to me, in the sphere of scenery any way, to be a more satisfying, tranquillising, and altogether bigger idea. Mr. Berenson speaks somewhere of the "noble

IN THE DESERT

spaciousness" of classic architecture. The noble spaciousness of the Sahara is one of its most tremendous characteristics. Nothing vertical counts here. Cliffs and crags seem of pigmy stature and hardly noticeable. One can imagine a fretful Alp quite lost and overlooked in this immense area.

The soft "crush, crush," of our camels' feet on the powdery, sugary sand is the only noise in the air as we jog on, our little caravan raised into unnatural relief by the surrounding smoothness. In all that barren landscape we are the only conspicuous objects, and as the last tufts of palms sink out of sight behind we enter into lonely possession of the globe. Was ever so vast a stage engrossed by so small a company? In my mind's eye I see our tiny procession from bird's-eye height; a little string of figures no bigger than ants, moving, or scarcely moving, on this vast expanse of yellow. We carry like a ship our own solitude with us. We are the centre of a circle that moves with us as we move, and the soft "crush, crush" of the camels' feet are the yards by which we carry the circle forward.

And, as the hours pass and the sandy slopes unroll, it seems to me that I am made conscious for the first time in my life of the meaning of the word *light*. There is no possibility here of any mitigation of it, of any shelter or refuge from it: the glare comes down to the level earth all round; the earth itself, yellow and crystalline, is a form, it seems, of mineralised light. I feel, as I ride on, as if I were saturated with light and penetrated by it; as if I lived in and breathed it as a fish lives in and breathes water. Nor is there anything in the least oppressive in such intensity of brightness. On the contrary, it seems as if what was heavy and opaque in oneself were burnt away, and body and mind were possessed by a new energy and alertness. It even appears that such light has a physically nourishing and sustaining quality of its own. The Arabs, in the way of food, manage on little more than a mess of rice and a few dates, and your own meals in the desert will be of the lightest. There is no need to run one's own little generator when one can draw supplies straight from the main power-station.

The total sterility of the desert does not come all at once. There is a margin of scattered scrub under the northern mountains. The parched bushes hold on to life with desperate tenacity, and adopt all kinds of queer shifts for treasuring up a little moisture and making their foliage sun-proof, yet turn wan and grey in the effort. They are images of silent despair. Their stems are thin and shrivelled, and their leaves exude particles of salt. The whole scene is one of great desolation, without motion in the air, and a sense in all you look at of almost stony immobility. The verdure of the place, to mock it by that name, the wiry grass tufts and bitter shrubs, look almost as lifeless as the burning sand and sun-blackened rock.

Such as they are, however, occasional flocks of goats and sheep find sustenance on them, cropping and nibbling at the leathery twigs, urged on and watched by ragged nomad Arabs, whose black camels'-hair tents we sometimes pass, spread upon and propped up by the bundles of white thorn bushes collected for fuel, and looking in the distance like clusters of great black toadstools growing in patches. They wander, these nomads, on the plain during the winter months, and, when summer comes and the heat dries even these guttapercha shrubs

THE LAST TUFT OF PALMS.

IN THE DESERT

to tinder, drive their flocks up the mountain slopes which we can still faintly discern, blue in the north. Even now they are setting in that direction with a tide-like motion; all slowly eating their way northward towards their summer quarters, sole moving objects in the desolate expanse.

"A disgusting place," the reader will think of the desert; "dry, burnt up, unwatered, monotonous, without interest, dead. What should take a man to such a country?" I will tell him.

The gipsy camp on an English heath, the camp fire, the kettle, and the tent, speak a language we all understand. Uncomfortable—impossible, as it may be—your first glance was a glance of envy. What sight in childhood fascinates one more than these wandering roadside bivouacs? What game is more exciting than "playing at gipsies?" I remember how we smug little scions of civilisation used to stare at the tan-faced, bare-footed gipsy children, with a handkerchief tied over their head instead of hat. With some such feelings birds in cages stare at birds on the wing.

But it is uphill work playing at gipsies in a country like England, where every field and wood and hedgerow bears the marks of centuries of careful discipline and control. I write this in a pretty little Sussex village, in the month of May, and near the end of it. The hedges are cream-laden with may blossom, the fields are yellow with buttercups. It is Sunday morning, and a bell out of a cluster of trees is calling the villagers to church. They plod obedient to its summons, each clad in Sunday best, and leaving a track of pomatum smell behind him. Fat cows lie on fat pastures; lambkins frisk and suck and twiddle their tails; the wind plays, but not too roughly, with the young corn; larks above spill out their little cups of song over the land. It is all sweet beyond words; yet when I went out, with my thoughts full of the desert, and walked among the sleek and gentle fields, I could not but feel a something too willingly submissive, and, as it were, spaniel-like in such a scene.

Among the many things Nature gives us in England, there is one thing she cannot give—sympathy with the old primitive original instinct of emancipation. She is on the side of the powers that be, the side of authority and routine and tradition. "Submit yourself," she says. "I submit myself, and see how I thrive." Hers is a tranquillising influence, not a bracing one. Under her tuition the mind is attuned to a kind of servitude. So that here, where the stifling influence of custom is so strong, and its ruts cut so deep, is just where there is no escape from it. You fly to Nature, but all that her docile fields and obedient rivers and inviolable park palings can do for you is to sweeten and hallow custom, and reconcile you to it, and strengthen and confirm its hold upon you.

The desert is of another order of scenery, and made of sterner stuff. It is as ugly as hell, to be sure. It has none of the English motherly fondness and gentleness about it. It hates you like poison, and will kill you if it can. But it is a landscape that has never bent its neck to the yoke of man, and its barren reefs and unploughed sands have the old, primitive, savage vigour about them still.

This is its potent attraction. We are rebels, all of us, but the odds are against us. We live the same day over and over again. We make our moves in a

A Bedouin Camp.

IN THE DESERT

trance. We talk of leading our lives, but our lives lead us. We are like quaint figures in a piece of tapestry, and daily routine is the busy little needle and thread that assiduously stitches us in. We belong to a "period." By and by there will come a professor and lecture on us. He will point out our curious attitudes and dress, so characteristic of Edward the Seventh work, and give an account of the extraordinary notions we had about things, and all the odd beliefs and sham little artistic and literary enthusiasms that made up the life we accepted so confidently. He will illustrate us with lantern slides, and people will say, "How interesting!" and "How real it makes us look!"

In the desert for the first time you have Nature with you in the old struggle for emancipation. The mind here can recollect and renew itself. It comes out from these solitudes, not, perhaps, with any great store of facts, but invigorated, and, as it were, retempered. The senses whet themselves on these crags and reefs. A new vitality and daring is infused into you. You step out of your tapestry for a moment, and stretch your legs and look about you.

There is a sentence in Burton's "Pilgrimage" which a little bears out my meaning. He says that in desert scenery, owing to the very few things to be seen, your attention is concentrated and vigorously exerted on the merest trifles. A rock, a tree, a track upon the sand, awaken instant curiosity, and invite the sharpest scrutiny. Observation, he says, is stimulated to the highest pitch by the mere capacity for grasping every detail.

Every one who has been in the desert will feel the

truth of that; every one will remember the strength and vigour of glance that comes from these vast spaces, so sparingly touched with points of interest. Every detail develops a sudden significance. I remember sometimes examining some desert plant, the exudations of gum and salt from its broken leaves, the manner in which it was rooted in the ground, the effect on its constitution of sun and soil; or, again, to have studied the formation of the rocks, the dark polish wrought by the scrubbing of the sand as it blew against them, their clefts and small fissures and splits, due to contraction by heat and cold, and the close graining of the crystals; or, at other times, to have noted the character and shape of the sand-dunes, the traces of old gales which had left the sand in wreaths and waves, arrested in the act of breaking, and stricken into a mortal stillness, yet with the presence of the wind still felt among them, like an animal's in its deserted lair. I remember, I say, noticing these things with an intense consciousness of their meaning which was a revelation to me.

There is in the desert, among the few signs of life there, a kind of enormous beetle that leaves in crawling a tiny trail in the soft sand. This trail, seen for the first time, I one day followed up, until I came at last to the poor pilgrim itself, whose progress of a few yards in the hour was in such pathetic contrast to the infinite space around it. And at this moment I can see exactly the action and look of the creature; the tiny splay feet, that at every step dislodged a few grains of sand, and sent them rolling down the slope; the crooked knees and bandy legs, the bent head, and in its broad back and hunched shoulders, and boorish,

IN THE DESERT

plodding gait, a suggestion of impenetrable prejudice and bigotry past all words to describe.

Woods and meadows at home, the clearness of English brooks, the smell of apple blossom, damp moss on rocks, the sight of cattle standing in water—these things remembered in this wilderness seem too beautiful for reality. The thought of them comes with a stab of recollection, and you say to yourself, "Why did I not appreciate them when I had them?" And yet you know that when you return to them again it will be as it was before. However fond you may be of them, they will not call forth in you the same emotion that these sands and rocks and few paltry signs of life call forth. The fault will be in yourself. You will not have the same power of realising them. The numbness will have settled down again upon your senses, the cloud upon your brain. You will walk in a lethargy, half the time not realising what is around you. Not all the rich variety and beauty of English landscape will ever bring back this inward deep delight with which you look at one poor shrivelled leaf, or a beetle's footprint in the sand.

CHAPTER VII

THE ARAB AND THE DESERT

Excitement of the desert—Its stimulus of the nerves, not of the mind—Corresponding excitability in Arab temperament and character—Their campaigns—Non-intellectual nature of desert scenery—Its deadness—Effects on the Arab—Lack of coherence in Arab character—Destructiveness of the desert—Its object to blot out all life and all form—Similar aim of all Arab activity—His history a history of destruction.

I WILL put together a few notes here on a subject which interested me much at the time—the relation between desert scenery and the character of the desert people. What I came to feel more and more strongly as time went on was the extraordinarily stimulating and exciting effect of the desert and the desert climate on the one hand, and its entire lack of anything substantial and definite to think about and feed the mind with on the other. The pureness and keenness of the air, and the wonderful brilliance of light in which you live, and which seems physically to invigorate and sustain you, enhance your consciousness and sharpen all your faculties. You are more susceptible to the least impressions. You see, hear, feel, move with an alertness quite new. Every sense is

THE ARAB AND THE DESERT

strung up, as it were, quicker, livelier, more express in its movements than heretofore. I may say that every sense develops on this account a distinct pleasure of its own. It is a delight to the eye to see and to the ear to hear in this atmosphere and with this sensitiveness. And if some of these pleasures are increased, others seem to be new altogether. The pleasure of *touch*, for instance, is quite latent with us, I take it, and scarcely recognised at all. In the desert it awakens, and becomes a source of positive feeling. The touch of things, the variability of their texture, their hardness, sharpness, roughness, or the degree of their flexibility and softness, the sense of intimacy, sympathy, knowledge of their nature, involved in the mere handling of stones, sticks, leaves, or sand—all this gives positive delight, and seems like the awakening of a new sense.

And as you live amid these surroundings this strung-up feeling grows to tension and breeds a sharp excitement. At the same time all this extra vigilance is very ill requited. If a twig rattles or a stone clicks in the sun, your ears shout the message to you as if it were a gun-shot, but for the most part they live an idle life. Your glance ranges these wastes like a wild beast. It delights in its freedom and in its own movements. Yet all the time it is sending in to the brain little news or none. In short, the stimulus that breathes in the air is addressed to the nerves and senses, not to the mind. It makes you feel intensely, but not think.

I used to think that the temperament I read in the keen face and glancing eyes under the burnous was the very temperament I felt in the glare and breath of the desert. All round one here quivers the nervous excitability of which one sees so much in Arab doings — the nervous excitability which inspired all their conquests and campaigns and invested them with their dangerous character of tremendous violence, suddenness, and unexpectedness. None of these outbursts ever seemed, or to this day seem, to be based on any intelligible cause or directed to any intelligible end. They are mere explosions of pent-up nervous energy, as vague, dangerous, and short-lived as an explosion of gas or dynamite.

And accompanying this excessive excitability, which was the spirit in which the Arab worked, and the impulse which in old times drove him forth on his career of destruction, we have round us here, too, the sense of that profound limitation which undid all his work and led him back eventually to the desert again. Though there is much here to feed feeling, there is nothing, as I said, to feed thought. It would be impossible to conceive a land more destitute of anything that can suggest a connected train of reasoning. No doubt a Professor Schirmer may find even in this lifeless solitude matter for study and reflection. But for ordinary mortals a scene must live if it is to command a reasoning attention. In most countries life and fertility are conditions of Nature. On all sides the soil brings forth its fruits and crops. The seasons succeed each other. Leaf and bud, blossom and fruit and seed are stages in an endless cycle. There is perpetual development, each phase the result of what went before, the cause of what is to follow. By every possible inducement, by the food we eat, the wages we earn, by our interests and occupations, and even our

THE ARAB AND THE DESERT 107

amusements and sports, we are invited to study a perpetual sequence of cause and effect. What wonder, our lives being woven into such a system, if a method of the same kind is encouraged in our minds, and a progressive and coherent mode of thinking becomes an intellectual habit?

This influence for the Arab is non-existent. The rich and varied scheme of development to which dwellers in other countries adapt themselves does not operate in these wastes. Here, day by day and year by year, everything remains almost entirely unchanged. Nothing, or almost nothing, we see invites us to reason forward or to reason back, but the mind is left in idle and stationary contemplation. It is difficult for us to tear ourselves out of our setting and imagine what such an existence as the Arab's must be like. But if we try to realise the effect that such an empty life must gradually produce on the mind, and conceive it operating on a race for countless generations, we can recognise, perhaps, the consequences of it in Arab character.

For what that character lacks is the capacity to think consecutively, to reason accurately on secure premises, and to go on slowly but surely, testing every step, in the knowledge that each phase can only be a sound basis for what is to follow if it is a logical deduction from what went before. This capacity the Arabs never have possessed, and it is owing to the lack of it that the whole mass of their achievement is to-day a crumbling ruin. If from that ruin, which rose so magically and collapsed so suddenly, we turn back to these sandy tracts, the similarity between the two stares at us with almost human significance. What is it this landscape of restless sand lacks? The question brings us face to face with the everlasting deficiency in Arab character and the Arab civilisation. It lacks that principle of cohesion which is the first condition of all progressive development.

So, I used to think, the strength and weakness of the Arab were alike displayed in the desert. All the influences that stimulated his nerves and starved his intellect were round one there. In his successes—his frantic conquests and frantic art and science—is the stored-up force of the desert's nervous energy. In the decline and disintegration of all his power and all his labour is the desert's fatal incoherence.

And the two are as like in conduct as they are in character. The Sahara is not altogether the motionless, dead thing it looks. It is carrying on a work of destruction all the time. The means it employs are the sand itself, helped by heat and cold and wind. The variation of temperature by day and night, often eighty or a hundred degrees, causes an expansion and contraction of the rocks so sudden as often to split them asunder as if a quarryman's hammer had done the work. "Sometimes," says Professor Schirmer, "a rock flies all to bits under the influence of the sudden contraction." And he quotes a passage from Livingstone, who used frequently to hear, after particularly blazing days, the black basaltic rocks exploding and the ringing of their fragments as they fell to the ground. In many places under the slopes of hills are to be seen heaps of broken stones which have been split in this manner and rolled down the incline. In the same way it is the common testimony of the natives that in the desert east of Damascus the black stones burst in summer. In the Sahara many of the plateaux are strewn with these sharp fragments, which cut the feet of camels and make walking difficult; and one explorer—Rohlfs, if I remember right—relates how he was forced to make little sandals for his dogs to prevent their feet from being lacerated by the splinters.

This rough quarrying, made easier by the dark, almost black, colour of the rocks, due, it is said, to the chemical action of the light upon their surface, which increases their heating capacity, is the first stage in the work. Where this process stops another begins. Apart from the newly-split fragments the common aspect of the desert is a surface scattered with stones and pebbles worn as smooth and glossy as if they had lain for ages in the bed of a river. This smoothness is due to the sand, which works upon the broken fragments, rubbing and wearing them away. No one who has felt a violent wind in the desert and the cutting force of the sand borne along on the wind will wonder at this effect.

Moreover the sand works not only on detached fragments, but on the permanent rock. The flanks of the cliffs near El Golea are worn and sculptured in some places to a mere lacework of stone. Some of the plateaux of calcareous rock have been rubbed till they are like sheets of ice, and between the Nile and Faragrah the lined and polished surfaces reminded Rohlfs of rocks that had been scored by glaciers. The varying degrees of hardness in the strata is a further aid to destruction. The soft stone yields first, and the result is that cliffs and hills are often undercut as if they had been hollowed out by waves, and often the overhanging strata are so completely undermined that they come crashing to the ground, where their fragments are instantly set upon by swarms of busy sand grains and gradually reduced to their component atoms.

Thus the hills and cliffs themselves yield by degrees to the sand's onset. The Sahara, it must be remembered, wears no covering of vegetation and earth stitched together by innumerable roots of plants and trees to protect it. It is open to all attack. At Nefsaoua there is a line of pinnacles crumbling rapidly away, of which one is still left of the original stature. This is protected by a topknot of shrubs and earth, nourished by a spring which flows from its summit. It is this patch of soil and vegetation, not the hardness of the rock, that has preserved it.

There are regions in which the sand has already completely triumphed. The dunes are calculated to occupy about a ninth of the whole Sahara. These are the districts where the sand has achieved its object, where all fragments of rock and stone, representing the last relics of structural form, have been decomposed. The plateaux and stony ground are the parts still in a transition state, having mostly become bare of all vegetation without being as yet finally dissolved. These tracts of firmer ground stand in the desert like continents rising out of, and washed by the gulfs and channels of a sandy sea. Slowly however, the dunes are gaining ground. The eastern ones are making progress towards Ghadames. In several places in the region of the Irgharghar, near El Golea, and between Sionah and Bahariah, they have invaded the old caravan routes. Year by year decomposition makes almost imperceptible progress.

A Dead Landscape.

THE ARAB AND THE DESERT

In all this, the object of the desert is clear enough, Its one endeavour is the destruction, blotting out, and utter decomposition of all organic forms. Every tiny oasis in the desert has to fight for its life. Each one stands a siege. Water, soil, a handful of palms give foothold for a little community. Individual property, social obligations, recognised responsibilities and laws, germinate and take root, keeping pace with the growth of plant and tree. But all around, constantly repulsed but constantly renewing the attack, the old blind monster fumbles and feels, like water round a ship, indomitable, persistent, assiduous, hankering to get back its own.

Professor Schirmer has likened the form and structure of the desert to the framework of a skeleton, losing shape and coherence as it dissolves into ashes. To bring about this dissolution is the one end of desert activity. For this purpose the sand exists. Volatile, restless, persevering; so weak that it is blown about by every breeze, and takes the imprint of a breath of air; so strong that the cliffs and rocks of basalt yield to its attack, it offers the best image I can think of, of the principle of dissolution in Nature; of the power which undoes and takes to pieces, which has declared a war of extermination against all life and all order, against man and beast and tree and plant, and even against the senseless shapes of rock and stone; which, in a word, is satisfied with nothing short of decomposition to the ultimate atom.

And all this is as true of the Arab as of the sand. He is a social solvent as the sand is a natural one. Fickle and unstable, a creature of impulse and blown about by every whim, he is consistent in nothing but his profound dislike of law and order, of fixed duties and responsibilities, and all that goes to build up a coherent society. If, instead of magnifying those fantastic attempts at creation of his which have had little real foundation, we turn to the field in which the power of the race has been displayed, we should find that destruction and the taking of things to pieces has always been the Arab's vocation. Those so-called conquests of his were really the taking advantage of a unique opportunity for destroying and pulling down. The collapse of the Western Empire, and weakness and paralysis of the Eastern, afforded the Arab a fine field for the display of his peculiar prowess. He took to the lumber and *débris* of these crumbling empires as fire takes to rotten wood. But if in the void that separates ancient civilisation from modern the Arab appears to advantage, there no sooner entered on the scene nations of solid character and creative genius than he retired before them, and yielded to their advance.

Since those days his efforts have all had one direction. Along the coasts of the Mediterranean the breath of the Sahara is felt in the hot south wind, and Arab activity has had about the same range. To all these coasts the siroccos of old brought the imps of the desert. Every town and village and hamlet learnt to recognise in them the sworn enemies of fixed society. With the progress of time every step in advance won by the civilising principle of law and order has been registered in a corresponding shrinkage of Arab influence; and the fall of Algiers and Tunis and the approaching collapse of Morocco are only logical issues of what, with the Arab, has been all along a perfectly consistent

THE ARAB AND THE DESERT

line of conduct. Even yet, to this day, restricted as his activity is, it remains the same in kind. Whenever one hears of any Arab enterprise we can always be sure of one thing about it, and that is that it will be a destructive one. It may take the form of a raid upon an oasis, or the surprise of a caravan, or the capture of a government official, or the breaking-up by slave gangs of a Sudan village; but in any case it is quite certain to have for its purpose the pulling to pieces of society in some way or other.[1]

Again, in Arab and desert alike the same outward manner of immovable composure masks a secret excitability within, and the immobility of the landscape is reflected in that iron self-control which is the favourite Arab affectation. The repose is the repose of a taut harp-string in both. So alert is the silence of the desert that you find yourself involuntarily listening. The hush seems a prelude to some important announcement. You hesitate to break it. It must be something more than usually worth saying that would claim so vast an attention. So, with a sense of having the same thing presented in a different shape, I have often noticed, on mid-day halts, or in the evenings in the caravanserai, how still and silent, hour after hour, the Arabs sit. Not lethargic, or sleepy, or inattentive; keenly attentive, on the contrary; but with only their dark eyes glancing from side to side; speaking never. It is the desert dumbness that is on them. You feel it yourself as you travel through these rigidly attentive landscapes. A man thinks twice before he breaks the silence of the Sahara.

One cannot help, then, I say, beginning to under-

[1] See Appendix, Note C.

stand something of Arab character here in the desert. Lie upon this hot slope. Pick up a handful of the warm grains and let them run through your fingers. Nothing can hold them. The tiny, rounded particles, each one distinct and separate from its fellows, slip like water through imperceptible chinks. They will take no form, for they have no consistency. You can make nothing of them.

Drink in this thin, scorching air. Can you not feel it refining all your senses, stirring every faculty to panther-like alertness? This is that desert *élan*, the most curious and terrible of forces, of which the world has had such memorable experience. When the Saracen hosts gathered for their rush, and—

> "On the wings of mighty winds
> Went flying all abroad,"

this was the stuff they were full of. This was the mettle of their pasture.

CHAPTER VIII

WHERE THE "ARGO" SAILED

Ahmeda's horse and horsemanship—The Shott Melrir—The old river system—The drying-up of the desert—Arab metaphors—The tradition of the sea—Greek cörroboration—Yarns of the Argonauts—Modern science contemptuous—Evidence of the inland sea—Arab and Greek tradition confirmed.

ALL our little caravan feels the exhilaration of this air and scenery. Our ponies break into a frisky gallop as we come to firmer stretches of sand; the Arabs from their camels glance about them with increased animation, and settle themselves contentedly to the familiar swaying stride; even the camels themselves, or so I fancy, are pleased at the bottom of their cold hearts to be adrift in the waste once more.

Ahmeda's exultation showed itself in a hundred fierce or gay signs. Something in his blood answered to these surroundings. His look changed. His eye, questioning these distances, was a changed eye. He was riding a tall, shambling nag with a lop-sided action like a cow, the result of hobbling of two legs on the same side together. When hurried it had to invent an action of its own as it went along. Its trot suggested the dislocation of every limb, and its gallop was sheer anarchy. You looked round instinctively as the brute passed to see what was left behind. "Never," I used to think to myself, as I watched the tangled heap of legs, tails, heads, and flying burnouses rushing over the plain, "never will that creature come together into the likeness of a horse again." Yet every time when Ahmeda pulled up the subsiding sandstorm of its own raising disgorged a steed apparently intact.

How its rider contrived to adapt his seat to its sprawling attitudes was always a mystery to me; but Ahmeda was perfectly at home in the saddle. When we found ourselves at last in the full loneliness of the desert, his joy broke out in all kinds of antics. Now he would scent the presence of an enemy and dart off to a knoll from which to spy out over the plain. He had a small, cheap telescope, quite without any magnifying power, and which obscured everything seen through its smoky little glass, but which he was never tired of gluing to his eye, as if he were reading the secrets of the desert through it. After these examinations he would assume a manner light-hearted and careless, or grave and preoccupied, according as the results of the reconnaissance had been satisfactory or sinister.

Sometimes, again, he would spur his horse to a frantic gallop, and then flinging the reins on its neck bring his rifle to his shoulder and fire across the plain as he tore along. These antics of his invariably took a warlike form. The unsuspecting prey, the cunning ambush, and the sudden onslaught were the themes he worked on. The number of caravans he plundered during these first two or three days must have been quite considerable. The old instincts were evidently not dead in Ahmeda. I doubt if they are quite dead in

WHERE THE "ARGO" SAILED

any Arab. As I watched his face on his return from his forays I used to think that a persuasive Mahdi would easily set fire to that tinder, and the vigilance of the ubiquitous French garrison became more explicable.

It was on our second day out that we came to a deep and far-reaching depression in the desert's surface. The stony ground broke away suddenly in a long irregular slant, and descended steeply to the bottom of the valley. Standing on the summit we had a view across to the low cliffs a few miles off on the opposite side. Eastward the flats, widening as they went, stretched to the horizon. That part which we were about to cross was but a narrow tongue; the last creek or bay, evidently, of this vast trough.

But the peculiarity of the view, and what arrests one in some astonishment, is that all the floor of the hollow is loosely paved with what at this distance seem like broken fragments of ice. The scales and pieces, twinkling and flashing in the sunlight and stretching away for miles into the distance, look exactly like the photographs and sketches one has seen of ice-floes in the northern seas.

This depression of which we stand on the verge is one of the most noteworthy features in the Sahara. From here eastward there stretches a chain of these salt lakes for over two hundred miles to the east coast of Tunisia. The Shott Melrir is the westernmost of the line. It is followed by the Shott Rharsa, the much larger Shott Jerid, and the Shott al-Fejij, which reaches to within about twenty miles of Gabes on the Tunisian coast. These lakes, which once formed a deep bay of the sea, are still considerably below sea-level, from which they are cut off by the sandbanks of the east coast. It has been shown that before the present total sterilisation of the Sahara a large river system, both from north and south, drained into this now extinct sea. It received the torrents from the Atlas range, and it received, what was far more important, the large rivers which drained the mountains and plains of Central Africa.

As the desert spread, and gradually encroached upon, and finally blotted out, the verdure of the country, these mighty streams dried up, or sank such waters as they collected from the mountain rainfall below the sandy floor of the desert. Unfed by tributary rivers, the arm of sea gradually contracted and silted up. The sandbanks grew and extended across its mouth until they joined, and, forming a continuous chain, cut if off from the sea altogether, and then under the fierce African sun its waters rapidly evaporated. In winter, when the streams come down from the northern mountains, a few reach as far as these lakes, which then turn into salt marshes dangerous to cross. With summer the streams fail, the water dries up, and a glittering field of white and scaly salt is all that remains.

Any one who knows the Arab love of metaphor will expect to hear that a sight so extraordinary as this dazzling view in mid-desert will have been made a target of by their metaphorical marksmen. Quite a number of pretty phrases have become embroidered round it. It is like a bowl of glittering soapsuds, like a cake of camphor, like a sea of opal, like a cake of florescent crystal, like a pail of molten lead and gold; and in the evening, when the peaks of the Aures fade away, purple and blood-coloured in the short twilight, it is like a leaf of blanched silver.

The habit of accumulating new images and new

WHERE THE "ARGO" SAILED 119

words is an appetite with the Arabs. They have a proverb that God's gift has descended on three things, the brain of the Franks, the hands of the Chinese

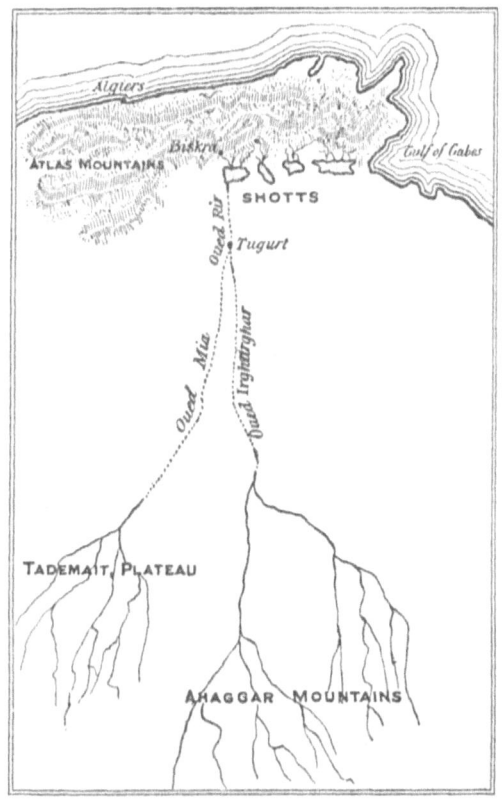

SKETCH MAP SHOWING THE FLOW OF THE GREAT
NORTH SAHARAN RIVERS TOWARDS THE SHOTTS.

and the tongues of the Arabs. Destitute as they are of other arts, they have made the naming of things and the description of things a subject of perpetual study and conscious endeavour. Speaking of the old competitions that took place between the poets of various tribes in the days of the Ignorance, Sir W. Jones says that they served to recruit the language with a supply of new words; "for," he says, "as every tribe had many words peculiar to itself, the poets, for the convenience of the measure, or sometimes for their singular beauty, made use of them all; and as the poems became popular these words were by degrees incorporated with the whole language."

The Arab is instinctively an artist in his choice of words. The exclamations Burton heard among his fellow-pilgrims at sight of the sacred grove of Al Medinah, read, as he has transcribed them, like a passage from an Arab poet. "Live for ever, O most excellent Prophet! live in the shadow of happiness, during the Hours of Light and the Times of Day, whilst the Bird of the Tamarisk (the dove) moaneth like the childless mother, whilst the West Wind bloweth gently over the Hills of Nijd, or the Lightning flasheth bright in the Firmament of Al Hijaz." Here is a gift of utterance indeed! We should have to wait some time before we heard an English peasant describe the cooing of a wood pigeon as the moaning of a childless mother; and as long, perhaps, before we heard a salt-marsh likened to an opal sea or a leaf of silver. But the Arabs, as I say, make a study of these things, and round every striking and peculiar natural object or feature there gathers in consequence a whole collection of epithets and images, the happiest of which find a place in the language, and are perpetuated in popular speech much as the words imported by the old poets used to be.

WHERE THE "ARGO" SAILED

It is a curious example of the persistence of tradition that, though for an untold number of centuries this bay has been silted up and the desert been in almost full possession, yet there still exists among the tribes of the south the legend of a sea across the Northern Sahara, with ports and ships, opening into the Mediterranean. Modern opinion has varied on the subject of this sea. Until lately it was accepted as a matter of course that the whole desert once formed the bottom of a sea. Where else could so much sand come from? Later, it was discovered that the Sahara was really a dried up continent. It was not sea bottom, but a tableland rather, with an average elevation of several hundred feet above sea-level. It had the usual mountain ranges and plateaux, now all dry rock, and the channels of rivers and torrents could still be traced, cut in its stony surface. Finally, it was discovered that the sand was the result of the action of the wind rather than of water, and that its manufacture was in active progress at the present time; and then the idea of the old sea was as absolutely rejected as it had once been absolutely accepted.

However, the no-sea theory would not do any more than the all-sea theory had done. Fossils were discovered in the desert which proved that the sea once rolled in certain parts of it. Some have been found in the neighbourhood of Lake Tchad, but the most plentiful and conclusive discoveries have been made in the north, in the valley of the Oued Rir, and in the depressions of the shotts. Consequently a mixed solution is now offered. The Sahara was never a sea, but it contained seas, and one of these seas ran under the Atlas where the shotts now are.

Of course, in pursuing its own calculations science paid no heed to the idle tales that were current in the country itself. Curiously enough, however, those tales were not of Arab or Berber origin only. Arab legend was supported by Greek myth. The story of the Argonauts vouched for an inland sea or lake somewhere in this very neighbourhood. The *Argo*, it will be remembered, is supposed to have sighted the mountains of the Peloponnese on her homeward voyage, and then to have been driven south by a northerly gale and wrecked somewhere, presumably, on the Libyan coast. Certain nymphs of the neighbourhood thereupon came to her rescue; but, being delivered from this danger, she was afterwards driven into an inland lake, from which she seems to have been unable to extricate herself, until, her usual luck holding, a Triton appeared who guided her into open water again.

Sailors are notoriously imaginative, but as a rule only in detail. They embellish, but hard facts are somewhere underneath. The writer was a sailor himself once, and has listened through many sultry night-watches to the strange mingling of memory and imagination that sailors weave into their yarns. From such experience he fancies he would have risked a guess that, though the Triton and the nymphs might be embellishments, the sandbanks and the inland lake were real.

At any rate, here was a curious tally in the way of legends. Here, in the mythology of the sailor people of the Mediterranean, is confirmation of the strange old fable that still survives among the

WHERE THE "ARGO" SAILED 123

Saharan tribes. Once there was a sea there, say the tribesmen. Once we sailed on that sea, say the sailors. Modern Science, of course, smiled superior. She knew what tricks imagination plays with poor weak human nature. Meantime she set to work to apply her own more reliable tests. She proceeded to question, not man, but Nature. She looked once, and declared that the whole place had been a sea. She looked again, and declared that none of it had ever been a sea. She looked a third time, and declared that there *had* been a sea just hereaway south of the Atlas; which is exactly what poor tradition has been saying all along.

The conclusion will recommend itself to every traveller in these parts. After visiting Gabes and the eastern coast of Tunisia, and seeing the narrow strip that divides the inland depressions from the outer sea, and watching the great cliff-like range of the Aures with their palpably sea-coast look, and taking into consideration the downward trend of the desert floor all the way from the Ahaggar range to the foot of the mountains, which would form a natural watershed and system of drainage towards this point, and remembering the still visible threads of the outlying tributaries on the mid-desert plateaux which bear witness to the course of ancient rivers down the centre of the basin towards this Triton's sea—in short, after grouping the facts in one's mind as they have appeared to one, and further propping them on Arab legend, Greek myth, and scientific fossils, one may allow oneself to suppose that in looking out from these sandcliffs over the glistening surface of the shotts we are looking across the very sea, or part of it, which Jason in his saucy clipper navigated in days of old.

What in remote antiquity was the aspect of this northern depression it is impossible to divine. But the existence of these great rivers is proof of the fertility of the regions through which they passed. And of the existence of the rivers there is no question. In the midst of this deadness and sterility one can still read, in the wide beds and chiselled rocks, the evidence of the force and volume of water that once poured through this waste. Still the upper Irgharghar, rising in the Ahaggar range in mid-desert, sometimes after heavy rains will carry a current as far as Amguid. The lower river carries no water at any time in the year, though its course is traceable in places by the rounded fragments of rock of its bed. Yet explorers have narrated that the old channels of the great Saharan rivers, like the Mia and the Irgharghar, sometimes after a rare, torrential downpour develop in an instant a majestic flood that rolls proudly in mid-desert with the strength of old days for a few hours and a few miles, and is then sucked down into the porous soil.

The Ahaggar range girdles the basin on the south, while the Tademait Plateau bounds it on the southwest. In these two mountain-formations the two main streams of the basin had their source. They united near Tuggurt and flowed thence to the sea. Curiously enough, it is the ends and feeble tributaries of these extinct Niles that still survive, while the main rivers they fed have long disappeared. The smaller streams, raised above the reach of the encroaching sand, still gather the occasional rains that fall upon the uplands; but betwixt those mountains and the site of the old sea

WHERE THE "ARGO" SAILED 125

stretches an ocean of tumbled sand-dunes, their rounded monotonous summits, unrelieved by a speck of green, not unlike the petrified billows of some ocean solitude. They have wiped out and buried the old rivers, whose course is now fitfully traceable where the surface is hard, or by the wells that have been sunk to tap the water beneath, or the moisture that rises in the depressions between the dunes and gives life to a grove of date-palms and an Arab village.

Enough, however, from these signs is discernible to reconstruct the dead river system as it once was. We must of course imagine the feebly-surviving puddles of the shotts infinitely enlarged. The shore-line at Gabes, and up the east coast of Tunisia, we must suppose to be in great part dissolved. It was, we may imagine, among the gradually silting up quicksands of this treacherous coast that the *Argo* first got into difficulties. There are writers who now contend that the sea into which it afterwards penetrated lay further to the north, somewhere in the neighbourhood of Monastir. Having been so long denied a Lake Tritonis at all, it seems we are now, by way of compensation, to have several. The point does not seem very vital. At their eastern end, in Tunisia, the Atlas mountains sink gradually down into the plain as once, in remote times, they sank down into the sea. The low-lying land of Eastern Tunisia, running in among the hills, was the arms and branches of that sea, which, as the sandbars formed across its eastern inlets, stagnated by degrees and gradually filled up. The contraction of the sea, first to a lake and finally to a few salt marshes, would cover an immense period of time. At what stage in the process the *Argo* appeared on the scene, to what dimensions the sea had shrunk by then, and what regions beyond the present shotts it covered, are questions best left to experts. If we add to all this the uncertainty as to the course of a vessel lacking chart and sextant, and steered by a Triton, the whole episode becomes more or less perplexed as regards detail.

Still there remains the basis of certain main facts, and what we may reasonably believe is that here, in the eastern parts of Tunisia and southern Algeria, replenished by great rivers from the south and overlooked by tall cliffs on the north, lay that sea, or part of that sea, of which the Arabs on the one hand, and Greek mythology on the other, still maintain the vague tradition.

We wound our way down the stony slope and held straight across the flats, ploughing at intervals through the crackling surface of salt. The spurs of hills came down round us, jutting forward like capes into the sea. As we climbed the opposite hills and turned to look back, the blue battlements of the Aures rose above us in the sky. We could well imagine the impulse of the French soldiers, who, on reaching the edge of those cliffs and looking out over the great expanse of desert, cried out, "The sea, the sea!" And once, we may think, the sea was actually here, and blue waves sparkled where the sand now sleeps.

As the processes of the change pass before one's eyes one scarcely knows whether to be struck by the vastness of these transformations, extending over such huge areas of time and space; or to wonder at the childlike pettiness of operations which are just the same, after all, as those which govern the dying puddles on the road's surface after a summer shower.

CHAPTER IX

WELL-SINKING IN THE DESERT

The underground water supply—Importance of the artesian process—Arab legends about water—Their notions of well-boring—Their fight with the desert—Invasion of their oases—"Dying" of their wells—Arab engineers—Their failure—The French intervene—Their success—Gratitude of the Arabs—Renovation of oases—Apparent happiness and content—The rising of 1870—Re-establishment of order—What the French have done in the Oued Rir.

THE old Lake Tritonis is dead, and the rivers that once flowed into it are dead; at least, they appear to be so. Their interest belongs to the past, you would say; present importance they can have none whatever. Yet, though their course is only to be traced here and there by the old channels which their current in bygone ages has sculptured in the rock, and though their beds are for the most part obliterated under an accumulation of sand and *débris*, these rivers are, nevertheless, not so dead as they look. Their waters, sunk beneath the sand, percolate along their old channels, or are collected and retained in the impervious strata deep below, circulating within which they give rise to that system of a subterranean water supply which is the most interesting and suggestive characteristic of the Sahara.

Oued means "river," and the reader, if he looks at a map of the Sahara, will be struck by the vast number of these rivers marked upon it. With the exception, however, of a few scanty streams which, among the mountain regions and for a certain period of the year, carry a fitful and uncertain current, the Saharan "rivers" have forgotten these many centuries what water looks like. They justify the name of river, however, by the fertilising influence, a feeble one comparatively, it is true, which they continue to exert. Indeed, in the Sahara the word *oued* means now not so much literally a river as the effects of a river. The river, being hidden, is thought of in the work it does, and *oued* comes to mean "fertile valley," or valley not totally destitute of some signs of fertility.

In this fact of a secret water supply lies the hope of the regeneration of parts at least of the Sahara. It appears that under its intractable exterior the desert hides some kindlier impulses after all; impulses that admit of being appealed to; springs of feeling that may yet be unlocked. It so happens, too, that just where we are, here by the Shott Melrir, facing the whole stretch of the Oued Rir valley to the south, is the best place in the whole Sahara for realising this fact.

For standing here we stand at the point where the drainage of a country as big as France once emptied itself in a single stream into the sea. The great depression reaching from the Ahaggar range in the mid-desert to the line of Shotts under the Aures possessed three main rivers, or rather two, which united to make a third. These were the Irgharghar, flowing due north from the

WELL-SINKING IN THE DESERT

Ahaggar; the Mia, flowing north by east from the Tademait Plateau; and the Rir, formed by the junction of these two, which finally emptied itself into the sea here where we stand.

The Rir at one time, then, was a stately stream. In no other part of the Sahara does there exist so large a watershed all directed to a single outlet. This region happened to be the one in which the French first made acquaintance with the desert. The amazing response received here to the process of well-sinking raised the most sanguine and romantic hopes. Enthusiasts saw the whole desert mantling with fertility. It was not for some time realised that the part they happened to have struck was a very exceptional part; that it represented a concentration of moisture from an exceptionally large area, and had supplies of water to yield much greater than existed throughout the desert generally.

When this was at last realised the disappointment was great, and many scornful and unkind things were said of the Sahara which had just now been the darling of the French imagination. However, it is beginning to be seen now that, though the desert may not have other districts so rich in water as the Oued Rir, it has plenty which may repay the sinking of wells. The artesian process will not, perhaps, transform the face of the country, but it may modify its character in many places. It is a very potent instrument for the furtherance of French occupation and settlement. It helps in the creation or maintenance of the little fertile islands scattered here and there through the waste, and these again support villages and a fixed population. They become centres in a small way of law and order. Moreover, the power of calling forth water is the surest claim the French could advance to the respect of the desert tribes. Every one, in the Sahara at least, understands the language of artesian wells.

The Algerian desert consists of two fairly distinct zones, the Western, or High Sahara, which is a rocky or stony plateau, stretching westward into Morocco; and the Eastern, or Low Sahara, extending into Tunisia. This Low Sahara forms the northern part of that great depression, seven hundred miles from north to south by from three to four hundred miles broad, the drainage of which, gathered by distant converging rivers, is concentrated in the Oued Rir; the Rir valley itself. leading down to the shotts, which are the deepest part of the depression and still beneath sea-level. These gradations are, of course, too gradual and on too vast a scale to be perceptible. You have no idea, as you gaze southward from the shott across an apparently level stretch of desert, that you are looking up a long gradual incline which culminates in a great range of mountains in the middle of the Sahara; nor that, from all round, the slope trends downward to this lowest point. Nevertheless, such is the fact, and it has proved a fact of enormous importance to the dwellers in this region.

The surface of the low desert consists partly of tracts of pure sand-dunes, partly of a dry calcareous crust of rock and shingle. Beneath this sandy and porous crust, however, there exist, often at very slight depths, impervious strata of rock and clay which may be called the true floor of the desert, on which the sand rests like an accumulated layer of dust in an unswept room. The rivers and torrents which descend from the mountains, partly from the great Atlas range, partly from the high Sahara on the west, and partly from the

WELL-SINKING IN THE DESERT

mountains in the mid-desert to the south, pass beneath the sand until they encounter the watertight strata beneath, within which they secretly circulate and extend for great distances. So that though, when in the midst of the desert and surrounded by blinding white sand-dunes, the very idea of water seems absurd, and its existence impossibly remote, yet it is often present at a distance of only a few yards underfoot.

This secret reservoir—so tantalisingly close, so difficult of attainment—of what in the desert are veritably the waters of life, is a phenomenon which has always haunted the Arab imagination, and has expressed itself in all kinds of legends and quaint theories and explanations. One tradition relates, what was no doubt the case, that the earliest oases grew round springs of naturally flowing water. These in time became gradually exhausted, and on this happening the Marabouts, or priests, confronted with a danger that menaced the existence of the tribes, united in offering up solemn prayers to the Almighty for guidance. It was in answer to these prayers that the existence of the underground supply of water was revealed, and the idea of tapping it by boring wells was suggested as a direct inspiration from heaven. Further south the tradition varies somewhat. It is there believed that a servant of the Prophet, having been inhospitably received by the people of the Rir, invoked a curse upon them, which sealed up the natural springs of their oases. In consequence of this ten of the most aged and venerable of the priests were chosen to go on a pilgrimage to Mecca to expiate the sin of the whole country. Their piety was rewarded. The springs were set going, and, in addition, the knowledge of the hidden water and of the means of reaching it was revealed. In both cases, it will be seen, the art of well-sinking is supposed to have had its origin in a suggestion from heaven. The dignity and solemn importance of the work were such that nothing short of celestial guidance could be allowed to inspire it.

What one has to remember—what traditions like these testify to—is that the constant war which the desert wages against any form of settlement and fixed abode is the dominating fact of desert life. Every inch of cultivated ground, and they are few and far between, has to be daily defended against the enemy. Sand penetrates like water, and just as the sailor has to be constantly at work caulking and overhauling every part of his vessel to keep it seaworthy and watertight, so the Arab in the desert has to guard and repair his oasis to keep it sandtight.

It is no easy task. The sand is constantly on the move. When the wind rises, the dunes, as the Arabs say, "walk." The word is very expressive of what takes place, for the rustling of the sand as it pours along the ground, and the rapid change in the shape of the drifts, give a strong impression of actual motion in the whole landscape. To prevent the obliteration of their gardens the Arabs plant rows of palm-leaves round the brims of the hollows, and along all the crests of the neighbouring dunes. It looks a childish expedient, but it is not without its effect. The sand is first set in motion along the sides of the dunes, and pours and rushes up the slope (each grain rounded to a marble in the process), and it is not till it reaches the crest of the ridge that it rises like smoke into the air. At this point the palm-leaf borders intercept it

WELL-SINKING IN THE DESERT

and lay it to rest. When, indeed, the dunes walk in good earnest, nothing can arrest them. The sand rises at every point under the lashing wind, turns the sky a uniform swarthy red, and blots out the view at the distance of a hundred yards. The spectacle of a landscape of dunes in rapid motion all around you, their crests melting and smoking in the wind, is one of the most curious, but to the husbandman or the traveller the most menacing, that the desert has to offer.

It will be seen that the tenure under which the Arabs of the desert hold their estates is a rather precarious one. By the middle of the last century the state of misrule, or no rule, in the desert, the perpetual incursions and forays of the tribes, had disintegrated the life of the fixed communities round the oases. With the Bedouins came the desert, symbol of chaos in nature as they in society. The discouragement or flight of the villagers was taken instant advantage of by the sand. Gently but assiduously it invaded the helpless plantations, just as on the banks of the Upper Nile the traveller sees it to-day encroaching on the strips of fertility that fringe the banks of the river.

But what, more even than the incursion of Bedouins and disruption of the villages, assisted the operations of the desert was the exhaustion, the "dying," as the Arabs expressively put it, of the wells. The boring system of the Arabs had been carried on from time immemorial by corporations of specially trained experts, among whom the office was hereditary, and who were held in universal honour and consideration. They were divided into the two classes of the *meallem*, or wise men, and the *r'tassin*, or divers. It was the business of the first to select sites for boring and construct the wells, and of the latter to clean them out and keep them clear of sand, with which they were liable to become choked. At the time of the French invasion these corporations had become almost extinct, the whole of the Oued Rir possessing only a dozen divers and three chiefs, all of whom were stricken with phthisis. One of these survivors is reported by Lieutenant Rose as lamenting the effeminacy of the later Arabs, who dared no longer face the dangers to which the excavators were exposed. "If God, the worker of miracles, does not come to our aid, in ten years the Oued Rir will be abandoned and buried beneath the sand." Divine assistance, as M. Jus gently hints, took the form of French intervention, and the Oued Rir was saved.

The danger of the Arab method of excavating was due chiefly to the sudden rush of water up the well shaft when the water-bearing strata were tapped. The engineers began operations by sinking a shaft which they lined with a rude timbering of palm-trunks, carried down to a depth where the sides became solid and not liable to fall in. This done, they erected a scaffolding of a couple of palm-trunks, with a third laid across over the mouth of the pit, from which two ropes raised and lowered the baskets which the workmen below filled. M. Jus, superintendent of the Saharan excavations, gives a lively account of the whole process, the one and only engineering feat practised by the children of the desert. He describes the patient artisan, sitting at the bottom of the pit, singing to himself the while, and chipping his way slowly downward with a small, short-handled pick, with which on off-days he worked in his garden.

WELL-SINKING IN THE DESERT

The strata enclosing the water are, according to the Arabs, the stone lid which covers a subterranean sea. It is commonly recognisable by its superior hardness and consistency. Arrived at this point the *meallem* ceases this operation, and before the final task of liberating the water is undertaken, the villagers subscribe what is called the *dia*, or " price of blood," for the workman who is to give the final stroke. The *dia* may average the respectable sum of £10. This point settled, the adventurous workman who is to complete the boring lets himself down by one of the ropes, and with his pick works a small orifice in the final layer of rock. It sometimes happens, M. Jus observes, that the water rushes with such fury out of its underground prison that the poor engineer is rolled over and suffocated before his companions are able to extricate him.

The work of the *r'tass* is somewhat different, but quite as dangerous. In some cases the water rises slowly and becomes choked as it rises with sand, which has to be removed before the spring can maintain a constant flow. Sometimes, too, wells silt up and have to be periodically cleaned out. This is the office of the *r'tass*. A party of *r'tassin* consists usually of four subordinates and a chief. To assist their operations a rope is made fast to the scaffolding above, its other end being tied to a heavy stone lowered to the bottom of the well, which keeps it taut. A second cord passed over the horizontal bar of the scaffolding lowers and raises the basket which is to receive the sand.

The *r'tass* who is to make the first plunge begins by warming himself thoroughly at a huge fire lit near the mouth of the pit. He then oils his body all over, and stuffs his ears full of well-greased wool. Then he jumps into the water up to his shoulders and stands with his feet on the timbers. He performs his oblations and says his prayers. "Then he coughs, spits, wipes his nose, draws in three or four long breaths, and blows the air out into the water with a bubbling noise, says good-bye to his companions, and finally seizes the taut rope and glides down."

The work is carried out in deep silence, every one being conscious of the danger run. The chief holds the cord by which the diver has descended, and which is his means of communication with the surface. A single jerk means that the diver is ready for the basket, and at a sign from the chief this is lowered. A second jerk indicates that the basket is full. On the *r'tass* reaching the surface his comrades embrace him, lift him out of the water, and take him to the fire, while a second gets ready for his dive.

When the *r'tass*, as not unfrequently happens, gets into difficulties, a succession of quick jerks gives warning to the chief, who with a particular signal communicates with the others, one of whom instantly dives to the rescue of his comrade.

The time usually spent under water by the *r'tassin* is from two to three minutes, while each *r'tass* makes from four to five plunges daily. Each basket of sand brought to the surface averages some ten litres, which would amount to fifty litres extracted as each man's day's work. When we remember that these two or three minutes of immersion are accompanied first with all the effort necessary to reach the bottom, and secondly with the work of collecting the sand and loading the basket, while the water itself, dense and

WELL-SINKING IN THE DESERT 137

turbid, is probably in violent agitation, such a feat of endurance must seem remarkable enough. The race seems to have an aptitude for the water. I am reminded of the Arab boy-divers of Port Said and other places, whose darts through the clear sea in pursuit of pennies I have so often watched from the deck of a P. & O.

The profession, however, of these divers, though highly honoured and highly paid, was open to such objections that one is scarcely surprised at its growing unpopularity. Blindness and deafness were apt to be the lot of the *r'tass* who escaped downright suffocation, and failing these he was pretty sure to be crippled by phthisis or rheumatism.

Besides this system there was, of course, and still is, the immemorial shadoof, so familiar to the traveller on the Nile, who watches the tall points sinking and rising along the river bank. It is easier to pull down than to pull up: that is the little bit of experience embodied in the shadoof. A tall pole like a fishing-rod is balanced on a crutch a few feet high, the butt-end being weighted with a huge lump of clay, and a rope and bucket suspended from the tip. Standing by the pit-edge the Arab hauls the cord down till the bucket reaches the water, when he lets it go, and the weight of the clay hoists the bucket up.

Such were the clumsy and inadequate systems in vogue when the French debouched upon the desert fifty years ago. A hydrologist of the name of Dubocq had, ten years before, drawn attention to the possibilities of well-sinking in this district, and General Desvaux seems to have been immediately struck by the possibility of bringing European science to bear on the problem.

The native pits being of wood were constantly wearing out and the sides falling in, and to clear out and revive one of these "dead" wells was always a work of great difficulty and danger. In consequence of this failure of water the oasis of Tamerna was almost completely dried up. The wells at Sidi-Sliman, Ourlana, El Harihira, Moggar, Tiguedidin, and others had become almost choked; while El Berd was totally overwhelmed in sand, and Sidi-Rached on the point of sharing the same fate.

It was, as it happened, at the latter place, Sidi-Rached, that General Desvaux first conceived the idea of introducing the artesian apparatus which has since then wrought such a change in this part of the Sahara. It happened that from the top of a sandbank he obtained a view of the entire oasis; on one side green with dense thickets of palms, on the other completely smothered under the encroaching sand of the desert. He was informed by the Sheyk that the northern wells had become choked; that they had found it impossible to sink new ones, and that in a few days the population belonging to that part of the oasis intended to give up the struggle and to disperse. The object-lesson of such a view was not lost on this practical Frenchman, and, thanks to the support of Marshal Randon, at that time Governor-General of Algeria, the immediate introduction of the artesian process was decided on.

Tamerna, in the Oued Rir, was the place fixed upon for the first essay. Sinking began on May 17, 1856, and on June 9th the water-bearing strata were pierced and a river of water, 4,000 litres to the minute, gushed forth. The joy of the natives was unbounded, and the news of this French achievement spread with incredible

THE IMMEMORIAL SHADOOF.

WELL-SINKING IN THE DESERT

rapidity throughout the south, bringing pilgrims from long distances to visit the scene of the marvel. The new well was solemnly christened by the assembled Marabouts, and received the auspicious name of the "Fountain of Peace."

Lieutenant Rose, who was in charge of the detachment working the pumps at Tamerna, sent to General Desvaux a report on the proceedings, which gives us a vivid idea of the excitement caused among the Arabs by this enterprise of the invaders, and of the mixed feelings of jealousy, astonishment, and delight with which the experiment was watched. M. Jus, the superintending engineer, had indicated the 2nd of June as the day when water would be reached. The hardness, however, of the intervening soil occasioned some delay. Several days were passed in mingled doubt, expectation, and uncertainty. The work grew harder and harder as the screw penetrated deeper. Parties of Arabs reinforced the gangs, and the work was kept going day and night. "But the Arabs, instead of seconding our workmen with all their might, were slack and ill-humoured. There was no mistaking the feelings of these men. They might calculate the great advantages they would reap in the event of our success, but one could read in their faces the intense satisfaction it would give them if we failed. Every time the pipe was drawn up fruitlessly they thought they saw the triumph of their process over ours. The partisans of the *r'tassin* looked hopeful, and Moslem prejudice evidently thought that the struggle against new ideas, of which they stood in dread, was won."

So amid disappointment and anxiety on one side and ill-concealed triumph on the other, the boring was pushed doggedly on till the 9th. At mid-day on that day the drill encountered more rocky strata, the depth attained being now 150 feet. M. Jus affixed a smaller and pointed drill to deal with the obstacle. The final scene we will give in Lieutenant Rose's own words :—" We worked two more hours without result, when all of a sudden the rod, after a continued encounter of hard rock, sank so suddenly that we thought it had broken ; but a moment later we saw the stream running stronger in the little canal that had been cut to receive the waste water, and then the strong shaking of the pipe told us we had achieved our object, and that a powerful spring had really been struck. Soon the water poured out of the outer pipe, and the flag run up to the top of the scaffolding and the shouts of the workmen announced our success to the natives. In two minutes every living soul was on the spot. They tore down the palm-branches that covered in the machinery. Every one must needs see with their own eyes this water that the Frenchmen had set running in five weeks, while they themselves would have required five years and five times as many workmen. Then up came the women of all ages, and those who could not get near the well managed to get water passed to them in the little cups of our soldiers, which they drank with enthusiasm. All the people were embracing each other, and the women fairly screaming for joy."

So for the moment, at any rate, the success of the "miracle" had silenced criticism. The champions of the old *régime* were obliged to conceal their enmity. The night is passed in dancing and festivity. A goat is sacrificed at the mouth of the well. The Sheyks and Marabouts of Tamerna, and the leading men of

WELL-SINKING IN THE DESERT

the neighbouring villages, gather round it to recite their prayers. The musicians of Tuggurt and Temacin range themselves in the midst. The young girls surround them dancing. The men, according to their wont, fire their guns in the air. All the inhabitants give themselves up to a manifestation of triumph and delight, such as only those, perhaps, who are acquainted by experience with what the word "water" means in the desert can understand. "And at last," adds our lieutenant, "I had the pleasure to see the covert signs of ill-will disappear from all faces, and I found myself surrounded with people who were blessing without any reserve the name of France and those who, in that name, had revived their groves, their sole fortune."

Let me turn back a moment to the case of Sidi-Rached, that oasis the pitiable state of which so appealed to General Desvaux. M. Jus gives some account of the scenes that occurred at the sinking of the well; scenes which were, he tells us, profoundly touching. "When the shouts of the soldiers announced that water was flowing, the natives rushed up in crowds. They threw themselves on this new spring we had set flowing out of the earth's bosom. The mothers bathed their children in it. The old Sheyk of Sidi-Rached, at sight of the current which was to restore a livelihood to his family, could not master his feelings, but, falling upon his knees with streaming eyes, he lifted up his shaking hands towards heaven and thanked God and the French."

Finally, let us hear the views of General Desvaux himself, after these early experiments. He points to the success, greater even than hoped for, which had crowned their efforts. "Public opinion among the natives," he says, "has been very much impressed by these useful undertakings, and by the energy with which they have been carried out. . . . French administration has entirely changed the aspect of these countries; instead of the anarchy, the injustice, of the old times, the constant acts of brigandage, it has instituted a just and beneficent form of government. It has restored security to the roads hitherto so dangerous. . . . The party devoted to our interests has grown stronger and more numerous, and it does not hesitate to declare that the French Government in two years has done more for the peace and prosperity of the Oued Rir than the Ben-Djellab through all the centuries of their rule."

There was, no doubt, at this time, while the benefits the French had to offer were fresh before their eyes, a strong wave of feeling in favour of the invaders. General Desvaux quotes the revered Marabout of Temacin, Sidi-Mohammed-el-Aïn, who had just returned from a pilgrimage to Mecca, as saying that he had passed through a great many Moslem countries, but that he had found tyranny and violence everywhere, and had never drawn a breath in freedom until he got back to French territory again. French officers could now travel freely, without escort, all through the Oued Rir and Oued Souf regions, so lately conquered, and would be everywhere welcomed with enthusiasm. Another significant sign of the times was the apparent willingness of some of the nomad tribes of the Sahara to abandon the wandering life and settle down to the cultivation of the oases. This was the case in regard to the Selmia tribe, which established itself at the newly-sunk well at Oum-el-

WELL-SINKING IN THE DESERT

Thiour. Such a change seemed to point to a modification of Arab prejudices, to a certain mitigation of their instinct towards the uncivilised life, which was full of hope for a permanent settlement of the country. It only needed a few years of French government, argued the General, and a few wells sunk in the desert to break up the old ideas of Arab life and open a breach for Western civilisation. Even Poetry lifted up her voice to celebrate the new era, and a native bard extolled the benefits of an alien government and described particularly the wonderful twisting machine which went down into the bowels of the earth to look for water, an operation which is likened to a diver diving to the bottom of the sea in search of pearls.

For some years reports continued to be of a most satisfactory nature. The 1860 report of General Desvaux dwells upon the sympathy, amounting to enthusiasm, with which the French and their miraculous pumps are being everywhere greeted by the native tribes. The old worn-out oases are being restored. New ones, flanked by happy villages, are rising, "as at the touch of the enchanter's wand," out of the desert. Feuds and brigandage are things of the past. The millennium seems suddenly to have alighted upon the Sahara, and we are edified by the sight of a happy and industrious people, who spend their contented days in cultivating the fruits of the earth and praising alternately the name of God and the French nation. Who could have foretold that ere many years had passed away this peace and prosperity would give place to revolt and massacre, and blood flow as plentifully as the new-found springs of water?

There is no need to follow the French well-sinking in all its detail. The enterprise was by no means confined to the Sahara. It extended to many regions of the plateaux, and even the Tell, where it seems to have been as welcome and successful as in the Sahara proper. Near the Shott-el-Hodna especially, a large number of wells were sunk. At El Fayd a feud between two villages, which appeared insatiable, yielded to the common blessing of a fresh water supply. At Aïn-Kelba, a position was selected for boring near the Kouba erected in honour of two much revered Marabouts. There was in the neighbourhood a natural spring of the same name, Aïn-Kelba, which means "the fountain of the dog," almost dried up, yet perpetuating a legend still repeated. It is said that two hundred years ago, at the time of a great drought, all the tribes of the Hodna had fled to such springs as still yielded a few drops of water, when there returned from Mecca a pious Marabout, on foot and followed by his dog, and finding no tent to shelter or person to succour him, he laid himself down exhausted and dying of thirst on the parched ground. His dog thereupon, seeing his master on the point of death, and guided by a divine instinct, set to work to scratch in the sand, and by and by a clear spring of water gushed out, and the pilgrim was quickly restored. This sacred spring had, however, in the lapse of years, almost run dry, and the people of the district in times of drought were reduced to the last extremity. Here the French successfully sunk a well, which they supplemented by another at Aïn-Nakrar, a little distance to the east. It is of the latter boring that we have some account by Captain Aublin, an account

WELL-SINKING IN THE DESERT

which coincides in every way with the description given of the wells already sunk among the Saharan tribes. "The miracle," he remarks, "has been repeated here which is already familiar to the Oued Rir." The importance of the work and the effect it is likely to have does not escape him. In particular he draws attention to an interesting belief, current among the desert tribes, to the effect that in remote times, when the Christians inhabited those regions, the rivers which are now dried up carried full currents and spread fertility through all the land. The present "miracle" would, he fancied, confirm that tradition, and would increase the prestige of the white race by associating it in the native imagination with the presence or control of water.

Yet Captain Aublin was sagacious enough to see that these blessings had another side to them. They would, he thought, end by accustoming the Arab to the idea of a fixed abode and a life of civilisation, and they would ultimately win his confidence and good-will. At the same time there must be the bitter thought in many Arab minds that the invaders were confirming their hold upon the country, that the old free and unfettered existence had passed away, and that the new one, whatever its amenities might be, was in fact subject to the government of a foreign race. Nevertheless, the final thought that remains is one of confidence. As he observes, the suspicion of the villagers turns to admiration and delight at the appearance of the water; as he watches their rejoicings and self-congratulations and prayers, and listens to their entreaties that the wonder-working machine may be transported into all their territories, the French officer forgets the dark, covert glances on some faces and declares that successes such as these spell peace between the races and cause the vanquished party to forget its defeat in the benefits heaped upon it. When a little later the *r'tassin* themselves, such as remained, seeing their employment at an end, begged to be initiated into the mysteries of the artesian process, and duly received an outfit and a French instructor to explain it, and set to work to strike some new wells at Tuggurt, it seemed past doubt that the tribes had been not only conquered but reconciled.

A few final words from a report of General Desvaux in 1860 will give an idea of the predominant feeling of optimism at that time: "The artesian wells begun in 1856 in the province of Constantine, by order of Marshal Randon, the Governor-General, have been continued without interruption from that time. Welcomed with enthusiasm by the natives, and followed with sympathy in France, these works have continued to produce the most satisfactory results. The oases of the Oued Rir have been saved from ruin; fountains and villages have sprung up in mid-desert; a part of the rich valley of the Hodna has been watered. In the Oued Rir (Tuggurt), confidence has become so general and so complete, that the natives, certain that they will reap the fruits of their labours, are working hard at new wells, planting palm-trees and rebuilding their houses; the tribes of the neighbourhood are renewing their trade with the villages, having nothing now to fear from the outlaws of old days. A change so marked in the social and political condition of the Sahara is due to the justice of French administration

WELL-SINKING IN THE DESERT

and to the blessings of the wells. Left outside the civilisation scheme which by the conquest of 1830 had been introduced into the rest of Algeria, the inhabitants of the Oued Rir, to whom the victory at Méggarine had been a revelation of France's strength, had found at last the justice and protection they needed. Instead of the Ben-Djellab, who were a burden on the people, and who shrank from no violence or crime, they had a Government which devoted itself wholly to the idea of administration, reorganisation, and to every possible means of redressing old wrongs."

The French soldiers were now to be seen, says this very optimistic report, as peaceful labourers "instilling life into the fainting oases, and mixing quietly with those who were lately their enemies, with all that devotion to duty which is so characteristic of the French army; they welcomed the roughest work, the most melancholy solitudes began to show signs of life, and after their artesian campaigns every soldier returned happy in the knowledge of that good to which he had contributed." The rise in the value of palm-trees is a significant sign of the change that had taken place in stability of government. A fine tree worth 5 francs under the tyranny of the Ben-Djellab was worth 30 francs in 1860.

It might, however, have been noticed that, whereas the rejoicings and congratulations were more or less superficial, the result of an appeal to such commonplace ideas as love of ease and plenty, the black looks that were sometimes noted bore witness to a discontent of far deeper origin. While the water first sparkled and the drooping palms revived, all other claims might be unheeded; but by and by, as the people grew used to, and heedless of, their benefits, the thought of the freedom they had forfeited recurred to them with growing importunity. In 1864 General Perigot succeeded General Desvaux, and in his report of two years later, otherwise as optimistic as ever, there is one ominous passage referring to the insurrection of one of the tribes in the Hodna, "blinded by fanaticism," which resulted in the partial destruction of two of the wells.

I will not attempt to describe the terrible revolt of five years later. It was due to those "black looks" we have heard of; to the growing discontent that was inflaming the Arab and Khabili imagination, and to the removal of the bulk of the French army, and especially of the experienced officers known personally to the natives, to take part in the Prussian campaign. It spread equally throughout the tribes of the Sahara and the Steppes. The Bedouins of the desert enjoyed a return to the old days of foray and plunder. Ouarla was besieged, Tuggurt taken, and the inhabitants massacred. The French were murdered wherever the tribesmen or the Khabilis could cut them off; a strong band of insurgents even marched on Algiers.

But this revolt, after all, like the lesser one that followed it a few years later, was a mere interlude. The French took up their task again where it had been interrupted. Their garrison returned. Their engineers got to work once more with their miraculous machinery. Their occupation confirmed its grip over the Northern Sahara, and extended far into its central regions. So far as the Oued Rir was concerned, the results of the well-boring surpassed all

WELL-SINKING IN THE DESERT

expectations. M. Jus, who for years had charge of these operations, made before his retirement a careful and exact computation of the work done throughout this district. Let me give an instance or two of the results.

In 1856 the number of inhabitants was 6,772, and had been decreasing yearly. In 1890 it was 13,302. The number of palm-trees, in which the wealth of the villages mainly consists, had increased from 359,300 in 1856 to 630,512 in 1890. This increase in the number of trees does not, however, express the increase in actual value, because it is invariably the case that when a district is deteriorating, as was the case with the Oued Rir when France took it over, the trees, from having to do with an insufficient quantity of water, became meagre and dwindled away, losing their capacity to bear good crops, and, consequently, their value. Such was the condition of the plantation in 1856 that during the following years it was found necessary to replant them almost completely. This was done. The 359,300 old trees of 1856 were valued at 1,300,000 francs. The 630,512 young trees of 1890 were valued at 10,097,160 francs. That is to say, though the number of trees had not quite doubled, the value of them had increased nearly eightfold.

To get at the cause of all this we must turn to the water account. In the Oued Rir the water supply shows an increase of from 46,000 quarts per minute in 1856 to 270,000 quarts per minute in 1890; an increase of nearly 600 per cent. in the thirty-four years. It may be added, too, that the number of fruit-trees, other than date-palms, rose in the same time from 40,000 to 90,000, and the value of dwelling-houses increased from 210,800 francs to 967,800. This was the effect of the artesian process. When France, by the treaty with England, secured the Sahara for her share of Africa, Lord Salisbury made the characteristic comment that "the French cock enjoyed scratching in the sand." The remark seems to have appealed to the French sense of humour, for I find it repeated in every book or article of theirs on the subject. I think, however, it will be agreed, so far at least as the Oued Rir is concerned, that the cock has scratched in the sand to some purpose.

CHAPTER X

TUGGURT

Arab love of display—Entering the town—A visit to the Marabout—Arab silence—An Arab *café*—Oriental colour—Colour emotional and belonging to the East—Form intellectual and belonging to the West—Incompatibility of the two ideals—Oriental colour an expression of Oriental life and character —St. Mark's the great artistic example—Its colour-effect obtained by banishing structural forms.

AS we neared Tuggurt, Ahmeda rode on in front to warn the inhabitants and arouse some little interest and curiosity in our behalf. Of all things the Arab dearly loves to make what Yankees call "a splash." To attract attention, to be watched and followed and make a sensation generally, is heaven to him. Ahmeda was easy-going and jovial enough in the desert, but when he put himself at the head of our cavalcade to ride through an Arab village or encampment he was a changed man. His gravity and dignity, and the haughtiness with which he stared round him, were quite alarming; but I think the performance was quite understood by the onlookers to be a mere bit of acting. They watched Ahmeda pacing proudly through their midst with critical acuteness, as you might watch an actor on the stage, to see how he availed himself of the opportunity for showing off.

When we saw in the distance the vast conglomeration of the mud roofs of Tuggurt I detected in Ahmeda signs of anxiety and restlessness I was already familiar with. After a bit he came to us and represented that it would be well if he went on and engaged our quarters for the night. This we agreed to, knowing well, of course, that his object really was to rouse the town and prepare for his own reception.

We entered by a narrow tunnel into the labyrinth of the town. The houses, or hutches, are of one storey, built of clots of sun-dried mud with low-domed roofs of the same material, over the tops of which we looked as we rode along the tortuous alleys. I was surprised to see such hovels roofed in this way, but no doubt the scarcity of timber explains it. The mud walls, unwhitewashed and unpierced by any windows, and the medley of narrow passages winding in and out, gave one the impression, stronger here than in Algiers, that one was in some haunt of insects or ingenious animals. The town seemed moulded out of the very slopes of the hill it stood on, and at a short distance attracted no attention, and could not be separated from its background. And when the silent-footed, mysterious Arabs began to well out through doors and alleys, swathed in their soft white garments and moving as noiseless as so many ghosts, though they seemed the right kind of inhabitants for these dim, blind walls, they looked a breed other than human.

Ahmeda had done his work well. At every entry and passage dark faces and white burnouses huddled,

TUGGURT

and keen eyes shot covert glances at us as we passed. He himself rode a little in advance and enjoyed himself like a child. As the crowd grew his stateliness and disdain increased. He told us he had arranged an interview for us with the Marabout of the town, and thither we went. The Marabout was a big, fat man—a good deal of the Turk in him, I thought. He was dressed very gaily in pale blue silk, if I remember right, and sat in a big, curiously-constructed chair in the open space in front of his dwelling, there awaiting us.

As we approached we heard the sound of music, but could not make out from whence it came. It sounded much like a barrel organ, but no instrument was anywhere visible. We had collected by this time in our passage through the town quite a crowd of followers, and as we debouched on to the open space I was aware of a sort of eagerness and expectation as they gathered closer up to us, as if they were awaiting some event of great interest. We advanced in a hush of expectancy only broken by the now loud and imminent squeaks of the invisible barrel organ. Where on earth did the sounds come from! Suddenly the truth flashed upon us; they came from the Marabout's chair.

The holy man got up to receive us, when the music instantly ceased. He pointed us to a lesser chair apiece on either side of him, and we all sat down. No sooner did his ponderous weight descend upon his own chair than it burst forth again into complaining squeals. We were, of course, struck with the expected wonder and admiration. It appeared that the French Government had made a present of this marvellous chair to the old Marabout, and it is certain that in so doing it showed its knowledge of the Arab character.

We sat in a row, the sky-blue Marabout in the midst, a circle of Arabs squatting round. Ever and anon, as I glance at the attentive ring, the dark eyes roll away to the horizon, but roll back, I feel, as soon as I turn my head. The conversation consists of an occasional grave inquiry about England, especially about the King; the number of horses and wives he has, and whether he too has a musical chair. What, however, interested me more than the talk was the silence. Talk among Arabs is not felt to be necessary It would be impossible for a circle of English people to sit, unoccupied, looking at each other and saying nothing. The discomfort would be unbearable. Arabs feel none of this. They sit on, vigilantly, imperturbably, and quite silently. The difference strikes one as much more than a difference of manner; it is a difference of temperament, the mark of a race which, as I said before, feels but does not think.

That night I strolled into an Arab *café*. It was a mere mud-hut of a place, sparsely whitewashed, with sand floor, having a big mud-built stove at one end, with little copper utensils gleaming on it. One candle stuck in a pinch of clay made the darkness faintly visible. A group of a dozen men sprawled or crouched upon the floor round a domino board. Several of them were Spahis in baggy blue pantaloons and short embroidered jackets; dark and handsome men, with reckless looks and keen, attentive Arab faces. One or two wore loose cloaks of dark crimson with big crimson hoods drawn over their faces. Others wore the dark chocolate-coloured burnous, and others, again, were in the usual white garments, their black faces blacker from the folds of white linen they peered out of.[1]

Huddled on the ground altogether they made an indescribable mix and blend of rich colour. There was just enough light to show it; to blacken the faces in the deep shade of hoods, or light up a cheek or forehead like a piece of bronze. Crimson, dark brown, and white were the chief colours, all low and together in large masses with the pale sand and walls as a set-off. Then their attitudes and features! One stretching back at full length and yawning; this one banging down his domino excitedly; that one as fiercely gesticulating dissent; another throwing himself forward over the other's shoulders to point advice; he in the corner crooning a careless carol to himself. All of it so unstudied, so loose and easy and unconscious!

I stood in the door some while, sipping coffee and looking. Outside the night was white as milk. The open space and the houses round looked as if they had been snowed on. There was a faint odour in the air of dust and spice, decay and sweetness mixed, the familiar smell of the East, always the same. A few ghost-like figures in their winding-sheets crossed the place and vanished into unseen openings. Then I turned my head, and beside me was this darkly-glowing interior and swarthy pomp of colour.

It is not enough to say of colouring like this that it is deeper, richer, stronger than ours. It is all this, of course, but it is more than all this. It is different in kind. In the East colour is a substantive, in the West

[1] See Appendix, Note D.

it is an adjective. We have coloured things; the East has colour.

Oriental colour is rich almost to gloom, but the gloom is like that of a ruby or sapphire, not on the surface, but deep and full of volume and power. And from this very depth of tone it derives a certain simplicity and gravity. Even a certain severity. It does not excite, it satisfies. The mind feeds upon it. In short, it strikes one as having an influence and character of its own, not as being the attribute of anything else. You do not, when you think of Oriental colour, think of any particular objects which it adorns; you think of the colours, not the things coloured. It exists in itself, not as an attribute or quality of something else.

Emotional rather than intellectual, the Oriental temperament finds in colour its proper vehicle for expression. The Oriental mind does not reason and does not construct. It does not, therefore, express itself readily in those arts which have a definite purpose and meaning, like sculpture and architecture. These belong to the intellectual West. What the East does express itself freely in is that medium which is itself emotional rather than intellectual, namely, colour.

And so when I find myself in a place like this *café* I feel myself in the presence of something new. I have been accustomed to think of colour as an adjective; to think, that is to say, of the object first and of its colour afterwards, as one of its several properties. And used in this way it seems natural that colour should be, as with us it always is, weak and powerless, not rich and satisfying. But here in the *café* that is not at all the use made of colour. There is not here any insistence on the idea of form. The burnouses and garments are all huge, loose, and unshaped. They make great full-brushed daubs of colour, but do not suggest form at all. And in all the surroundings the same idea is borne out. The interior itself, far from being of exact dimensions, is rounded and blurred in outline. The walls bulge, the angles are rudely turned; the roof is a low ponderous curve, the great oven protrudes a shapeless rotundity into the room. Darkened shadows fill the space, and the feeble candle-rays have only power to show a vague suggestion of whitewashed creamy wall, somewhat of the colour of old stained ivory. Shape there is none, form none; all is vague and indefinite.

And the use of this in setting off the mass of colour in the midst is incalculable. If that mass were set in any ordinary room, let it be as plain as you like, but a room as ours are, correctly and exactly built, with level walls, flat ceiling, accurate windows and doors, it would, I am sure, lose three-fourths of its effect. The suggestion of distinct architectural form that would exist in the room, the definite purpose expressed in all the surroundings, would go far to kill the effect of the colour altogether. It would rouse in your mind that kind of intellectual perception which exact form always appeals to, and in so far as it was able to do this, it would weaken and cripple your emotional perception of the colour. As it is there is no such clash. That passively receptive attitude of the mind, so directly opposed to the reasoning and thinking attitude, is encouraged here, ministered to and sustained by the whole *mise-en-scène*. The surroundings and background all bear out the same impression, and powerfully carry the suggestion of the colour itself deep into your mind.

But at the same time there is nothing of the happy accident kind about this setting. This ill-constructed and shapeless interior is just as significant of the race that built it as the heap of colour in the middle is. Let the reader glance at any available illustrations of Arab construction, and he will see that the Arabs have not got it in them to build a flat wall or a symmetrical arch. They do not think or feel in terms of form at all. It is, indeed, impossible that they should, since, as we see when we imagine this colour in an exact setting, the process of thinking in form is itself destructive of thinking in colour. The whole effect of this *café* is of a piece, harmonious and spontaneous. It all comes out of one impulse of the mind, and is the expression of a homogeneous character. Even the dimness of the light is wholly characteristic. An English public-house, how mean and poor soever, will make an effort to light itself up brightly, because it is the English wish to see things clearly ; an instinct which is natural to a character based on the sense of form. The Oriental wish is not to see things clearly, but feel them deeply, and to Orientals a clear light is not a recommendation, but the reverse.

One could multiply instances. What makes the fascination of such places as the bazaars of Constantinople, or those of Kairwán, a town which we shall be coming to by and by in the course of these travels? The same elements are all present as in this *café*. The little shops under their arches make heavy blots of dark colour; the light is shaded and dim, a soft twilight; and, most essential, but most often overlooked, there is nowhere the obtrusion of the idea of exact form. The niches or tunnels which

TUGGURT

contain the wares, the walls, supports, roof, and architecture generally, are inexact, indefinite, almost formless. As architecture it is all beneath contempt. As a vehicle for colour, harmonising with and deepening the impression of the rich colours massed beneath, it is beyond all praise.

The advantage of seeing these things amid their natural surroundings is that it is only thus that they attain to the significance of an interpretation of life. The colour achievements of Orientals, their stuffs and carpets and tiles and glass, torn from their surroundings and seen in a London shop, have no power in themselves to depict character. It is when you see them in the setting which harmonises with their own character that their interpretative power is felt. They stand here for something more than a gift, a tradition, or an accomplishment. They stand for a temperament. They make up with the things about them a spontaneous, consistent expression of life and character. Transplant them and this significance dies out of them. He who attempts to estimate Oriental colour by studying it in a museum attempts an impossibility. Better would it be if he were just to let the fire burn low in his own study, and, sitting in the twilight, let his mind attune itself, if it will, to the rich obscurity round him. He will be nearer to understanding Eastern colour in that hour than all the museums will ever bring him.

But, best of all, let him, if he can, visit the villages, homes, or bazaars of an Eastern people. Here, and here only, does colour exist for its own ends. Here only has it the richness and the strength which it gains from being the expression of racial character. No helpless parasite of form, no decorative quality attached to this or that; here it lives its own life, here it rules supreme. This is that kind of artistic expression which has in it the character of a people. This is what you read or feel in these gliding figures, in these dark, speculative eyes, in these breathing silences, in these gusts of scorching passion. The handiwork interprets the man. To stand amidst the dim splendour of that hovel yonder is to be offered the soul of the East to handle.

And yet there is one other place where, in a different way but still more completely, the same idea is brought home to us. When the Greek architects built St. Mark's they built it out of the consciousness they had of what the sense of colour meant to the East. They did in St. Mark's for the Eastern sense of colour what, in the Doric temple, they had done for the Western sense of form. Every one must feel the depth, solemnity, and power of the colour effect of St. Mark's; and feel too that colour here is not treated in the Western fashion. It is not treated as something subordinate to form. In St. Mark's you think not of coloured things, but simply of colour. This is the secret of its power; but observe how this end is achieved. Every single feature suggestive of form is banished from St. Mark's. The very race who, when they were dealing with form as their ideal, insisted on and developed every structural feature with such severity and precision, directly they came to use colour as their ideal entirely discarded those features. They let their architraves and cornices and pediments and friezes all go, and fashioned their interior out of a flexible mass of soft and ductile gold, indented, rounded, undulating, drawn up into hollow domes or curved into apses, but

TUGGURT

never for a moment evincing anywhere the sharpness and precision of form.

What they thus turned into laws of art is precisely what we have round us here in life in this village *café*. The Greeks had seen and felt, in daily observation, what colour meant to the Oriental. They had realised that for him it had a significance of its own, and a significance incompatible with the significance of form, because appealing to opposite faculties; to the emotional and sensuous faculties, not to the intellectual. They perceived that the two cannot coexist; that colour, if it is to be its own sufficing end, must exist independently of form. The knowledge they acquired and the sources they drew from are still scattered through Oriental life. It is not too much to say that any one who feels the profound colour-effect of this little twilit *café* I have been describing will, if he analyses his feelings, find that they are similar in kind to the feelings evoked by St. Mark's. It would be odd, indeed, if they were not, for the very same means are employed in the great basilica as in the little hovel. In both there is the use of rich masses of colour used for its own sake; in both all suggestion of exact form is banished, all sharp edges and clean-cut angles are avoided, and deep, heavily rounded ceilings bound the interior; in both a dim twilight heightens the effect of mystery, and adds to the richness and depth of colour. In short, the laws which the Greek artist worked out with such splendid audacity in his architecture were merely matters of common life, and are being exemplified, as blind instincts, by Orientals every day and all over the world.[1]

[1] See Appendix, Note E.

CHAPTER XI

THE OUED SOUF AND ITS OASES

The region of dunes—Aspect of the scenery—Difficulty of judging size and distance—The several kinds of oases—The hope of well-sinking—The "cup" oases—Our stay in an Arab village—The Souf dates—The census of palm-trees—The date harvest—The cares of desert husbandry—The source of desert life—The attack of the sand.

THE Oued Souf, lying eastward of Tuggurt, forms a portion of the Grand Erg, the region of pure sand-dunes. The decomposition of the desert's structure—of rock and cliff and plateau—is here completely carried out. The last pebble has been resolved into the grains that composed it. The whole landscape is a testimony to the successful perseverance of the sand, and bears witness to its victory.

Hour after hour, and day after day for several days, the curved slopes of sand lay round us as pure as drifts of snow just fallen. Not a blade of green marked their surface. The whiteness of the sand was dazzling, and its absolute monotony and sameness, combined with the deep, equally unvarying blue of the sky, produced an effect of eccentricity not far removed from the grotesque.

THE OUED SOUF AND ITS OASES 163

The dunes succeed each other in an endless array of hillocks, rarely divided, in my recollection, by any appreciable flat. The caravan proceeds by winding in and out between their bases. Let the reader picture a field sprinkled, as thickly as they can be set together, with molehills. Let him, if he can, by an effort of the imagination, turn those molehills pure white, and see with his mind's eye a string of black insects making a corkscrew progress by winding in and out between them, and he will have a bird's-eye view of our caravan among the dunes.

As we entered into these white defiles an unutterable deadness, emptiness, and mortal stillness seemed to close about us. The unreality of the landscape was added to by the loss of all sense of proportion. The scenery is mountainous on a diminutive scale. It suggests an endless array of chains of hills and mountain summits, the similarity of which in shape to formations of real ranges gives the idea of considerable size. Crest beyond crest and ridge beyond ridge, they stretch away into the distance. It is impossible to judge their dimensions or the width of the valleys that separate them. Nothing exists that can supply a standard of measurement; no tree, or house, or rock, or other object gives scale to the picture. No atmospheric effect softens the further outlines and suggests their distance. In this pure air you see all things, as it were, in a vacuum, and the distant ranges are as clear and white as the nearer ones.

Under these circumstances the instinct of a European is enormously to exaggerate the size and distance apart of the hills. The peak you see some way off, lifting its head above its fellows, will seem a Mont Blanc, to be measured in thousands of feet. The last range you can distinguish on the horizon will seem a day's journey off. In five minutes you are passing under Mont Blanc, which turns out to be a hillock of two or three hundred feet high, and in another five are crossing the range where you thought to camp for the night.

In spite of constant correction I never could get the hang of this scenery. Again and again I rubbed the illusion of great size and great space out of my eyes, but it always returned. Our caravan itself was the only object that could give a standard, and this it sometimes did with very startling effect. Repeatedly, after riding forward, H—— and I would sit on some blond summit and watch the vast tumbled expanse that lay around us until we had all unconsciously received the impression of its vastness. Then through a gap far away would come a terrifying spectacle— gigantic beasts, half as big as the hills themselves, with curved, outstretched necks, and huge men lolling on their backs. They came bearing down upon us with leisurely gait, that somehow left hills and valleys behind in a few steps. For a moment one was aware of a struggle between scenery and camels as to the correct size of scale. Then as the realisation of Ahmeda's cooking-pots asserted itself the scenery would give in and collapse pitifully to its real dimensions.

To a stranger's eye the existence of water in this country of the Souf would seem hopelessly out of the question. But it is never safe in the matter of water to judge the Sahara by appearances. We are now in the trough of that great depression which

THE OUED SOUF AND ITS OASES 165

drains towards the shotts, and the water-carrying strata here approach nearest to the surface. Frequently among these dunes there is but a crust of earth dividing the water from the surface. The gardens of these regions fill small hollows excavated by hand between the dunes, so that the palms have their roots in the soaked strata. The oases look like round bowls of green plants set in the earth, the tops of the palms reaching to about the level of the desert.

There are three kinds of oases. First, the river oases, which are confined to the neighbourhood of hills sufficiently big to attract a rainfall. The descending water quickly sinks beneath the sandy floor of the desert, but during the winter and spring its bed will frequently carry for some distance a torrent which in summer either dries up entirely or shrinks to a slender line of stagnant pools. The oases are planted sometimes in the bed of the river, sometimes on its bank, and the water is intercepted by barrages and conducted by an elaborate system of watercourses to the palms. These are, however, not the most prosperous oases, the water being apt to fail just at the season when the palms have most need of it.

The second kind are those fed by wells, whether bored by the Arabs themselves or by the artesian process, which is now steadily supplanting the native method. Of these I have already spoken. They represent the only possibility or hope of mitigating the awful sterility of the desert. To what extent the system may be generally applied is a question it is impossible to answer fully as yet. Southward to Ouargla and the furthest French outposts wells have been pierced, and oases planted or renovated, and in many places, from points of vantage, the windings of the hidden river may be traced by the spots of green which mark its course, each one of which is secretly sucking at the buried stream. Through parts of the Tunisian desert, and especially along the eastern coast, where forests of palms have been planted in the last fifty years, the artesian apparatus has been used with signal effect. There is reason to suspect that in many districts in the Sahara it can be employed. The signs and cuttings of prehistoric rivers are traceable in places throughout the central and southern deserts, and these are held to indicate the presence of subterranean water. Certain mountain ranges, as the Borku and Tibesti groups in the east, the Ahaggar and Tademait in the centre, and the Adrar in the west, attract a rainfall and encourage hopes of irrigation. The great oases of the central desert at Tuat, Tidikelt, and throughout the Gourara valley are rich in water, and capable, probably, of considerable extension Several artesian wells have already been sunk there. And there are numbers of other spots where villages and a restricted fertility already exist, and these it is expected may be enlarged and their number added to.

It is, in fact, in the artesian process that the optimists see a hope of the Sahara undergoing in time such a change as will fit it to be included in a scheme of civilised organisation. A settled population may, through it, be increased, the trade of the old caravan routes may be revived, travelling may become safe and comparatively easy, a trans-Saharan railway may link the Sudan with the north, the control of the Government over the predatory tribes may become more tangible and effective.

A RIVER OASIS.

THE OUED SOUF AND ITS OASES 167

There is something so attractive even to the mere traveller in the creation of oases—the work strikes one as so purely beneficent, and the appeal made to the eye and the imagination is so emphatic—that any one who has travelled in the desert and who remembers—and who can forget?—the change from these blazing wastes of sand to the dense thickets of palms, and the delight of being received from the outer glare into the green embrace of these groves, must always think of the work with sympathy, and be under the temptation, perhaps, to exaggerate its prospects. The Sahara is the ultimate problem with which all the French North African colonies are concerned. Follow up any one of them and it brings you to the desert. The desert forms the vast core of this great empire, and before the separate colonies can become united in anything but name, the question how to span these almost uninhabited wastes, how to extend the oases, and how to curb the enterprise of Bedouin marauders, will have to be dealt with. There are pessimists in regard to the part that well-sinking may be made to play in the scheme of union as well as optimists. The moderates, however, while they agree that the hopes of the Sahara must not be pitched in the key of the Oued Rir, are sanguine that the work of irrigation may be so extended as to render French occupation of the desert effective.

Much hangs on this issue. The permanent nature of the artesian borings has already introduced, wherever it has succeeded, a quite new sense of security into Arab life. The French wells apparently do not "die." The villagers, not being haunted by the fear of having to abandon their homes and push off into the waste, and not being bullied and plundered and even actually enslaved by their nomad brethren, as was the happy custom in days of yore, attach themselves permanently to the soil and range themselves on the side of law and order. It must be remembered, too, that the stability of the Government which protects them depends itself on the creation of habitable centres, since it is impossible to exercise efficient control over the desert except from points of vantage within it. Thus the mitigation of desert sterility by means of oases and springs and the pacification of the desert tribes are aspects of the same process. Pacification depends on fertilisation. The Arab and Touareg nomads are fierce and dangerous races, but it is not by armed expeditions and flying columns that they will be finally dealt with, but rather by weakening those natural conditions which sustain them. The desert stands for the principle of incoherence in nature. The Arab stands for the same thing in society. He may be trusted to flourish and exercise his peculiar gifts, to pillage and rob and plunder and generally disintegrate every existing form of social structure, so long as the conditions favourable to such an existence reign in the Sahara. What it comes to, in short, is this: the tribes can only be subdued by subduing the desert; the desert can only be subdued by planting oases; and oases can only be planted by sinking wells. To realise this sequence is to understand the part which an engineering process may be called upon to play in the consolidation of a great colonial empire.

And then, besides the river and the well oases, there exists also the excavated or "cup" variety.

THE OUED SOUF AND ITS OASES

This, though a small family, is the most exquisitely lovely of any. I have been faintly reminded of them by those little villages, nestling among orchards and elm-trees, which you come to suddenly in deep nooks among the smooth sweeping outlines of Exmoor, or look down upon from the rolling bare downs of Dorsetshire; nooks which seem to have collected and appropriated all the fertility which by right should be outspread over the surrounding country.

But in the desert the effect is heightened by the utter barrenness of the sand and the extraordinary richness of the fertile spots. These little "cups," an acre or two in extent, clustering in groups or strung out in an irregular chain, are filled to the very brim with verdure. The palm-heads form a roof above, supported by the slender columns of their stems. Below fruit-trees, peach, apricot, almond, fig, open their blossoms and spread their paler green leaves, while the ground itself is thickly covered with succulent crops and vegetables. Seen from the top of some taller dune, the view of the desert floor, inlaid with these patines of bright green, combines into one view, with extraordinary effect, the extremes of barrenness and fertility.

We stayed among these villages nearly a week, being kept partly by the bad weather. It blew continuously, and to travel in this country of loose sand during a wind is difficult, if not dangerous. The nights were calm, and then the murkiness died out of the air and the stars shone out. At dawn the wind would gradually rise and the air slowly become obscured. First there came a milky tinge along the horizon, obliterating its sharp outline. Gradually the whiteness spread over the sky, and, as the wind lashed up more and more sand, it grew darker and darker, until it became a dull murky red, almost like a London fog.

During these days we lived in a disused, or unfinished, little hut in the midst of one of the villages which are huddled on the slopes above the gardens. Our lodging consisted of a small walled enclosure, with, in one corner of it, a roofless hut:

> " Four naked walls
> That stared upon each other."

Here we spread our rugs and saddles. From here every morning we watched the sky above the low roofs of the village grow sickly white and yellow. There was no escaping the sand. Everything we ate and drank was gritty with it, and the thickness of the atmosphere brought on a feeling of almost unbearable weariness and oppression. It was a blessed change at evening when the wind died and the moon came out. Our little camp looked snug enough then. The ponies tethered to their footrope; under a white arch opposite the flicker of a fire where the men are sitting; above, the clear sky and sparkle of stars.

Sometimes we braved the weather and went for rides and walks among the villages and oases. We skirted, or climbed, the smooth sandbanks, and came every now and then to hollows, or dells, between them, or narrow ravines winding round their bases, all filled with date-palms, whose heads as we stood on the slopes above came to the level of our feet. These

IN AN ARAB VILLAGE.

THE OUED SOUF AND ITS OASES

cups, full of verdure, were usually unsuspected until we got to the brink of them. Each came as a fresh and delightful surprise. Sometimes they appeared in the distance like a fringe of dark green feathers, just rising above the sand.

These Souf plantations are famous for the quality of their dates. Indeed, the natural conditions here are most suited to the peculiar needs of the trees. The date-palm has this odd and apparently contradictory habit—that it loves moisture yet cannot bear rain. Great heat and extreme dryness of atmosphere are necessary for it to ripen its crop. It only prospers when, in the Arab phrase, it has its feet in water and its head in fire. The difficulty of fulfilling these requirements constitutes the date-palm the exclusive perquisite of the Sahara. It is formed expressly to profit by that subterranean supply of water which is the curious characteristic of desert agriculture. It is the desert tree as unmistakably as the camel is the desert animal.

Here in the Souf the trees stand with their roots permanently in moisture. In the oases depending on springs and wells the trees are watered at regular intervals, just like cattle, and the supply allowed to each is carefully measured. The waterings should be at intervals of five to ten days, and the allowance for each tree should, if possible, attain to half a litre per minute. It has been tried in lesser quantities, and careful experiments have shown that the half-litre tree yields a 20 per cent. larger crop than that nourished on a third of a litre. The least stinting of their drink is immediately registered in a diminished harvest, and the deterioration of the tree soon follows.

The decay of the palms is the most significant and conclusive testimony possible to the impoverishment and dwindling numbers of the population of the village. So much are dates the staple of food and commerce that it is always customary among Arabs, and, indeed, I think among all who are familiar with desert life, to compute the wealth and strength of a village by the number of its date-palms. It is easier to census these than to census the people, and the result is more reliable. Instead, therefore, of speaking of a village of such-and-such a population, as would be customary with us, you will always in the desert speak of a village of so many palms. The equivalent in human numbers will be understood. The village of Elim, "where were twelve wells of water and three score and ten palm-trees," is described in this way in the Book of Genesis. The people are not mentioned.

I have met with an account by A. E. Pease of the date harvest, answering to the vintage of a wine country, which makes one long to be among these oases at that season. "In October," he says, "the bunches of golden and brown fruit hang in great clusters on the gaudy orange stems from the head of every palm. Towards the end of the month and early in November the Arabs and negroes may be seen daily climbing the high trees and cutting down the great white masses. Then follow, during the succeeding weeks, all the other operations of the date harvest, the stacking of the dates in the houses, the packing in the shops and warehouses, the loading and unloading of the camels." A novice will divide all dates into the two classes of dry dates and glutinous. There are, however, a great number of varieties of both classes. The

THE OUED SOUF AND ITS OASES

most prized of all, I am told, is the deglat-nour, a delicious, semi-transparent date that melts in the mouth.

More clearly here than elsewhere, since the oases are smaller and the sand more mobile, can one realise that state of constant feud in which the villagers and the desert live together. When first I saw the fringes of dry palm-leaves stuck like decorative friezes along the contours of the dunes round the hollows, I fancied that the village children had been playing here at a little gardening on their own account. Later, when I noted the effect of these puny-looking obstacles, and the way in which they caught and stilled the rolling sand before it could take wing from the dune's summit, I saw them as part of the tactics of a prolonged campaign.

The cares of the desert husbandman do not end with the finding of water. That finding is the signal for the beginning, not the ending, of the strife. It is the first requisite, indeed, and that on which all hangs. Its preciousness is a commonplace, a truism; you say it and have done with it. And yet, living in the desert you are bound to recur to it. Again and again you are made to feel how water measures life. Yonder, in the hollow, a tap is turned and a spring set flowing. The gardens gather round it, the heads of the palms throng taller and thicker, the village spreads along the slope. Human life with all its vicissitudes is here. The little drama, ever old and ever new, is played and played again; the web woven and rewoven. There is the gossip in the village above, the toil in the garden below, the friendships, quarrels, and daily cares, the love-making under this big moon. And all this hangs, as palpably as a coat upon a nail, by that jet of water in the hollow. There is the source of all life, from the old greybeard who saw, maybe, the first palm planted, down to the last-arrived brown baby tossed out to kick in the dust and flies. Let that be turned off, and instantly life fades from garden and village, and the desert resumes its sway.

And the oases once formed must be maintained. The desert never despairs or gives in; you can never say you have conquered it. Now it comes at you like a roaring lion, all its dunes charging in mad commotion, with yellow manes flying in the wind, as though they would carry the position by a *coup de main*. But even on tranquil days it is never quite idle. Look at this tiny thread of new sand that has slipped down the slope, and is, innocently and all unconsciously as you would say, gliding in between these onions. Come to-morrow and you will find it advanced another few inches; come next month and your onion bed will be a thing of the past. Innocent as it looks, that thread is the advance-guard of the desert. It represents a settled and constant purpose which can only be met by an equally steady resistance.

CHAPTER XII

A HAVEN OF REFUGE

The desert in a rage—A rough ride—Arrival at Nefta—Fertility of the oasis—Composure of camels—Death of one of our camels—Their adaptability to the desert—Their beauty amidst this scenery—Our camp in the oasis—A night scene—Sensuousness of Oriental scenery—A scrap of poetry.

OUR worst experience of the desert in one of its mad fits of rage was on a morning when, luckily for us perhaps, we were nearing the large oasis of Nefta, near the Tunisian frontier. The flapping of the tent and the drumming of rain-drops upon it woke us, and Ahmeda, in some excitement, with his haik bound about his face, hurried our departure. He explained that, so long as the rain lasted, it would keep the sand quiet, and that this was our opportunity to press on.

Accordingly, in a very short time we had struck tent, loaded camels, saddled ponies, and were under way. It seemed to us a somewhat purposeless proceeding. The rain was, and had been, heavy, the ground was saturated, and there seemed no prospect of its drying in a hurry. As Nefta, we knew, was only half a day's march, it seemed unnecessary to start off in this frantic hurry, in the middle of the night and the pouring rain, to reach it in safety. Ahmeda, however, made no answer to these representations beyond loading up the camels and flinging saddles on ponies. The other men, wretched as they appeared, and as Arabs always appear in rain, seconded his efforts with all their energy. It was evident there was a motive in their haste which was not as yet apparent.

Morning broke wan and sickly. As the light grew the rain slackened. The big warm drops became less frequent and at last ceased. The dull, opaque sky was of a pasty-faced white, and the air was hot and oppressive; but the wind still blew as hard or harder than ever.

Hardly had the rain stopped than I tasted between my lips and teeth the familiar gritty texture of sand. Hardly had the light increased sufficiently to disclose to view the drifts when all their hedges and crests could be seen crawling and flickering in the gale. Already there was that droning sound in the air which meant the beginning of the "walking" of the dunes. We saw now the reason of all the hurry. The rain cannot hold the sand for more than the instant it is falling. So soon as it strikes earth, it sinks in. One moment you may be streaming with water like a drowned rat, the next you are choking in clouds of sand.

Ahmeda ranged up alongside and waved to me to follow him. "How far to Nefta?" we shouted at him. "Two hours," he screamed back. The air was growing darker and darker, and the roar of the sand as it rushed along the desert made speech, except by shouting, impossible. I could just distinguish our tall camels in the gloom, their ungainly action giving them some-

A HAVEN OF REFUGE

thing the look of ships pitching and tossing in a gale of wind.

However, it was no use to stay with them. Ahmeda led the way, pushing his tall and shambling beast along at a great pace, and guiding himself by some mysterious instinct which was to us totally incomprehensible. We followed as best we might, breathing sand as we went, and with our unprotected faces bent to escape the cutting sleet. My recollection of the next two hours is no more definite than would be the recollection of being rolled over and over by a huge breaker. A singing and roaring in the ears, almost total blindness, a sense of something not very far removed from suffocation, and the feeling that you are in the hands of elements very much more powerful than yourself—these are the only vague and general impressions that remain to me.

I have heard, and can well believe it, that the Arabs in many regions look upon these sandstorms with a superstitious dread and horror as being the work of evil and hostile spirits. They convey that impression. They seem to express an almost humanly malignant rage and spite. The shrieking of the sand, the bewildering fury of its attack, the sudden darkness, the chaos of mingling earth and sky, suggest one of those mad instincts of hate so fierce and definite as to be unaccountable for as an unconscious process of Nature. This rage you feel is meant. This is intentional spite. Only devils could act thus.

I have a clearer recollection of our appearance when at last we got into Nefta. If we had been buried in sand and dug up again we could not have been more saturated with it. Hair, ears, clothes, were full of it.

Our cheeks were scarlet and sore with the ceaseless battering, and on them had formed hard crusts of sand, cemented by the water that had streamed from our eyes. To penetrate into the green recesses of the oasis and leave the tumult and storm behind, was an experience never to be forgotten. The oasis we were in was an extensive one, with many flowing streams and dense throngs of palms that, sheltering each other, shut out both wind and sand. Far in the distance by the edge of the grove the long leaves were weeping and tossing; but here all was tranquil. Beneath the palms a quantity of peach and other fruit-trees made clouds of white and pink blossom, and the earth beneath was green with crops. With senses still half bewildered, we led our ponies into the midst of this tropical vegetation and camped, by permission of the owner, in a green plot near running water.

It was hours before our camels turned up. We strolled through the oasis, following the narrow tracks of hard-beaten mud which led into the green glades. The large heads of the young palms springing from the ground made clumps of dense and glossy foliage, mixed with the flowers of almond, peach, and apricot trees. Corn and rice, and onions, and other vegetables grew knee-high on the ground. Far above us the starry heads of the taller palms shook and whispered in the passing currents of air. Occasionally, the faint tinkle of water sounded. We were soon completely enveloped in this delicious underwood, the view showing nothing but green labyrinths on all sides, the surrounding desert completely shut out and forgotten, so that we might have been wandering in an interminable jungle.

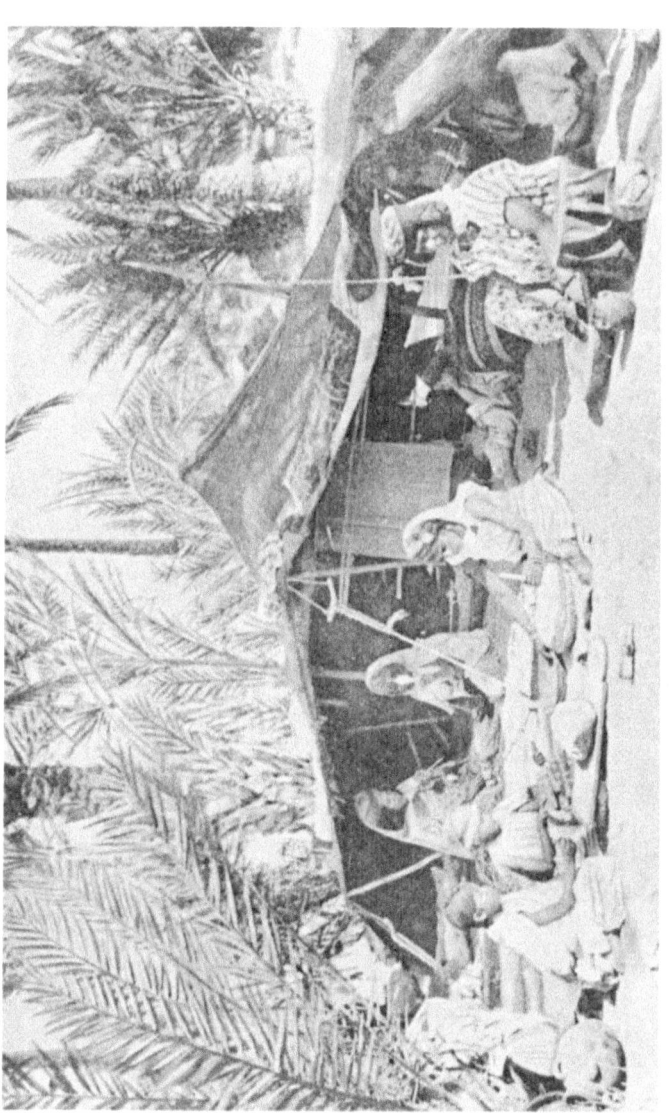

Camp in an Oasis.

A HAVEN OF REFUGE

Returning, we climbed the hill to the village, built as they generally are on the slope overlooking the oasis, for the alluvial land is too precious to be used for building purposes. We visited an Arab *café* spread with grass mats, where we sat and drank delicious sweet coffee out of tiny cups, and then returned once more to our grove.

At length, much to our relief, we saw our belated caravan approaching, gliding through the trees with its usual stealthy, undulating movement. The Arabs were much buffeted and dishevelled, and proceeded to shake the sand from their garments and clear it from their faces with many groans and lamentations. The camels preserved their usual air of impenetrable tranquillity. They gazed at the delicious verdure about them with the same *sang-froid* with which they gaze upon the desert wastes.

It seems as if nothing, painful or pleasant, had power to ruffle a camel's serenity or disturb his slightly cynical composure. Just before reaching Tuggurt one of our camels fell sick. By some mysterious signs the Arabs knew it was bad, but to an ordinary eye, except that it was inclined to lag a little, there seemed nothing the matter. Calmly it walked into the village and sat down in its place, and calmly, with the same cold indifference as it had lived, it died.

I was told a story by our guide of a camel which, after being cruelly ill-used by its driver for a long time, turned upon the man, threw him down, killed him by crushing him with its sharp breastbone, and then proceeded to tear him up into the smallest pieces. One can imagine that if once that iron composure of theirs were broken down some such frenzy might ensue. They have, I think, that sort of attraction that belongs to a curious, whimsical piece of mechanism which is yet wonderfully adapted to its own special purpose and place. In cities the very houses laugh at them. But watch them in the desert, slinging forward with tireless, stealing action, and see how every gift they possess is brought out and applied. How well the soft sand upholds those ridiculous, great, spongelike feet! How admirably the slack action, which consists only of a swing of the long, pendulum-like legs, is fitted to deal with these vast spaces! How marvellous, above all, is that arrangement of an internal pouch, or "extra stomach," whereby the animal can carry its own supply of water. The camel needs a Sahara to set it off. Its very temperament seems caught from the desert. It has the desert's reserve. I never saw an Arab caress or pat his camel, or a camel that seemed to know its own master. It has the desert's aloofness and cynicism. It blends in colour with the desert's tawny hue.

Millet once wrote in a letter to Pelloquet, "I desire that the creations which I depict should have an air of being dedicated to their situation." He adds in the same letter that everything is beautiful provided it turns up "in its own place," and he ends, "This, then, is my conclusion: the beautiful is that which is in place."

So I have seen a camel coming from the town into the desert, and, by the act of placing itself in harmony with its surroundings, put on beauty like a garment. I have seen the uncouthness of form and shape and the awkwardness of gait disappear and perfect propriety and comeliness take their place.

A HAVEN OF REFUGE

I have seen the whole character of the beast change under my very eyes, and, from being a grotesque and a monstrosity, become perfectly natural and a delight to look at; and so I conclude with Millet, "the beautiful is that which is in place."

Our camp was pitched that night in the grove. Towards evening the storm went down. The curdled, murky air gradually cleared. The noise of the desert ceased. Above the palms the great, languid stars looked down at us, closing and opening their saucer eyes. Our fire lit up a little space, showing the groups of hooded Arabs, the ponies, and the crouching, teapot-shaped forms of the camels. The twigs and branches round us projected into the light, and the upward-arching leaves of a young palm glittered. Beyond this illuminated spot all was mystery, deep recesses veiled in shadow throwing up the groups in the foreground. One caught whiffs every now and then of musky scent from almond or other flowers. The whole scene—motionless palms and big stars, snake-necked camels and crouching Arabs, the flickering beams of the camp fire, the velvet-shadowed spaces beyond, and the warm and perfumed air—all seemed charged and loaded with the same deep emotion. Somehow, Wordsworth, the poet of English wood and meadow, has managed to put into three lines more of this emotion of tropical scenery than is to be found in all Byron's or Moore's Eastern tales put together—

> "The breezes their own languor lent,
> The stars had feelings which they sent
> Into those gorgeous bowers."

Nights passed in the low country of Ceylon came back to me. I remembered the droning chants and spicy smells of Cingalese villages, the dull throbbing of tomtoms, the yellow light, the deep surrounding gloom, the polish on the slow river, hardly moving between masses of overarching foliage. There was the same feeling there as here, the same wonderful depth and richness of light and shadow, the same suggestion of hidden splendour, of wealth and luxuriance felt rather than seen, the same languid, warm, and scented atmosphere. These are the things that make up that elemental force, an emotion, not a thought, on which the character and life and art of the East are founded.

According, however, to Ahmeda, the morals of the neighbourhood were by no means equal to its beauty. He announced his intention of keeping a vigilant look-out, and proceeded to post a sentry between us and the village and carefully to secure all the animals. We were inclined to take a light view of the danger to start with, but when he returned with his firearms and proceeded to load and prime them the gravity of the situation made itself felt. Heaven defend me from my friends! I remember thinking as I watched the barrel of an old revolver staring impartially round as if in search of a victim. However, in spite of our precautions, the night passed bloodlessly away.

Next morning, standing in the grove and watching the daybreak bring its details into view, I endeavoured to describe the scene in a kind of Arab chant, with the following result—

"Soft and light as foam the almond-blossom breaks; the white tufts of it appear in the shadow of the palms.

A HAVEN OF REFUGE

The camels are loading; through the fruit-trees pass moving figures.
It is a green twilight in which I stand; the slender columns of the palms shoot upward,
Bearing their delicate heads like clusters of ferns against the sky.
A bird sings near me a note or two and is silent; now through the grove steals the first yellow sunbeam.
The spell is broken—a dove wings its way through the covert, straight and fast, as if on an errand;
The leaves shake in the breath of morning, an Arab passes, a dog barks.
The spell is broken—the indescribable hush and silence, as of sleep surprised, is over,
As I turn to go, through all the countless heads of palms breaks the yellow sunlight.
When I read this let me recall this hour, this scene in the Sahara."

CHAPTER XIII

SCENES BY THE WAY

The evening camp—Birds—A moonlight start—Cold nights—Instincts wakened by desert scenery—Sunrise—The sound of it—A desert landscape—Arab poetry—Its insistence on shade and water—Arab society—The spring grazings—Their poetic treatment—A scene in Devonshire—Tendency of the imagination to recall such scenes in the desert—The mirage—The desert's sense of humour.

THE coldness, silence, and starlight of the start before dawn and the gathering when the day's march is ended round the evening camp fire are the two hours best worth remembering in desert life. We camped, as a rule, in some dell or hollow, sheltered from view and from the wind. On the march, unless there was water near our destined halting-place, we would have filled our water-skins at the last well; and sometimes we had to carry with us a supply for more than one day. "Drinking water" is a *façon de parler* in the desert. Threepennyweight of salt to the quart is enough, as the reader will find if he tries it, to give it a strong briny flavour. Such water, however, is freely drunk in the Sahara. Horses, camels, and donkeys even thrive on water containing nearly half an ounce of salt to the quart. It varies very much in different neighbourhoods, but is always distinctly brackish and

SCENES BY THE WAY

generally impregnated besides with potash, magnesia, sulphuric acid, and other delicacies, to such an extent that the old custom of poisoning the wells always struck me as a very superfluous one.

All things, however, adapt themselves to it. Water that will appease the thirst of an Arab would only aggravate that of a European. The date-palm, *pièce de resistance* of Arab life, has the capacity of living with its roots in a solution of brine that would try the constitution of anything but seaweed, and all such bushes and grasses as struggle for life in the desert are saturated with salt and have a strongly salt and bitter taste. The Arabs distinguish carefully between the degrees of brackishness of the water, and a good well is widely celebrated, caravans often going miles out of their way to strike it. Even the purest, however, is strongly tinctured with the sulphur imbibed from the soil, and the blackest coffee only partially disguises its flavour and smell.

If possible we would halt where some tussocks of dry grass, or scanty scrub, or low, twisted thorn-bushes, with long white thorns like bayonets, gave a supply of fuel. These, easily pulled up and piled in a heap, were lit by the touch of a match, and instantly the fire blazed up, jumping from twig to twig with a rapid snapping noise like volleys of tiny musketry. The little coffee-pot was then thrust into the blaze and cups and sugar set out on the sand. The camels were let loose to graze, the ponies tethered and given their forage, and the little tent pitched. By this time coffee was ready, and we gathered round the fire to sip it, while we rolled our first cigarette and looked round with great satisfaction at our small encampment, ensconced so snugly in its dell, with the white sand-dunes spreading for leagues all round.

I used to walk up the slope above camp and enjoy from there the view across the desert in the last half-hour of sunset. There is a moment's feeling of relaxation, and the desert seems to sigh with relief, as the sun drops like a golden ball into the west. A few birds sometimes chirp from the plain below, though of these there are very few. The commonest is the desert lark; a pale dove-coloured little thing with black marks on wings and tail. It has a clear, melancholy call of one note, and loves sitting on the topmost twig of a bush or grass-tuft and there uttering this low, soft cry. Every now and then it goes through a curious performance of shooting straight upward some yards into the air, and then pitching over and coming down head first. This is done in a languid and woebegone way, as if the performance had long outgrown any interest it may once have possessed. Both song and flight still keep a faint memory of lark traditions. The flight is a lark's flight broken off at a few yards. The single note of song has the lark's sweetness.

Even for that single note, however, one is grateful in the desert. You must live for weeks in the midst of a dead silence to appreciate the singing of birds. Your thoughts go back then to English lawns, mornings and evenings, with the long shadows across them, and the clear calls of blackbirds and thrushes echoing in the shrubberies—

> "In Devon woods at break of day
>   The birds sing clear;
> Oh, burning land of desert sand,
>   No birds sing here."

SCENES BY THE WAY

I find this note in my diary, jotted down on the spot one evening. "The last beams of the sun come to me across a broken sea of sand-dunes. At my back, in a saucer-shaped hollow, already in shade, the camp fire snaps and sparkles. Figures run about with pots. The call comes up that supper is ready. On the slope opposite our camels browse, stretching their long necks left and right to the coarse grass-tufts, their coats lit to a warm yellow by the sun's last rays. How solitary our speck of a camp looks on the face of this vast solitude! I stop a moment and look out across the sand. The sun's last spark flickers and disappears. The awful blue pallor settles down on the face of the desert."

England and English life used to seem remote at these times to the verge of unreality. One saw it as something from which one had become, for the moment, wholly detached. The things that were so important —Piccadilly and its omnibuses, "the old crush at the corner of Fenchurch Street," Parliament and politics, Mr. Chamberlain and Mr. Balfour, grave literary schemes and consultations, the slings and arrows of outrageous editors, and all the pushing and pulling, and scolding and arguing, and sweat and dust of that compressed and tangled little state of existence—somehow all these things no longer seem important at all. You have won clear of it all for a little, and drift at ease, the bare soul under the bare sky, relishing its solitude and calm.

There was an arrangement of the sand and grasstufts, which I remember, here and in most of our desert halting-places, which seemed purposely designed to bear out the weird loneliness of the scene. The wind in the desert blows with the regularity of the trades, almost always from one quarter, and of course drifts and carries the sand to a great extent along with it. The big tussocks of grass, growing a few yards apart, arrest this flow of sand, and the wind sweeping past either side leaves a mound perfectly rounded and symmetrical, exactly like a grave, with the grass-tuft for a headstone. The effect used to be just as if we had come to camp in some vast cemetery, and the countless graves scattered around seemed to account, to my fancy, for the solitude and lifelessness of the scenery.

But better than camp even was the morning ride before sunrise. Whether it is the way you live in the desert, the wholesome, light food, chiefly dates, figs, and rice, or the pure air, I do not know, but anyway the misery of the "getting-up" process, the blinking and groaning and stretching and yawning, are entirely and absolutely obliterated. Instinct or some slight sound rouses you, and with the opening of your eyes sleep has vanished. Instead of struggling for half an hour with the fumes of it, you wake, as animals wake, to an instant and full consciousness of all around you.

The moon still rides in crystal clearness, and the great stars are scattered thickly over the sky down to the very edge of the desert. The nights are extraordinarily cold, compared with the great heat of the day, for the sand, light and porous, radiates its warmth away directly the sun's rays are withdrawn from it. There is something rapier-like in the thin piercing cold of a desert night, matching in sharpness the steelly glitter of the moonlight. Coats and rugs are flung on shoulders while the hot coffee, invariable accompaniment in the desert to every halt or start, is got ready. Preparations for the march take but a few minutes. The sleeping mats are rolled up, the tent struck and packed, the ponies saddled, the grunting, protesting camels loaded and corded, and in a few minutes the little caravan is winding in single file through the white drifts.

As these preparations are carried out on sand they are, of course, carried out quite noiselessly. The white figures of Arabs, the crooked shapes of camels, the ponies, and ourselves move and mingle without a sound, like ghosts. This gives an appearance of great stealth and secrecy to our proceedings. You would say, watching us as we steal away, that we were planning a night attack, or fleeing from a pursuing enemy.

One has some such feeling, a sense of cat-like vigilance and cunning, answering mysteriously to such surroundings. I used to feel abnormally crafty at this time of day. To waylay a caravan and pillage it would have seemed quite a natural and obvious thing to do. I should not have minded its being wrong, or cared what people said about it.

I used to imagine that such promptings might be the legacies of long-past actions; a secret tingling and response of deep buried instincts to the suggestion of their appropriate environment. Somehow the scene suggested experiences. It did not look familiar, perhaps, but it felt familiar. You could not say you remembered such a landscape, yet something in you responded to it, was secretly thrilled by it, sometimes seemed almost, or quite, to recognise it.

I am sure that where Nature is entirely primitive and savage she whispers little furtive suggestions to the savage in each of us. " Don't you remember," she mutters, "you felt thus, and thus? Wouldn't it be nice to go back to those days again?" And then the what you were a million years ago cocks an ear and stirs in its sleep. Ah, well it is the pretty Sussex fields and dumpling hills of Devon cannot hear the wicked whisperings of the desert.

The flats and salient features of this strange landscape are quite formless in the moonlight. The shadows look like crooked pieces of jet inlaid in a white surface. Even by day the desert is weird enough, but laid out in black and white with the vacant glitter of starlight hanging over it, it seems to have no connection with the earth you know of.

By and by we are watching the beginning of that tremendous spectacle, played for our sole benefit every morning—sunrise in the Sahara. As the moment approaches the air darkens, as though for fuller effect of contrast, and the cold sharpens. There is a breath heard that comes from nowhere and dies away. It is the desert turning in its sleep, as they say. Then a tuft or two of loose cloud in the east catches the first suggestion of colour, so welcome after the watery whiteness of the night. It appeals to what little life there is, and the low wail of a lark is heard near by as he pitches his first melancholy somersault for the day. Now a spark catches in the lower edge of a narrow cloud that lies along the horizon and runs along it like fire along paper. Next moment the sky is all ablaze. The clouds dissolve away. Two or three arrowy spokes of light dart to the zenith. The molten rim comes over the desert edge, and the first beam hits you full with marksmanlike precision as though you were a target.

These desert sunrises used to remind me of some great orchestral performance. First the note or two and tuning up; then the *bâton* raised, the one, two, three, and the crash of instruments all together. One does not usually talk of listening to a sunrise, but those in the desert used to strike me as distinctly audible. One could even characterise the music. It had the sound of cymbals and gongs.

By degrees comes the test of endurance. As the sun gets higher and hotter you feel the desert set its teeth and settle down for long hours of silent endurance. Slowly and deliberately the sun scans its face, with such a searching scrutiny as if it had dropped a half-sovereign here the day before and had come back to look for it. The air scorches your face, and you sip it through closed lips as you sip too hot tea. Your eyes burn, and you press your fingers on them now and then to give the relief of complete darkness.

And what a view the light discovers as it lays bare the face of the desert! An endless plain—

> "Forlorn and wild
> The seat of desolation,"

made up of whitish-brown or yellow sand and grit and rock, stretching to a horizon that seems a thousand miles away, so far can your glance penetrate in this pure atmosphere; broken by rocky plateaux or irregular chains of low hills, seamed with reefs and strewn with black fragments of stone worn smooth and glossy by the friction of blown sand; a landscape utterly dead and mineralised, from which everything suggestive of the possibility of life has fled.

And yet, strange as it may seem, it is out of this sterile scenery that the Arabs have evolved their songs of green bowers and shade. Perhaps that poetry can only be understood in the desert. No other has allusions so thrilling to groves, foliage, the scent of flowers, dew, moisture, and the murmuring of water. Their treatment of these subjects is even apt at times to strike one as morbid, as excessive. But it does not seem so when you are in the desert yourself and when your thoughts of shade and water have the poignancy the desert gives them.

A translation must miss the force of the original, but I will quote a specimen of the Arab treatment of these things:—

> "The shades have spead their canopy, and the flowers spread their pillows.
> The streams roll along their shores of flowers, some white, some red, some yellow, some sweet-scented.
> See! the waters gliding through the gardens, and the trees and their fruits resemble bracelets and chaplets;
> The birds sing melodiously upon them in every variety of note.
> The nightingale and the dove pour their plaintive strains, and make every lover weep.
> The gentle zephyrs whisper, and the branches move in softest measure.
> The boughs dance in the groves, among the trees, in the graceful movement.
> The dewdrops fall, and the flowers and the trees are studded with their pearls."

The reader will feel a certain exaggeration of sentiment here; an exaggeration which is due to the influence of the desert.

But what brings home to us, I think, most strikingly

SCENES BY THE WAY 193

the need the Arabs felt for dwelling on, in their poetry, what was so stinted in their lives, is a recognised rule of theirs, which laid it down that all considerable poems, whatever their subject, should open with a description of the spring grazing-grounds to which the tribes all resorted for a certain time in the year. The two main divisions of ancient Arab poetry were the Ode, or Kasîdah, and the Fragment, or Kitah, and of these the former, which was the longer and more important, was strictly formal in its development. Whatever the event might be which the poet wished to celebrate, he must begin by describing the bygone love-affairs, and the romantic meetings and partings of lovers which had taken place during the time when the tribes drove their camels to their common pasture-grounds.

No passages in Arab poetry are more touching, more romantic, or contain keener thrusts of pathos, than these recollections of vanished springs and vanished loves. But to understand them aright it should be remembered that they deal in experiences which were common to the nation. The Arabian late winter and early spring, when the scanty rainfall encouraged some growth of herbage over many parts of the land, was the time of social intercourse. At this time the camels were driven far and wide to common grazing-grounds, and acquaintanceships and friendships sprung up between the tribes. It was, moreover, a time of peace. The blood feuds of the Arabs were pursued with so much industry that it was found necessary to temper their thirst for justice with certain restrictions, and by mutual consent four months of the year were set aside as a close season, during which the taking of life under any plea was illicit. Of these peace months the first three coincide with the grazing season, an arrangement which was obviously indispensable if the benefits of that season were to be enjoyed.

Here were the makings of romance on a national scale. All lovely influences combined to foster it. The sights and sounds of spring were in the air. The herbage sprouted, flowers blossomed, water sparkled, the songs of nightingales resounded in the glade, the herds browsed, while over all an unwonted peace reigned, and enemies who had been seeking each others' lives but a little while before and hoped to be doing so again but a short time hence, might now associate freely and enjoy the pleasant season in full security.

Such interludes must have seemed like a glimpse of the Elysian fields. How deep they sank into the national consciousness, the Kasîdahs remain to tell. By and by the draughts of summer came again, the desert resumed its sway, the days of peace drew to an end, and each tribe sought the distant and permanent wells round which were its headquarters, and which afforded it a scanty supply of moisture through the summer heat. Imagination may suggest the melancholy partings, the breaking-up of camps, the farewells of friends, the more agonised farewells of lovers. Sometimes for lovers it was not farewell. A fleet dromedary might lurk in the darkness of the grove, a noiseless shadow flit across the empty desert, and the disappearance of the dark-eyed damsel with her daring lover might furnish a vendetta to start the summer upon.

Tradition demanded that the Kasîdah should, to begin with, revive the memory of these sylvan scenes

SCENES BY THE WAY 195

and romantic episodes, so painfully sweet to the Arab imagination; and only when that standing demand was satisfied might the poet go on to deal with the matter he had in view, which was most probably a panegyric on himself or his tribe, interspersed with boasts of his camel's fleetness or the breeding of his stallion.

There is something touching and pathetic in this endeavour to supply by poetic description the kind of refreshment which one is meant to derive from Nature, but which in the desert is so entirely lacking. And yet this demand on the poet's imagination is really only a typical example of what each individual's imagination is trying to do for itself. It seems a natural instinct, amidst such surroundings, to attempt to conjure up visions of coolness, foliage, and shade, so as to allow the mind to feed upon them. And never do such scenes seem more real and vivid to the mind's eye than when one is surrounded by scenery most alien to them. The shepherd in Wordsworth's poem, who had turned sailor, drew a vision of the life he missed out of the waves and foam round him, and—

> "Even with the organs of his bodily eye,
> Below him, in the bosom of the deep,
> Saw mountains—saw the forms of sheep that grazed
> On verdant hills."

In something the same way imagination in the desert plays such tricks with one that I can almost be said to have seen with my "bodily eye" in those wastes the kind of features which most one lacked there.

There is a spot in the valley of the River Exe, in Devonshire, which might be singled out as typical of the greenness and moisture of that most green and moist of counties. The river here divides, part of it diverging to act as a mill leat. The mill, however, was burnt down a good many years ago, and the leat's occupation being gone, it seems to have occurred to it of its own accord to abandon that enterprise, and it has accordingly broken across the neck of land which separates it from the main river, and in doing so has cut off an angle and made an island of it. A feeble trickle only continues in the old path of duty towards the mill, through a dense tunnel of hazels and alders.

These changes happened more years ago than any one can remember. The mill and the mill leat are practically things of the past. Only an extra richness in the bushes, and the thick growth of willow herb and meadowsweet, show the dampness that lingers along the hidden course of the leat. The island is a dense covert of alder and ash-trees, some of which have been cut off by the cross-current, and now stand, coated with moss, in mid-stream with channels of water, shaded by their branches, gushing and bubbling round them. Trout and water rats and moorhens haunt here. Sometimes a water ousel will light on a snag, and bob and curtsey at the foam below, or a kingfisher draw its line of blue up the long dark pool.

Water is seen or heard here on all sides, and speaks from each side with a different accent. There is the deep murmur of the mother river, the agitated clamour of the leat hurrying to rejoin it, and now and then the low, bell-like note of the few drops that, with impossible loyalty, still proclaim their faith in the vanished mill. The place had always, from the days I used to bathe there with other village children, been a favourite haunt of mine. For suggestions of coolness, dense foliage shade, and water tinkling and gliding in all directions it could not be beaten. As a rule, water with us runs in fixed beds and channels, which gives it a stereotyped and sophisticated look. Here it ran wild, following its own gipsy impulses. This was what, perhaps, gave the sense of naturalness to the place. One could imagine it a haunt of dryads or water pixies.

Well, this place now forms a part of my recollections of the Sahara. There was a pool just below an overhanging tree-trunk, where great blobs of foam, just the colour of the meadowsweet, went round and round perpetually, and the water always looked as black by contrast as stout in a tankard—that pool I have seen in the desert as clearly as ever I saw it in Devonshire.

In the case of the Arabs the endeavour to recreate such scenes as their spring pasturings must have been a normal imaginative condition. It expressed itself, as I have said, in that established regulation which required that every important poem was to open with a realistic description of these scenes. No matter how disconnected the subject of the poem might be with such associations, the first portion of it must be dedicated to the few glimpses the Arabs ever obtained of greenness and shade. To us, of course, a regulation of this kind would seem like an arbitrary forcing upon the poet of an absurd irrelevance. But in the desert it is not an irrelevance. Thoughts of shade and water are never irrelevant there. Had I been obliged to attempt a Kasîdah of my own, on the prowess of Ahmeda and his steed, let us say, it would have seemed to me perfectly natural to introduce, preferably at the beginning, an account of that spot on the Exe I have described. Had there been a party of us with the same recollections it would have seemed perfectly natural to make a rule that all our poems should begin with some such description. Never to the Arabs could an account of their spring pastures seem irrelevant, for their imaginations were so constantly at work correcting present sterility with the image of those scenes, that the scenes themselves were always, in a sense, present, and could always make their claim to notice felt when it was a question of the poetic treatment of any subject whatsoever.

And besides what there is of pathetic in this dwelling of the Arab mind on the little it ever experienced from Nature of kindness and motherly love, there is also something that gives one a great idea of the power and influence of the desert. It is difficult to define and limit an influence like this, even though one is perpetually conscious that it counts for a great deal in Arab character. It is, therefore, useful to be able to point to a concrete example of the working of it; a definite effect which it had on the mind and imagination of the Arab race, resulting in fixed and arbitrary rules in regard to the form and matter of their poetry.

A somewhat similar illusion of the desert's own inventing is the mirage, which tantalised our aching eyes on many a burning day's march. It is an attempt of the desert's own to reproduce the appearance of water and freshness in these wastes, and certainly, as a bit of counterfeiting, it beats the poets hollow. In some valley, perhaps, where the stony hillocks break down abruptly to the plain there lies a glittering pool of blue water. A breeze plays upon it, for the surface is silvered with a slight ripple. The hoax is sometimes

SCENES BY THE WAY

kept up until you are on the verge of the pool. Then the water shakes. Its edges begin to dissolve. The brink recedes as you advance. It breaks up. Parts seem to rise and float in air, and you ride in among the dissolving fragments and find nothing but unwetted sand and hot stones.

This is the desert's idea of humour. It is impossible for any one knowing it to doubt that it enjoys doing this sort of thing. The mirage is the smile that flits over its haggard face, and a wholly characteristic expression it is. Many a poor wretch, no doubt, dying the desert's death, has writhed under the irony of its bitter joke.

CHAPTER XIV

ARAB POETRY

Its portraiture of Arab life and character—Its genuineness and vigour—The type it describes—The death of Rabîáh—The traits it dwells on—Limitations of the type—Arab love-poetry—Its contrast with modern—Lack of depth in the Arab—The type common among Moslems—The Afghan—The Turk—The Albanian—The Moslem stage in civilisation.

BUT I have another reason for wishing to recur to Arab poetry. That that poetry gives us a vivid picture of the Arab in his great days every one knows; but the picture is a picture of more than the Arab. It is a picture of the orthodox Moslem type, which has never varied for twelve hundred years, and exists to-day wherever orthodox Mohammedanism prevails.

The great age of Arab poetry belongs to the time when the Arab race was gathering up its strength, like a great wave for bursting, for the effort which was to carry El Islam through the world. The forming of the nation and of a common language were the means to that end, and in both processes Arab poetry played an important part. Its tremendous popularity among the tribes, its stirring descriptions of scenes and a country general to the whole race, its insistence on universally recognised virtues and ideals, its appeal to the same passions and memories and prejudices, tended to bring out what all Arabs had in common and nourished a national sentiment. It was through its poets that tribe spoke to tribe. In the same way the honour in which poetry was held, the annual recitative competitions to which the tribes sent their most popular minstrels, and, in this way, the transmission from tribe to tribe of words and expressions sanctioned by fine poetry, all helped to spread a common language.

Moreover, it is important to notice that this common language and common nationality were a language and nationality entirely of the central or true Arabs, of the Ishmaelites, the Arabs of the sand. The waxing strength of the nation was marked by the decline and final extinction of the authority of the settled agricultural states. The nationality that arose on the fall of the Himyarite dynasty—settled in the fertile regions bordering on the Indian Ocean—was a nationality solely of desert tribes. The language which became universal was a purely desert language. The poetry that flourished was desert poetry. The warriors who carried the faith east and west were desert nomads. In short, the whole Mohammedan impulse, poetic, religious, and national, was of exclusively desert origin. It had to thrust aside everything that was not of the desert before it could satisfactorily exhibit itself. It came burning hot, so to speak, from the sand.

And of the breed of men who championed and swept forward this great movement, Arab poetry speaks with absolute clearness and precision. It describes the details of desert life with a vigour and realistic truth there is no mistaking; it throws the same fiery passion again and again into incidents of a similar kind. The

Arab poetry of this time has the merit that belongs to our own early ballad poetry. Whatever else it may or may not be, it is real. It deals with real events and real men.

Poetry was more a popular possession of the Arabs than, perhaps, it has ever been among any other people. The pains taken to preserve and perpetuate it bear witness to the almost sacred character which this, their sole art, had attained to. The duty of thus preserving it, in an age ignorant of writing, was entrusted to a special order of *rawis*, or reciters, often themselves poets, whose business it was to learn by heart each poem of their master, as it was composed, together with any special meaning or interpretation which any doubtful passage was intended to bear. Each poet had his *rawi*, and each *rawi*, in his turn, transmitted the poems and interpretations he had received to a disciple; and thus they were handed on by a literary class consecrated to the purpose from generation to generation.

That shows us the profoundly popular character of the art. And to that I will add this testimony of Ibn Rashik, translated by Sir Charles Lyall: "When there appeared a poet in a family of the Arabs the other tribes round about would gather together to that family and wish them joy of their good luck. Feasts would be got ready, the women of the tribes would join together in bands, playing upon lutes as they were wont to do at bridals, and the men and boys would congratulate one another; for a poet was a defence to the honour of them all, a weapon to ward off insults from their good name, and a means of perpetuating their glorious deeds and of establishing their fame for ever. And they would wish one another joy but for three things—the birth of a boy, the coming to light of a poet, and the foaling of a noble mare."

We may rely upon the reality and genuineness, hence the trustworthiness, of poetry of this kind. An unlettered and wandering race, without fixed habitations or written literature, whose architecture was the tent, and who in their passage through the world left no trace deeper or more durable than their footprints in the sand, it seems as if the Arabs turned instinctively to poetry as their only means of self-expression, their only rescue from oblivion and claim on the memory of future generations.

So that, in dealing with Arab poetry, and attempting to extract from it a living presentment of the Arab of that age, it is not as though we were set the task of deducing from the poetry of Rossetti or Swinburne a picture of contemporary English squires and farmers. Arab poetry is not imaginative and abstract, nor is it the outcome of a complex civilisation. It portrays the habits of a primitive people, and portrays them in direct and forcible language; and so unanimous and consistent is it in its testimony, so strong and vigorous in its strokes, so outspoken in all it loves and all it hates, that the typical desert personality jumps out of it at us, so to speak, and we see in it, as we see in nothing else he has left to us, the living Arab as he was in the great days of El Islam.

What was he like? We see a man physically, perhaps, as perfect as any type that has existed; a figure spare and lean, but sinewy and vigorous, with movements which betray, under the control of a natural dignity, the keenly sensitive nervous organisation of the character. With that a face and features fitted to express the kind of emotions by which such a form should be governed; an alert and fierce sensibility, haughtiness and pride, a swift, instinctive readiness to vindicate his own rights and resist the claims of others.

A favourite legend in Arab poetry is that which describes the heroism and death of Rabîáh, son of Mukaddam. The chief, convoying a party of women, is pursued and attacked by hostile tribesmen. Seeing the following cloud of dust, he turns to reconnoitre, and his sister, misinterpreting the action, cries out upon him for deserting his womenfolk; Rabîáh haughtily rebukes her —

> "Sayest thou, my sister, I am one to quail?
> Hast thou not known me join with spear and sword,
> And bring my blade back red with men's life-blood?"

He gallops to meet the enemy, and a desperate fight ensues, Rabîáh striking down several with his arrows. Then he spurs after the caravan and urges it on its way, and again turns to meet the pursuing enemy. Again and again he turns to beat off his assailants, and when his arrows are spent he attacks them with sword and spear. At last, in one furious encounter, Nubaishah, son of Habîb, gives him a fatal lance thrust. "I have slain him," he cries. "Thy mouth lies, O Nubaishah," answers Rabîáh. With difficulty, mortally wounded, he extricates himself from his enemies and rejoins his party. He bids his mother bind him up with her veil, which she does. He says to her—

> "A horseman hast thou lost like burning gold—
> A hawk that drives the throng like frightened birds,
> Deep diving with his blows before, behind."

ARAB POETRY

Still the enemy follow, and once more Rabíáh turns to bay. Where the track enters the mouth of a pass he reins up his mare, barring the way. His pursuers hesitate to attack him. At length, while he still fronts his enemies, death steals upon him, and as he feels its approach the indomitable chief thrusts his lance head into the ground and leans upon it as if resting. So he dies; but still, propped by the long lance in the saddle, the motionless form guards the pass. Day passes and twilight descends, but the well-trained mare never moves, and the dead knight sits as rigid as the surrounding rocks. At a bowshot off the enemy confer together. At last one of them, approaching closer, looses an arrow at the mare. She starts aside, and Rabíáh's body falls with a crash to the ground.

This theme has been several times treated in Arab poetry. Indeed, scarcely a better one could be thought of to illustrate the qualities which the Arab most ardently admires. In mere scenic effect the situation is striking and fine. The gathering twilight, the timid and distracted foe watching and whispering, the gap in the gaunt rock, and the motionless steed with its dead rider, make up a composition which might well stir an Arab's blood. But stronger still was the appeal to his sympathy. Every trait of Rabíáh's is a trait sacred in Arab eyes. The courage that despises odds, the fortitude that smiles at wounds and death, the prowess that even in death is terrible to the enemy, these are the greatest of Arab virtues: and these are the virtues that the dead horseman, with his rescued women behind him and his shrinking foes in front, immortalises.

Every hero we meet with in Arab poetry is of this same type. By far the most important and vigorously treated subjects are war, revenge, slaughter, the *mêlée* of hostile tribes, or combats between deadly enemies. The ideal Arab character is such a man as this—

> "Lean-sided and thin, but not from lacking,
> Liberal-handed, keen-hearted, haughty,
> He journeyed with Wariness, and when he halted
> There Wariness halted, herself his comrade."

The desert wariness is particularly insisted on—

> "A man must be crafty and wise when peril is round his head."

Again—

> "Yea, his is the wary soul, on whom lights a thing to do,
> And finds him alert, intent, his end straight before his eyes."

He who would prosper in the desert must "watch like a warder," must carry with him "the heart of a wary man and bold."

The leanness and hardness of a warrior, tireless and in perfect training, is the corresponding physical attribute. He should be "slender of flank and lean." In speed and endurance he—

> "Outstrips the sweep of the wind as it drives in its course along:
> It blows but in gusts, while he still journeys unresting on."

Generosity is an Arab virtue, and no less a one is a certain dignity and stateliness of bearing—

> "A rushing rain-flood when he gave of his fulness;
> When he sprang to the onset a mighty lion;
> In the midst of his kin flowed his long black hair; and
> His skirts trailed: in war a wolf's whelp with lean flanks."

ARAB POETRY

Throughout all these poems there rings an immense boastfulness, the boastfulness of men living in small and ever-conflicting societies, and holding their own by sheer strength of arm—

> "If there should be among a thousand but one of us, and men should call 'Ho, a knight!' he would think that they meant him.
> When the fighters blench and quail before the deadly stroke of the sword-edge, we leap forth and catch it in our hand."

Vainglory was counted no slur when men had to make good their words with deeds, and the more direct the boast the better—

> "If thou givest the cup to the noblest, reach it to us,
> And if thou callest one day to a mighty and valiant deed
> The chiefest of noble men, let thy call go forth to us."

To outface others, to trample down opposition, is the finest thing possible—

> "We say nay whenso we will to the words of other men;
> But no man to us says nay when we give sentence."

And again—

> "Our swords have swept throughout all lands both West and East,
> And gathered many a notch from the steel of hauberk-wearers;
> Not used are they when drawn to be laid back in their sheaths
> Before that the folk they meet are spoiled and scattered."

To die by the steel is the only death worth having—

> "Our souls stream forth in a flood from the edge of the whetted swords;
> No otherwise than so does our spirit leave its mansion."

The poet gives the rein to his profoundest emotion when he speaks of revenge wreaked on the tribe's enemy. "Never is blood of us poured forth without vengeance," cries one. Another thus describes the treatment accorded to the slayer of his uncle—

> "To Hudhail we gave to drink of death's goblet,
> Whose dregs are disgrace and shame and dishonour.
> The hyena laughs over the slain of Hudhail,
> And the wolf—seest thou—grins by their corpses,
> And the vultures flap their wings full-bellied,
> Treading their dead, too gorged to leave them."

I have taken these extracts from many different poems in Sir Charles Lyall's collection of translations. One after the other these poems are as like as peas in a pod. They are all perfectly agreed as to the kind of man they admire, and what those characteristics are which form an ideal character. And the man they paint is a man strongly marked with the aggressive and virile virtues; full of pride and valour, fiercely militant, vengeful, courteous, too, and dignified and generous; in all respects what we should call a gentleman—one who is himself his own standard, and whose demand upon conduct is that it shall be worthy of himself.

Not an ignoble ideal, certainly; on the contrary, so noble a one, or at least so spirited and attractive a one, that anything set against it will be apt to seem dull and colourless by comparison. Nevertheless, the

ARAB POETRY

reader will certainly find, if he takes the trouble to think it out, that the aggressive and purely virile ideal, however picturesque, is essentially unsatisfactory. It is so because it results in an inevitable stupidity. The qualities which give depth to character are not the Arab fine-sounding and showy qualities at all, but a much more sober and much less striking lot. They may be said to be directly opposed to the Arab traits, for they are concerned with the negation rather than with the assertion of the sense of self, and they bring depth because every act of understanding of whatever kind is in itself an act of sympathy, that is, an act of self-obliteration. The self-assertive or unsympathetic attitude is, in short, wearisome because of its inherent shallowness. Now the reader may search through every one of these poems, and of any praise of such virtues as patience, gentleness, modesty, humility, and the like, virtues which are all concerned in some form or other with the act of self-negation, he will find not one trace. More even than that, he will find these virtues treated as despicable weaknesses. To forgive an injury, to count himself as nothing, to go down lower when he can go up higher, are not to the Arab counsels of perfection, not things which he would do if he could, or at any rate knows that he ought to do; they are the marks of abject worthlessness. One of their poets, after taunting his associates with their slackness in coming to his rescue, sums up his scorn and detestation of them in the words—

"They requite with forgiveness the wrong of those that do them a wrong,
And the evil deeds of the evil they meet with kindness and love;"

words which have a curious ring in our ears as an expression of contempt and condemnation.

If it were a mere question of the poetry itself it would not be difficult, I dare say, to show what this loses by its limited range of vision. It would be easy to show that, though it has great rhetorical vigour and great directness, though its descriptions are trenchant and telling and every word hits the mark, though nothing can be more vivid than the picture it draws of all the vicissitudes and adventures of a desert race, yet it gives us such a merely literal interpretation of nature and life as is only saved from being wearisome by its historical interest. The Arab's thoughts about nature are the thoughts of the man of action only. He conceives all things as relating to himself, as deriving significance from himself. Friendly aspects of nature are to be praised and commended, hostile aspects are to be defied and overcome. But he himself is the only source of meaning or interest in each case. The thought of another never crosses his mind. The question never shifts for a moment from What is this to me? to What is this in itself?

Next to war the Arab poet's chief topic is love, and this too he treats in his own characteristic way. His passion unlocks for him none of Nature's secrets. Nothing that he sees is endowed with any added meaning or emotion of its own. All Nature is subservient to his own affairs. The winds are to carry his messages to his beloved, the streams murmur her name, the flowers are poor imitators of the brightness of her eyes or the fragrance of her breath.

Contrast such a method with the same subject

ARAB POETRY

treated with real depth. What is the secret of the passion in lines like these?—

> "On such a night,
> When the sweet wind did gently kiss the trees,
> And they did make no noise; on such a night
> Troilus, methinks, mounted the Trojan walls,
> And sighed his soul towards the Grecian tent
> Where Cressid lay that night."

It lies in the first lines, in the idea given us of emotion, not as something human and finite but suffusing all nature and existing in nature quite apart from man. The wind would be kissing the trees that night as gently if Troilus and Cressida had never been heard of. The instinct of a great poet is to deepen the human emotion by making it cognisant of the natural, universal emotion. The instinct of a shallow poet is to make the human emotion dominant and nature subservient to it, by which means he kills emotion altogether. The consequence is that, while second-rate love-poetry is always prating about its own passion, and using a kind of language which has more emphasis than meaning, first-rate love-poetry often scarcely alludes to its own passion directly at all, yet keeps us profoundly conscious of it from the emotion in which it steeps everything it touches. When Lorenzo says to Jessica—

> "Look how the floor of heaven
> Is thick inlaid with patines of bright gold:
> There's not the smallest orb which thou behold'st
> But in his motion like an angel sings,
> Still quiring to the young-ey'd cherubins,"

though there is no word of love spoken, yet its presence

is felt in the consciousness it brings to the lover of what is deep and inward and profound in nature.

So, too, in the passage I have already quoted from Wordsworth—

> "The breezes their own languor lent,
> The stars had feelings which they sent
> Into those gorgeous bowers."

What a depth of passion enters directly the emotions are thought of as nature's own! We have only to compare Wordsworth's "The breezes their own languor lent" with Shakespeare's "When the sweet wind did gently kiss the trees" to see how precisely similar the standpoint of the two poets was. It was a standpoint which to the Arab was simply incomprehensible.

I will quote one further example for the sake of the contrast in the two styles it affords. In the lines—

> "The slender acacia did not shake
> One long milk-bloom from the tree,
> The white lake blossom fell into the lake,
> And the pimpernel dozed on the lea,"

we have a fine specimen, as every one will feel, of emotional poetry. The silent summer night, the still, deep water, the heavy blossom falling of its own weight, are images all charged with emotion. Immediately following these we have the lines—

> "But the rose was awake all night for thy sake,
> Knowing thy promise to me;
> The roses and lilies were all awake,
> They sighed for the dawn and thee;"

ARAB POETRY

in which we are conscious of coming suddenly to the surface, and exchanging with shocking abruptness the language of emotion for the language of compliment. What has happened is that the poet has shifted his standpoint in regard to Nature. In the first passage he thought of her, as Wordsworth and Shakespeare did, as having her own feelings and being full of a deep sentiment of her own, while in the last she is treated as entirely subordinate to the human beings, with no other office but to fetch and carry for them. The result of this transition is that the poetry drops into a mere jingle, and the sentiment of love it is meant to convey becomes quite superficial, and even, by contrast with what was first suggested, vulgar.

Verse of this rose-was-awake order we should have no difficulty in finding plenty of in Arab poetry. Such conceits are a habit of the Oriental mind, and occur frequently enough in common speech. I read the other day in a French newspaper an account of a visit of the Governor-General of Algeria to some Arab chiefs at Beni-Ounif, at which the Arabs assured their visitor that "les palmiers et les pierres elles-mêmes s'agitent pleins d'allégresse à votre arrivée"; a compliment precisely similar to the lover's in "Maud." We have plenty of this in Arab love-poetry, but what we look for in vain in that poetry is any trace of a conception of love as of something that confers initiation, that is less eager to speak of its own affairs and refer everything to itself, than it is to speak of the new meaning and beauty it feels and sees in nature.

The test of good writing with us is that the writer does not stop at the outward and obvious. Wherever he settles he penetrates, he draws blood. But the

Arab's treatment of all subjects is merely a literal treatment. He judges of everything only as it affects himself. In short, Arab poetry, like all ballad poetry, though direct is hard, though vigorous is matter-of-fact, though sincere is superficial. And these limitations in his poetry are the limitations in the man. The man we have been looking at in Arab poetry, despite all his directness, vigour, and sincerity, is hard, matter-of-fact, and superficial. In conversing with average Europeans one is conscious, as a rule, of no strict mental barrier separating obvious and outward things from the inward and profound. Their minds shade off. You may come pretty quickly to insensibility or indifference, but you do not run your head against a brick wall. With the Arab you do. It is not that he lacks capacity. It is that his allegiance is already enlisted on the side of a merely outward and obvious interpretation of life. A fierce believer in everything that is self-assertive, virile and boldly overbearing, he is an absolute stranger to the idea of self-effacement in any shape or form. What he can pluck by force he takes; but he has no other idea of conquest. Heaven itself, he thinks, can only be carried sword in hand.

It is interesting enough to be shown, as Arab poetry shows us, what manner of man it was who carried fire and fury through the world twelve hundred years ago, and who has left behind him on the page of history a mark and an impression so utterly unlike those of any other race of which it bears record. But Arab poetry shows us a great deal more than this. It shows us the Moslem type not only as it existed in Arabia in the days of Mohammed, but as it exists to-day all the world over.

ARAB POETRY

If the reader will imagine himself to be standing in a Ceylon or Indian village, he will probably see come striding through the crowd of slender-limbed, languid natives a great tan-faced Afghan with long, glossy hair and curled moustache, dressed in swinging white garments, with half a dozen crooked knives stuck in his sash. Look at that gait and swagger. Watch those keen glances darting right and left among the crowd. Note the pride and curbed self-assertion of manner, the haughty and arrogant bearing that says as plainly as if the words were spoken, " If thou givest the cup to the noblest, reach it to me!" You do not need to be told that the man is a Moslem; you can see it.

Or stand, as I remember once standing, among the motley crowd of the Constantinople streets, and see a regiment of Turkish cavalry file by. The similarity of type will strike you in a moment. The lean, sinewy figures, the careless, easy seat, the keen, roving glance, the look on each tanned face of fierceness and pride, all these are traits that seem to you familiar, that you cannot mistake. Where did you see that look and bearing before? Why, in the Afghan stalking through the Ceylon bazaar.

Or, for a third example, come to the craggy hills of Southern Albania, and mix, if but for half an hour, with the armed shepherds, as wild and intractable as their own crags, or as the gaunt dogs which guard their flocks from the wolves, and whose attentions to strangers you are apt to find such a nuisance. You will understand from the first glance at the men more of the interminable Balkan difficulty than newspapers and books can ever teach you. These are the fellows who swoop down from their peaks on the mixed races of the plains and carry fire and slaughter through village and valley. Their natural aptitude for fighting and foraying, for bearing things with a strong hand, for cowing the weak and feeble, for vindicating the old "might is right" theory, is written all over them. You see it in their gait, glance, walk, and manner, you hear it in every accent of their voice, you feel it in their individuality and presence.

These are specimens of the Moslem type, the type that stops short at the virile virtues, that makes the best host and worst neighbour in the world, that has many splendid qualities to recommend it, but to which all that makes life profound and inexhaustible is a dead letter. It is the most strongly marked and salient type I have ever met with. There is the Moslem walk, the Moslem scowl, the Moslem courtesy, the Moslem dignity, the Moslem carriage and attitudes and features, the Moslem composure, and the Moslem fury. All these traits and characteristics, inspired by the same temper, expressing the same ideal, conspire to depict a figure so notable that you must be a dull observer indeed if you cannot pick him out from a mixed crowd as you would pick out a Chinaman in the London streets.

Some people say it is the religion that creates the type. "There," they say of Mohammedanism, "is a religion that breeds men." It would be truer, I think, to say that Mohammedanism recommends itself to men at a certain stage of their development, and has for that stage a natural affinity. Every race goes through a time when the virile estimate of life and the splendour of self-assertion seem the finest things possible. It is at this time it is open to the attack of El Islam. The

ARAB POETRY

Moslem religion answers all its needs at this stage, and lays good hold of it, and having once laid hold of it, it sanctifies the ideas belonging to this stage, and so tends to restrict the race to it. There is no instance on record of a people having embraced Mohammedanism and afterwards achieving a complete, or what gives promise of ever becoming a complete, civilisation.

For my part I think we may well thank our stars that we, too, when we were passing through the Moslem stage of civilisation, were never caught in the Moslem net. There was a time when it would have suited us well. The ideals of European society in the mediæval age were the ideals which are the regular Moslem stock-in-trade. The same love of action, the same type of manhood, the same dominating and virile qualities were common to both. The same achievements were held in honour and the same customs recognised. Woman's place in life in feudal or Moslem society, immured in the castle or the harem, was similar. In the usages of chivalry there was the same correspondence. The ideas that suited them suited us, and were largely and freely assimilated by us. We know how forcibly Arab poetry influenced the early ballad poetry of Europe. It was, indeed, of precisely the same quality.

Our crusades and the Arab conquests, again, were events identical in character and perfectly typical of the Moslem stage of civilisation. A simple faith in strength and steel animated both. What sent men crazy about the crusades was not the Holy Sepulchre, but the thought of dedicating the exuberant vitality and energy with which they were overflowing to the service of God. The Holy Sepulchre was the object alleged; but if it had not been the Holy Sepulchre it would have been something else. What we wanted to do was exactly what the Arabs in their great national irruption wanted to do—we wanted to sanctify and make holy what we most believed in and gloried in. And what we and they most believed in and gloried in was physical strength and courage. Conquests and crusades alike mark an age in which this ideal rules paramount. This was what Arab and Christian both felt to be the best they had to offer and the most worthy heaven. The age of the crusades was, in fact, our Moslem stage of development. It was the age when the ideals of Arab poetry were our ideals, and the standard that satisfied the Arab would have satisfied us.

It was so long before the special character of Christianity could unfold itself! It lived through so many centuries not by what was best in itself; centuries during which a quite outward religion such as Mohammedanism would, as far as general society was concerned, have met all needs. Suppose that our rugged Germanic ancestors, instead of coming in contact with a religion which made it its special business to sanctify the deeper virtues built upon the idea of self-sacrifice, and which managed to entrench itself and hand on to calmer ages the teaching of a faith at that time little understood, round which, as round a central core, might gradually form in successive envelopes a whole system of civilisation, with all its manifold activities, intellectual, imaginative, scientific, all partaking of and working out in their own departments the same quality of inward depth which existed in the central moral idea; suppose, instead of this happening, we had been met at the outset, as the Turks were met, by a religion which sanctioned all that we then knew of good, but contained no promise of after-development. Should we not have accepted it? And, having accepted it, should we not have found it a millstone round our necks ever after? Should we not have been entangled permanently among the ideals of a half-way stage of development?

That, at least, is what has happened to all other Moslem races. They have walked gladly into that religion, and, once in it, the key has been turned on them and they have never got any further. Let the reader recall for a moment the figure of Rabîáh, the hero of Arab poetry. Match that figure with every Arab celebrity mentioned in history. They are identical. Match it again with types of every race which holds by the strict and orthodox teaching of Mohammedanism to-day. Again they are identical. Now look around, among all these races so rich in warriors, and ask, Where are the leaders in other lines of activity? Where are the St. Francises in piety, the Wordsworths in poetry, the Newtons in science, the Bacons in philosophy? Where is there a trace of insight or depth, spiritual, imaginative, or intellectual?

No such trace exists. The energy of Mohammedanism is still merely a militant energy. It has stopped short at the masculine, self-assertive virtues, and every race that has embraced it has stopped short with it. One result of this general stopping short is, of course, the prevalence of a single type, and it is, as I began by saying, one of the great merits of Arab poetry that it reveals this type so clearly. That the poetry was written twelve hundred years ago or more makes not the slightest difference. The type has never changed or varied. The orthodox Moslem of Arab poetry is the orthodox Moslem to-day all the world over.

CHAPTER XV

MOHAMMEDANISM

The desert religion an incentive and a bond—The Arab as propagandist—The sects of Islam—Conservatism of the orthodox faith—The Shiites—Their efforts to infuse emotional depths and warmth into the religion—Fruitlessness of the attempt—What backs up the orthodox party—The influence of the desert—The standard of life it maintains—Mecca the Mohammedan Rome.

IMMOBILITY is surely the most extraordinary trait of the Arab race. If it is true that all races have their ballad-poetry stage, it is true also that, with most of them, this passes. The poetry of thought succeeds to the poetry of action. The Shakespeares and Wordsworths come in their season. But the Arab has remained always in the ballad-poetry stage. The ideals of that stage are the only ones that have ever had any meaning for him.

In a measure those ideals are indigenous to the country. He who lives in the desert lives in an enemy's land. He makes his way here by force. He must foresee his needs, forget nothing, and press on to his destination. He must fight with nature for every well and palm-tree he possesses. His whole life is a training in wariness, vigilance, courage, endurance. Such are the qualities called forth by this scenery and which are indispensable to existence in it. But beyond this nothing. The stable conditions which develop social life are altogether wanting. That life is here unknown. The influence it exerts is an unknown influence. And since to these surroundings the Arab has been inured for immeasurable lapses of time, what wonder that the limitation, here so marked, should have become in time a fixed limitation in character, and that the only virtues applicable to such a country should have come to seem to him the only virtues worth having?

But the influence of the desert does not stop at the Arab. The desert ideal has become much more than an effect upon a particular race. It has translated itself into a dogma and a creed. It has become a teaching and an idea. It is a bond of union between races in the same stage of development all the world over. And this result it has achieved through the religion it has propagated.

Mohammedanism gave the Arabs two great things. It gave them for the first time a kind of national unity, and it gave them a tremendous incentive to action and conquest. By temperament and precept the Arab is a propagandist. Every movement to-day of any consequence that agitates the desert has the spread of Islam at the root of it; the features of the first great mission are reproduced in miniature in every rising and under every Mahdi in turn. Only whereas these later ebullitions are sporadic, and agitate only scattered and weakened tribes, the original outburst was a solid national effort, towards which the Arab race had been concentrating its strength for centuries. In that effort the desert delivered its shock and scattered its seed.

Its religion was carried east and west through the world, but the exertion drained the desert itself of its store of energy. Apparently Arab nationality was forged and cast for the delivery of one tremendous blow, and having delivered that blow it collapsed.

And yet, spent and exhausted as it seems, the remarkable thing is that the birthplace of the faith still exercises a distinct influence over the creed it propagated; still watches over it and guards it and protects it.

Mohammedanism was not everywhere accepted without protest, nor was it everywhere persevered in without some attempted modifications. Matthew Arnold, in his essay on a Persian Passion Play, speaks of the "fierce and militant" character of the faith. "It is not a feeling religion," he truly says. "No one would say that the virtues of gentleness, mildness, and self-sacrifice were its virtues; and the more it went on the more the faults of its original narrow basis became visible, more and more it became fierce and militant, less and less was it amiable." The Arab possesses no impulses that can respond to gentleness and mildness, while he has a vivid appreciation of everything fierce and militant. It is in accordance with the character of the race, therefore, that these latter qualities in the religion of Mohammed should have been developed, and that the gentler ones should drop out of sight. Offer the Arab any religion, and the same modifications would occur; the fiercer traits would grow and expand, well nourished by the soil, until they altogether eclipsed and crowded out the gentler ones which received no nourishment at all.

But if the tendency of the Arab was to develop the

sterner side of his religion, the tendency of some other races was to lay stress on whatever there was of gentleness and mildness in it, and even to add to this. In the essay I have already quoted from the touching story is told of the martyrdom of the grandchildren of the Prophet. Matthew Arnold dwells on the gentleness and self-renunciation of these pathetic figures, whose spirit of meek endurance is so unlike that of the usual strenuous soldier-saint of Islam, and he speaks of the warmer current of emotion which the sanctification of their story tended to introduce into the colder and harder parent stream of Mohammedanism.

No doubt the story does form an exception in Islam traditions, and the dwelling on it and development of it into a religious ceremonial is a kind of protest against Mohammedan austerity. But who was it who felt the need of this protest? It was not the Arabs, but preeminently the more sedentary, more peaceable, and more civilised Persians, who sanctified the story; who seized upon it and made it a part of their religion. And not only that, but who made it by far the most revered and cherished part, and a part that appealed to them more intimately and touched them more closely than any of the precepts of Islam. It was they who lingered over all that was moving and pathetic in the legend, and who elaborated it into those Passion Plays which excite such enthusiasm and attract such sympathising and deeply-stirred multitudes. Moreover, these dramas are constantly tending to enlarge their boundaries. Other incidents and stories of the same emotional character are introduced, which are commonly taken from Christian tradition, or the Bible, where they are to be found in greater abundance than in the bleak history of Islam.[1]

I should soon lose myself if I were to try and disentangle the various heresies and sects of the faith; but I imagine that the same endeavour to supply emotional warmth was at the root of most of the innovations. The Mohammedan religion, as the reader probably knows, is split into the two main bodies of the Sunnite and Shíite sects. Of these the Sunnite is the orthodox sect and represents the centre of Mohammedanism. And the distinctive note of it is that it rejects and repels all attempts to soften and enrich the faith by working up the emotional side of it. On the other hand, the Shíites are heretics. They have little in common with the austere Sunnites. They prevail outside the Arab nation, and especially in Persia, though there is a tendency for the more educated and cultured Moslems to be of this sect in all nations. And the point on which, under various shapes and guises, they are always insisting, and their insistence on which drives them into heresy, is the need which, from their point of view, exists for impregnating and suffusing the faith with emotional warmth and feeling.

The sanctity surrounding the persons of the Caliph Ali and the martyrs of Kerbela, which forms the subject of the Persian plays, is a main tenet of the Shíites. But their work of innovation did not stop there. Sufism has been another influence of the same kind which has been especially fathered by the sect. Professor Guyard defines Sufism as the mystical element in the Moslem religion, and he says, "Mysticism is rather a way of practising religion than a distinct

[1] See Appendix, Note F.

MOHAMMEDANISM

religion in itself; it depends on the temperament of the believer and is able to accommodate itself to any dogma. Tender and dreamy souls are particularly drawn to it. And so it is that we find among the Mussulmans that it is a woman who has the credit of having initiated Sufism."

This woman, who took the first step towards steeping the new religion in the tender and dreamy light of mysticism, was named Râbia. She lived in the first century of the Hegira, and her tomb is still visited at Jerusalem. "Her doctrine," says Professor Guyard, "was simply the theory of divine love. She taught that God alone is worthy to be loved, and that we must make an act of sacrifice of everything pertaining to this world to Him, in the hope of one day being reunited to Him in the world to come." This idea of self-effacement in the contemplation of the Eternal brought the new sect into touch with the Gnostics. Gnostic thought had, as we should have expected, already made itself at home in the Shíite party. Accordingly, for that party Sufism had a double recommendation. It had the recommendation that it was a teaching of pure love and absolute self-surrender, and it had the recommendation that it was allied in principle with a philosophy which was already familiar. The natural result was that Sufism identified itself closely with the Shíite heresy, and made particularly rapid progress in Persia, where that heresy had its home.

Here, then, are two clearly distinguishable and rival influences at work in Mohammedanism. One an expansive influence, an influence bent on harmonising the new religion with the subtleties and depths of the human mind and human spirit, and which welcomes to that end the mystical visions of the Gnostics, the absorption of self in the Infinite as taught in the doctrines of Sufism, and a passionate love and devotion to saints and martyrs; the other intensely conservative and bent on maintaining the faith in all its rigorous and cold monotheism. The two influences are quite distinct from each other, and a certain method in their distribution is apparent. Wherever conditions favourable to barbarism prevail, there the sterner sect predominates. Wherever more civilised conditions are found, there the party of expansion has influence.

Throughout India Mohammedanism has completely changed its character. It has been impregnated and soaked by the converted population in the rites and legends of their ancient faith until Mohammed himself would not recognise it. This is particularly the case throughout the plains. In Sind, the Punjab, and Kashmir some of the old primitive vigour still survives, and plays and flickers freely about the great rampart of the north-west frontier. North of this the sterile, waterless hills of Beloochistan and Afghanistan's almost inaccessible mountains afford it the kind of foothold it needs, and it flourishes among the deserts of Eastern Turkestan and the desolate steppes of Samarkand and Bokhara.

In the east, then, the haunts of orthodoxy are those isolated and remote states which form part of, or lie adjacent to, the lonely region which is known as the Roof of the World. Further west it comes under the protection of a race which, like the founders of the faith themselves, has never been able to advance far along the path of progress or to shake off altogether the instincts of barbarism, the Turks. Between, how-

MOHAMMEDANISM

ever, the semi-barbarous Asian states and the semi-barbarous Turkish Empire lies Persia—Persia, old in civilisation and religion centuries before this new faith had ever been heard of. The raw, external religion of Mohammed, with its fierce insistence on action and outward things, its lack of depth and gentleness, and what Christians call grace, might satisfy the shepherds of the Oxus or the nomads of the Pamirs, but it entirely failed to meet adequately the Persian conception of life, and Persia has remained in consequence the hotbed of all those innovations of which we have been speaking.

In short, in a glance from east to west over the whole region traversed by Arab influence, let your eye seek out those spots naturally rude and barbarous, the mountain fastnesses of the Balkans in the west or of the Himalayas in the east, the deserts of Africa, Arabia, or Turkestan; there, where advance in civilisation is slow or impossible, is where primitive Mohammedanism flourishes. These are the strongholds of orthodoxy. In the very types that accept the sterner faith there is an extraordinary similarity. They are all framed on the same model. They are all emphatically *men*. They have the virile virtues—pride, courage, courtesy, a natural independence, warlike instincts. But you are no sooner among them than you feel a something lacking. They have not an atom of real inward depth, not a trace of that quality in the mind which answers to grace in the spirit. To associate with them is to be made vividly conscious of what a real and terrible want the humanising and liberalising sects have been all these centuries struggling to make good.

All religions have a tendency to expand and become

modified by time to answer to wider and more subtle spiritual and intellectual needs, and there is nothing extraordinary, therefore, in the efforts of the Shíites to expand Mohammedanism. On the contrary, it was a natural and inevitable process, the more natural and inevitable when we remember the original coldness and narrowness of the creed. What is, I think, extraordinary is that this tendency should have been so sternly and successfully resisted. Not its desire to expand but its refusal to expand is the peculiarity of the faith. One seems to be aware here of an influence at work more reliable and dependable than the human mind and human intelligence. How comes it that central Mohammedanism, the orthodox party, as it has the right by numbers and influence to call itself, has maintained so consistent and successful a resistance to the natural widening and completer application to life of its doctrines? By what authority has it been enabled to repel the liberalising tendency at all points? What is it that gives to Mohammedan conservatism its tremendous consistency and endurance? It pretends to no infallibility, and yet it maintains a unity which, one fancies, it never could have derived from so changeful a source as the human mind, and which gives it an authoritative air resembling certainly in some degree the aspect of the Roman Catholic Church.

The fact is that if Mohammedanism has not got infallibility it has something that, up to a certain point, supplies the place of it. It has, in the desert, a tremendous influence, physical only and natural it is true, but permanent and unchanging, to back it up. The desert not only conceived and launched the Moslem faith on the world, but it keeps watch and ward over it

THE ATTRACTION OF MECCA.

still. It is the desert which maintains the obdurate orthodoxy of primitive belief. It is from the desert that the heat waves occasionally issue which reanimate the old dogmas. It is to the desert that yearly pilgrimages bring hosts of the faithful from all parts of the earth to reimmerse themselves in the original enthusiasm. It is to the desert that the thoughts of all Moslems turn when, facing towards Mecca, they prostrate themselves in prayer. The sanctification of Mecca was a master-thought. The drawing together of believers to one spot, the concentration of the Mohammedan mind on this spot, must, one would suppose, facilitate a certain agreement and a certain unity. Only it is essential that this spot should possess a definite character of its own, and be capable of exercising a definite influence. Mecca does this. It is not only the capital of a religion, it is the capital of the desert. The local influence here is tremendous. To be in the desert oneself and among Arabs is to be at once conscious of it. There is here, in nature and in man, a spirit fierce and strenuous, but narrow and bigoted; a spirit strong to impose its own rigid and zealous will, but inflexible, and as it were cast in an iron mould.

Every one who has been in the desert must be more or less conscious of this influence of the place, and every one who has read accounts of the great pilgrimages will be able to form a faint idea of the tremendous power and dominion which this spirit has over masses of men. Mecca, in a word, is the centre of a very narrow and limited, but, just because limited, distinct and well-defined influence. It is this influence which the sanctification of the city imposes on the faithful, and which, in fact, constitutes in their imaginations what Christians call the odour of sanctity. It is to this influence that in pilgrimage and prayer they constantly submit themselves; and consequently it is this influence which comes to exert over the faith a certain control and which ensures a kind of unity.

It is difficult to imagine that any other region in which the spirit of Mohammedanism may be said naturally to dwell ever could have fulfilled this *rôle*. Others, one can easily suppose, might have given birth to such a creed. What nobler nursery could it have had than the tremendous mountain system that girdles North India? Here, in that fierce and lonely isolation, is the atmosphere, here is the temper and spirit of Mohammedanism.

But to breed or foster an idea is one thing, to propagate it is another. The spirit of the great mountain groups is an isolated and self-contained spirit. Mountains retain their children, locked in their embrace; the desert pours forth its brood into the world. There is much likeness in the essential temper of the two. Each fosters a direct, virile view of life, and brings into prominence those virtues which make for immediate personal efficiency, and so yields plentifully the kind of nutriment that the Moslem religion thrives on. But the desert as a centre of the faith has this decisive advantage, that its character is exactly the reverse of self-contained. Its impulse constantly is to expand or explode, to overflow its own boundaries, to rush forth and scatter itself through the world.

Travelling once on the Upper Nile, in days when Wady Halfa was the front, they showed me the slopes along the river at Toski where we fought Wad el Negoumi in 1889. The Arab leader evaded Wady

MOHAMMEDANISM 231

Halfa and marched south by the hills, and the English boys who told me the tale brought out their Nubians and gave chase along the river, knowing he must strike water at last, like a deer, to soil. At Toski he swept down upon them, and a mound between the trees on the river bank is where they buried him. What adds interest to the incident is that Negoumi had issued what we should call a "proclamation" announcing that he was about to purge not Egypt only of the unbeliever, but that all Europe should be made to yield to Moslem arms and the Moslem faith. That is the desert's accent, and it is an accent that every great propagator of Islam has caught. It is the voice of Kaled or of Omar, and had Negoumi's adversaries been as theirs, the same result might have ensued. It needs but a certain measure of weakness, or degeneration, in the surrounding powers to put the activity of the desert into effective operation. The gap between the fall and rise of Roman and European civilisation was the great opportunity of the race. In our day the weakness of Egypt in the Nile valley, and the withdrawal of France's Algerian army in 1870, have been its two chances ; and it showed itself as ready to profit by them as ever. The tribes have weakened, but have changed little in character during the last thousand years. The fiery desert spirit is all for expanding and overflowing. It is as anxious as ever it was to put down dissent and carry its Koran through the world.

This is what, it seems to me, gives the desert its advantage over all other naturally Moslem regions. It is the desert alone which is capable of setting up and maintaining the connection between detached fragments of Mohammedanism. I forget how that familiar saying, "If the mountain will not come to Mohammed, Mohammed must go to the mountain" originated, but it seems to sum up neatly enough the part the desert has played in the propagation and maintenance of the faith. It was because the desert could go to the mountain, while the mountain could not go to the desert, that the desert was able to assert its place as the common binding link between those centres of the Moslem spirit whose natural isolation it has overcome. It is this that makes Mecca the Rome of the Mohammedan world.

Only with a difference. The unity, such as it is, of Mohammedanism is obtained at the price of one of the two things that make a religion efficient, its power of adaptability to the needs of man. The test of orthodoxy is the fiercely literal view of life which the desert so unvaryingly maintains. Beyond that it cannot go. Let those satisfied with such a view come to it and accept its standard. Never will that standard change, never more especially will it admit one of those deeper thoughts of gentleness or self-sacrifice which are heresies to the desert life before they are heresies to the desert religion. It is this inability to expand, to open up the depths in the human mind and spirit, which seems to mark it as so hopelessly sterile. The immobility of the desert itself seems to rest on the Moslem religion. It keeps a certain consistency, but it produces nothing. It is durable, but it is barren.

CHAPTER XVI

KAIRWÁN

Approach to the town—An ideal bathe—Arab roads—Aspect of Kairwán—Loneliness and desolation of its surroundings—The beginnings of the city—Choice of a site—Early miracles—Warlike character of the town—Its luxury and culture—Fanaticism of the town—Early visits and reports—Violation of the sanctuary—French occupation—A broken spell.

THE night before reaching Kairwán we camped on the banks of what for North Africa might be called an important river. Its bed occupied a width of several hundred yards, and was composed of dry white shingle interspersed with strips and clumps of evergreen which formed dark green islands in the midst of it. This wide white bed was conspicuous enough, but the current was more difficult to find. At last, parting the leaves of a thick covert of oleander, I came upon a narrow stream, ankle-deep and a few feet wide, all that was left of a flood which during the winter rains evidently swelled to a furious torrent capable of tearing up shrubs and bushes and whirling along rocks.

We had seen no natural stream since the El Fedala ushered us into the desert. Now I sat down and watched the water that came running and dancing towards me. Its whiteness bore testimony to the limestone masonry of those blue ramparts in the north. I could trace it a long way in that direction, its bright threads of water, for it often broke into many streamlets, glistening among the white stones and making a network on the flats of sand. Its murmur and motion as it came dancing and singing along were inconceivably pleasant after these weeks of the desert. After a while I undressed and lay me down and let the white creamy water run over me, and cuddled down upon the smooth stones, like Keats's minnows that—

> "Nestle
> Their silver bellies on the pebbly sand";

and felt the heat and fatigue and stains of desert travel washed away by the cool and cleansing current.

This ideal bath I looked upon as the right Moslem preparation for entrance into the holy city. It is advisable, indeed, for several reasons, to approach Kairwán as we did, from the south. Most of the few people who visit it come by railway from Tunis. Such a transition, however, from a bustling and cosmopolitan port to this worn-out, solemn old place, which has never had any thought but religion, and whose fallen fortunes seem symbolic of so much more than its own decay, is altogether too abrupt for initiation. One should come into Kairwán from the desert, trailing some of those gradually-gleaned impressions and ideas, wanting which the sacred city is as closed to strangers to-day as ever it was.

There is much that is appropriate in the position and surroundings of Kairwán as a holy city of Islam. It stands in a greatly lonely and desolate plain, a plain sprinkled with a few sparse tufts of sage brush, and

KAIRWÁN

with scarcely a sign of man's presence to be seen for hours of riding on its vast expanse. Great roads lead towards the city. Roads that have carried the pilgrimages of many centuries and are padded and worn by the feet of countless generations of worshippers. Venerable roads, yet still retaining, somehow, more the character of the runs of animals than the regular and permanent tracks of human beings.

That one we came in from the desert by was in many places, perhaps, two or three hundred yards wide. Hardly could you call it one road. It was a compound of a great many little paths. In some places these tended to unite and combine to make a single track of it; in others they unravelled and fell apart like a lose skein of thread. If they joined, it was accident and blind contact that did it. There was no intention to make a road.

The weary plain and these worn tracks, the distant hills, and in the midst of the plain the domes of the sacred city, made me think of the approach to Rome. But this is far sadder. The feeling here is not of venerable antiquity, but of desolation. The thought of an influence still exerting itself, a heart beating in the midst of all this antiquity, is wanting. The place is very melancholy and lifeless. Along these much-worn roadways are no *osterie*, or rest-houses, for the refreshment of travellers. No mule carts laden with sacks or wine barrels jog along on their way to the town. No groups of drivers and peasants gather at tables in the plane shade. A long way off the hills rise out of the plain, with that solemn clean-cut outline never to be dissociated from Africa; but there is no glint of white villages on their blue slopes.

The sun rises in clear unclouded air, and as I look across the landscape suddenly revealed, for dawn here is like the drawing of a curtain, it seems to me that it expresses the same vacancy and emptiness that is in the sky.

Such desolation seems sadder here than elsewhere. One misses instinctively the signs of security and peace that should surround an ancient citadel of religion.

The soil is not altogether unfertile, nor unwatered. Streams and torrents have brought down some of the earth from those hills and spread it over the plain, and in the beds of some of them water still flows. The fault is not in nature; more likely, I fancy, it is in the character and practice of that stern faith which has never known how to set any value on the duties of citizenship. It was impossible not to read in this melancholy waste, this loneliness, this sterility, a comment on that creed whose sanctuary these things had come to embrace and surround.

The tomb of Okba ibn Nefi stands in the desert at no great distance from Biskra. It bears an inscription which in one sentence expresses for us that spirit of greatness that lasted among the Arabs for so brief an interval: "This is the tomb of Okba ibn Nefi. May God have mercy upon him."

Okba was a great soldier, and, what among Moslems is pretty much the same thing, a great saint; but he was also, as Kairwán proves, and which is much rarer among the Arabs, something of a statesman. He divined exactly in what the strength of Arab character consisted, and what were the best means, or only hope, of bracing and sustaining it and giving it the stability it lacked. Thanks to this clear knowledge, he was able to found a city which was as terrible as it was holy

KAIRWÁN

and as much feared as it was reverenced; which poured forth its conquering armies into Spain and Italy and Sicily; which was a menace for centuries to all the South of Europe, and of which to-day very few people, even among the educated, have ever heard the name.

Kairwán was founded in 670. It was intended to be a great garrison town, a rallying point for the strength of Islamism in Africa. "Neither was it, they say," writes Leo Africanus, the Arab historian, "built for any other purpose but that the Arabian army might securely rest therein." The difficulties and risks of campaigning in North Africa with Egypt for a base had taught the Arabs the need of a great military depôt somewhere midway along its extent, and Kairwán was the answer to that need. The choice of the site, however, and the process of foundation seem to have depended entirely on Okba. Leo expressly says that it was he who "persuaded the citizens of Tunis that no army or garrison ought to remain in any sea town." This point he carried, and the new city was founded 120 miles south of Tunis, and thirty to forty from the Gulf of Gabes. When he had reached the proper spot, Okba struck the butt of his long lance into the ground, which is still the habit of chiefs when choosing their camping-ground, and cried to his men, "Here is your Kairwán"; meaning here was their caravanserai, or resting-place, and naming in the word the future town.

This condition of an inland and secluded site was a vital one. The Arabs are those people who mix worst with the world, and who most quickly lose their strength of character when blended with other races. A seaport is fatal to them. In securing this lonely position Okba secured the first great condition necessary to his city's greatness. Kairwán felt the advantage of it all through her history. She kept to the end something of the fierce, fanatic spirit which is the spring of Arab action. The Arab cities of the coast quickly lost their character. Such towns of theirs as existed in the desert or on the margin of it—as Zinder and Timbuktu in the south, Tuggurt and Biskra in the north—were merely trading centres, built where the caravan routes converged towards the Sudan or the northern settlements. They embodied nothing of that fiery spirit which for a brief space made the Arab so irresistible. Kairwán alone of the cities of North Africa engrossed that spirit and with it a certain strength and durability.

But other influences came to foster it. War and sanctity are twin instincts with the Arab. Religion as they understand it is vindicated and propagated by war; war is inspired and sanctified by religion. The Arab is not able to separate the two in his mind, and so it is quite appropriate that a city formed for war should have become invested with a peculiarly sacred character.

Indeed, religion was on the scene as soon as her ally. Miracles rocked the cradle of Kairwán. It is narrated that a thick jungle in those days clothed this plain, and that Okba's men were scared by the number of wild beasts and serpents. Thereupon Okba, "whose intercession," says Novairi, "was all-powerful with the Divine Being," addressed himself thus to the wild beasts, his warriors seconding his words with earnest amens: "Oh, you serpents and savage beasts, be it known to you that we are the companions of the Prophet of Allah. Depart from the place we have

KAIRWÁN

chosen to establish ourselves in. Should we find any of you henceforth on this spot ye shall be put to death;" upon which the offending animals immediately began to depart, and "the Mussulmans saw with astonishment, during the whole day, the venomous reptiles and ferocious beasts retreating far away, and carrying with them their young, a miracle which converted a great number of Berbers to Islamism."

The same divine sanction attended the foundation of the Great Mosque. There being a doubt and difficulty as to the correct Orientation of the mosque, Okba dreamed a dream; and in his dream a voice spoke to him, saying: "When the morning shall have come, take the Standard, place it on thy shoulder; thou shalt hear before thee a recital of the *Tekbir* unheard by any but thee; the place where the prayer will end is the spot chosen for the *Kibleh*, there place in the mosque the holy niche for the Imam." Okba carried out these instructions. He shouldered the banner, heard and followed the voice, inaudible to other ears, and, at the spot where it ceased, marked the sacred niche which directs the gaze of the faithful towards Mecca. Of all the *Kiblehs* of North Africa this one has to this day a peculiar prestige. It is common in most mosques for the Imam when praying to turn a little to this side or that of the *Kibleh*, as though to correct a slight inaccuracy in the indicated direction. None venture, however, to take such liberties with Okba's mosque. The Imam there invariably faces straight towards the niche which was so wonderfully revealed. When all is borne in mind that Kairwán owes its founder, the choice of the site, the early miracles, its religious and warlike prestige, it will be agreed that a city has seldom been more indebted to the exertions of one man than Kairwán was to Okba.

Thus was established the holiness and sanctity which grew with the city's growth, until the religious consciousness of the whole of North Africa concentrated itself on Kairwán. Many legends and traditions stimulated this enthusiasm and curiosity. One was that the stones of which the Great Mosque was built had found their way to their places without aid of mortal hands. Another was that a certain pair of superb columns which embellish the mihrâb were so miraculously adjusted that no person with the taint of mortal sin upon him could pass between them. What, however, decisively raised Kairwán to the rank of a holy city and place of pilgrimage was the burial here of Abdullah ibn Zemäa, the Companion of the Prophet. He lies buried with three hairs from the Prophet's beard, which were his talisman living, now interred with him dead; one under his tongue, another under his right arm, the third upon his heart.

The sanctity and influence of this stronghold of the faith are thus described by Guérin in 1860: "Les caravans qui s'y rendent constamment de tous les points de la Tunisie viennent s'y retremper en quelque sorte dans l'Islamisme; sa Grande Mosquée . . . est sans cesse visitée avec un profond respect par les adeptes du Coran, les sanctuaires de ses santons sont également le but de pélerinages fréquents; tout cela entretient dans l'esprit des masses un fanatisme que rien jusqu'ici n'a pu affaiblir."

Meantime every advance in holiness was registered in a corresponding growth of militarism. Half the great feats of arms of North Africa seem to have

KAIRWÁN

emanated from Kairwán. We in Europe have good reason to remember Tarik, who marched an army from here to the invasion of Spain; to whom Granada, Cordova, and Toledo yielded their gates, and who has stood godfather to that most important of all British rocks—the Rock of Tarik, Djebel Tarik or Gibr-al-Tar. Numbers of the Moors when they were finally evicted from Europe returned to their holy city, and it is said that still in many Moorish homes in Kairwán there hangs the antique key that once opened a door in Spain.

I need not enter into the city's exploits. She sent frequent expeditions into Italy and Sicily, she captured Malta, she founded several towns along the Tunisian coast, and besieged and took Tunis. Her armies ravaged Lombardy, took Genoa, and dominated Sicily. All her power and splendour seem to have culminated in the eleventh century, when, according to Richard Ford, the city held 300 mosques, 900 baths, 600 caravanserai, and a million inhabitants. In luxury and refinement it rivalled Cordova and Granada. Philosophers, poets, mathematicians, and all those various architects who combined to build up the many-coloured dream of Arab civilisation, spread its fame in literature and science. Its writers have handed down to us the memory of the olive groves and orange gardens, with rills of water murmuring in their shade, which once surrounded the city and turned it into an earthly paradise.

There is something fascinating to the imagination in the growth of this lonely and isolated city, which seems to have courted with care and forethought all the circumstances that would be fatal to the prosperity of a civilised town. If such prosperity usually depends on a central position and facilities in trade and commerce, the success of a Moslem town depends on exactly opposite conditions. Algiers is an instance of the fate of an Arab town that opens up relations with the world. What the Arab spirit demands, if it is to retain any of its virtue, is absolute seclusion and isolation. Endow the Arab city with every advantage that a town can have, and it falls to cureless ruin. Handicap it with the most overwhelming disadvantages, and it grows and flourishes. Here at Kairwán, remote from human intercourse, gathered and concentrated, as time passed, the dregs of that fierce, militant zeal which had carried the current so far. And still as it shrank and diminished, bitterer, as the condensing pool grows salter, became its fanaticism and intolerance, more closely, strictly, and jealously did it guard itself from the approach of the world.

This seclusion is the note of orthodox Mohammedanism. It is as safe to track a tiger to its lair as a Moslem to his sanctuary. Mecca and Medina, as they are the only places that excel Kairwán in piety, so they are the only two where a stranger's presence was more savagely resented. Kairwán retained its intolerance intact almost to the last moment. In 1830 Sir Grenville Temple, with the help of a strong escort and carrying an order from the Bey, managed to pass hurriedly through its streets. He calls the town the "hotbed of all the bigotry of Mohammedanism in Africa." He was only allowed to go out after sunset, and then disguised as an Arab, and there were some parts of the town that he might not enter lest he should be torn to pieces. Ten years later the Marquis of Waterford's attempt at exploration ended in his being

KAIRWÁN

stoned and nearly killed by the townsmen. Dr. Tristram, in 1857, explored much of the country south of the Atlas, but he did not venture to enter Kairwán, though he passed near it. Even down to 1877 there were many formalities and some risk attending a visit. Edward Rae describes his expedition in that year; the suspicion, dislike, and occasional rage which his appearance excited, and the threats and insults which were now and then lavished on him, guest of the Kaid though he was.

Five years later the French army in three columns converged upon the city. From the accounts written at the time by the French officers it is evident that a strong resistance was expected. The army was, however, too strong. The city lies in a plain. It is easy to surround, and a force once entrapped in it could never make good its escape. The Arab horsemen accordingly abandoned it before the troops could reach it, and fell back upon the hills. Summoned to surrender, the city calmly opened its gates. A white flag fluttered from the great tower of Okba's mosque, and, in solemn silence, for the first time since the foundation of the city 1,212 years before, a Christian force filed through its streets.

Such is the character of a Moslem metropolis—fiercely aggressive in its prime, fiercely exclusive in its decline. It is in keeping with the nature of the place that, once violated, its sacred character should have fallen from it. Exclusiveness with the Arabs not only guards sanctity, it *is* sanctity. Guérin more than fifty years ago described the peculiar inviolability of this town, which had "remained virgin to the contact of any faith but that of Okba." And he adds, "*hence*," and I underline the word, "the sort of holy and mysterious aureole with which the Mussulman religion surrounds it." But, once the French had occupied the place, it was in Arab eyes desecrated. The mosques of the cities of Tunisia are, as a rule, very jealously guarded. A stranger may with difficulty enter any of them. But there is one exception. The mosques of Kairwán, the most sacred of all, are open to all comers. Rae, whose visit took place in 1877, tells how he once suggested entering the Great Mosque to a group of idlers who were seated at one of its gates, and whom his own urbanity had apparently put into a good humour, and he describes the snarl of hatred which the proposition met with and the instant preparation for resistance. Any visitor may enter now as he wills, and no Arab will trouble to turn his head. It was, I believe, a stipulation of the French Government that the mosque should be open. But the entire indifference of the people proves how much its character is shaken. That "holy and mysterious aureole" which used to surround it has faded since strangers have been allowed entrance. It was holy because it typified the fierce isolation of the race. Not the miracles of its Great Mosque, not the sacred tomb of the Companion, but the fact that never in all these centuries, except by stealth and at peril of his life, had an unbeliever set foot within its walls, was what vouched in the eyes of Moslems for its high sanctity. On the day when the French army entered the town three-quarters of this sanctity departed. The tomb and mosque remain. They guard their miracles and sacred relics still, but they no longer symbolise to the Arab that lonely and strict seclusion in which lies, as Okba knew so well when he founded Kairwán, the secret of his strength and stamina; and accordingly their glory has departed from them. Kairwán is a broken spell.

CHAPTER XVII

ARAB ARCHITECTURE

The romance of the Arabs—Quality of their architecture—The early mosques—Difference between Moorish and Arab architecture—The Great Mosque—Fine effect of the whole—Slovenliness of detail—Indistinct arches—Arab and Gothic architecture compared—The Arab lack of purpose—Quality of his masonry—Decorative design—Corresponding mannerisms in life—Arab crowds and streets compared to English—Fickleness of the desert.

A CHARM and enchantment clings to everything Arab. Taking Europe's history as a whole, the events of it all seem natural and commonplace with one exception; and that exception is the Arab invasion. This is bathed in an atmosphere and a light of its own. Wild legends and ballads are its only histories. Dark eyes and snowy turbans and desperate deeds of love and valour are its incidents. These things make up the spell that surrounds the Arab. He is poor old Europe's romance. And yet, child of impulse as he is, what a dashing figure he cuts! A dreamer of ineffectual dreams, an actor of terrific energy, to-day a Sybarite, to-morrow an anchorite, it is impossible to make head or tail of him, and yet it is impossible not to love him. He retains always, through all vicissitudes—

"What he had received
From nature, an intense and glowing soul."

He is never commonplace or vulgar for an instant. Even in his vices he is not ignoble. He is sometimes a hero, often a devil, but never a slave.

No wonder that all he ever did is steeped for us in that poetic glamour which effectually rebuts criticism. Even his architecture, and his architecture especially, is lifted out of the sphere of reason and analysis, and the vision of the dark-eyed maidens who have glanced from these lattices, and turbaned warriors who have pranced through these courts, is sufficient to disguise the weakness of the structure and the trivial originality of the forms employed.

In some ways this is a pity. The interpretative quality in architecture is its main fascination. There is no form of art which so faithfully portrays the character of its creators as this does. An Arab building is, indeed, a signally graphic presentment of Arab life and history. Look at this masonry, with its blocks of stone, probably filched from some earlier classic building, and fitted hastily and feebly together with wide joints of inferior mortar. Look at these irregular, nodding arcades, with their air of insecurity, their lack of symmetry and precision. Note the eccentric forms of arch used, the horseshoe, the stilted, the ogive, the foliated. Commonly enough the arch-ribs, intersecting at the apex, expand, then meet, then expand again, and so go wobbling up the wall with something of the fluctuating motion of tongues of flame. Naturally most of these buildings are falling into decay. They were not built to endure. The columns are generally old fragments stuck together. The Roman capitals, of all shapes and sizes, are often put on upside-down and heightened, where necessary, by rude fragments of

ARAB ARCHITECTURE

stone, or even by billets of wood. Even where some care was taken and more regard for symmetry observed, the fantastical nature of the forms employed was an element of inherent weakness. Simplicity is the essential of strength, an essential in which the whimsical structures of the Arabs were wholly wanting.

And yet it is perhaps in its very drawbacks that that architecture's value lies. As architecture it is indeed worthless. It has taught us nothing that we had not better never have learnt. But as a human document it is among the most interesting, and it is in its very deficiencies that its interest is embodied. All this furious speed and zeal, this straw-fire energy and whimsical extravagance, are a humorously exact personification of the very qualities we meet in Arab history. They have the Arab expression. They have his look and way. In them the evolution of Arab civilisation, a civilisation defying the ordinary constructive rules, fanciful and feeble, is reproduced to the life. The heat, the haste, the luxuriant imagination, the lack of all common sense and sound judgment, are all there. Neither civilisation nor architecture was made to cope with time. The fatal instability that is the root of Arab character possessed them.

No, if we are to look for anything of real value bequeathed to us by the Arabs, we shall scarcely find it in their buildings. To this day the Arab talks of "building" his tent when he pitches it; and very rightly, for it is the only kind of architecture he has ever understood. It is his weakness that shows itself. His real influence is felt, not seen. Nothing he ever built or fashioned gives us the best of him, unless perhaps it be some of those beautiful gardens where the nightingales still sing among the odorous orange bloom and in the tangle of roses birds build their nests. His influence survives, but not in art. It survives in the character of southern races. It has introduced a strain of sentiment and manners for which the West is the richer. And to us, to poor, prosaic, middle-aged old Europe, it is a pleasant memory, the memory of our one romance.

Still, let us see if we can put aside this glamour that enwraps the subject, and get something definite out of Arab architecture.

That architecture is like everything else the race ever did in this—that if you wish to find the most expressive and only really imposing period of it you must turn back to that brief interval when the national tie held. It was in the century or two immediately preceding and following their tremendous irruption that the Arabs accomplished everything with any touch of power or character in it—whether in art or literature or action—that they ever did accomplish. Their after-civilisation has ingenuity, fancy, luxury, but it has not the sincerity and simplicity of the earlier work.

Okba's Great Mosque was one of the first, as it is one of the most sacred, mosques built. The reader will see a plan of it on the opposite page. It is sufficiently clear to be understood at a glance. It consists of a large open courtyard with a double arcade of arches round it, which, on the eastward or Mecca side, however, are deepened to ten arcades, making at that end an immense dim hall, very low for its extent, and upheld by a forest of several hundred columns. This is the plan of all the early mosques, and it was adopted because it most closely corresponded to the habits of

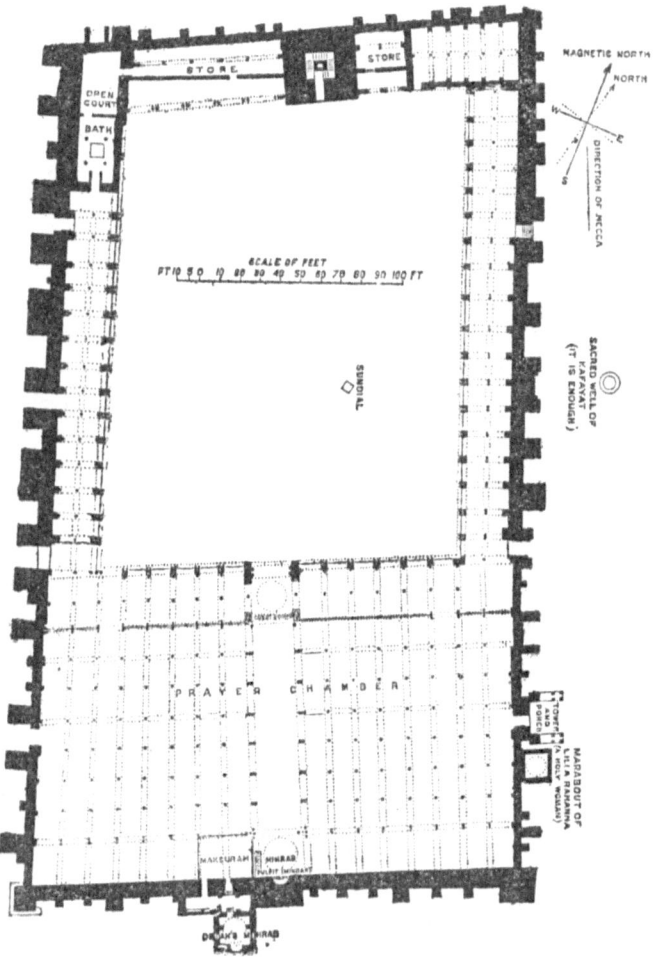

PLAN OF GREAT MOSQUE OF KAIRWÁN.

desert life. It is, indeed, neither more nor less than a caravanserai, identical in general configuration with many that are to be found to-day on the desert routes. These "resting-places" consist, just as the mosque does, of a large open space into which camels and goats may be driven at night, and of a portion at one end, or sometimes all round, arched over to afford shelter and shade for travellers to rest in.

In towns these caravanserai, now called khans, soon became more complicated. The great central space diminished in size; the surrounding buildings increased in height to several storeys, and were divided into separate apartments. Exactly the same change occurs in the mosques. The great square shrinks and shrinks till it becomes an insignificant courtyard. The body of the building is divided into a number of chambers of greater or less sanctity and very involved and complicated architecture.

The caravanserai mosques, as they may be called, only maintained themselves for about three centuries. But during that time they were fairly universal. They are to be found wherever the Arab penetrated: in Syria, in Spain, in North Africa. In all the countries he conquered, so long as the Arab remained an Arab, he remained true to the caravanserai mosque.

And the reason is evident. The caravanserai mosque gives him all that a building possibly can give a man of the desert. To a wanderer there is bound to be something repugnant in all constraint and all confinement. Gipsies hate houses. There is that in their intricacies, in their passages, stairs, and doors, bolts and bars, that suggests the feeling of being trapped.

CORNER OF THE GREAT MOSQUE.

ARAB ARCHITECTURE

But the caravanserai mosques hardly suggest constraint at all. The open space in the midst, bare to the sky, is the dominating feature of the whole. The arcades form but a fringe round it. Nor are these cut off. There is no mystery. As you enter you can at a glance take in the entire place. The arcades lie open to your eye in all directions. The air blows softly through them, free to come and go. The most shy and wild of mortals could find nothing here to alarm or perplex him. Here are the things he loves. Here is water for him to wash in, and deep shade for him to rest in. Here, too, is something of the amplitude of space and largeness of the desert itself.

So long, then, as the Arab retained any feeling for the desert this was how he built. And it may, I think, be said that he retained his feeling for the desert as long as he retained the right to call himself an Arab. The various names indifferently applied to the race and its doings are a cause of some confusion. Saracen, Arab, Moor, are the words used. Saracen we may strike out as being of romantic origin merely and of no specific meaning. Moor and Arab we want to express the difference between the town and desert people. The line of demarcation is by no means distinct, for the Arabs naturally did not turn into Moors at the mere sight of bricks and mortar. They retained the desert spirit some little while, and when it went, it went gradually. It is the going of it that is shown in these mosques. For as long—that is to say, about to the tenth century—as the Arab remained true to a form of building which derived all its merit from its close association with desert life, so long did he keep the Arab heart in him. When he took up with the cribbed and cabined style of architecture he was becoming a Moor. The remembering or forgetting of the desert is the difference between Moor and Arab.

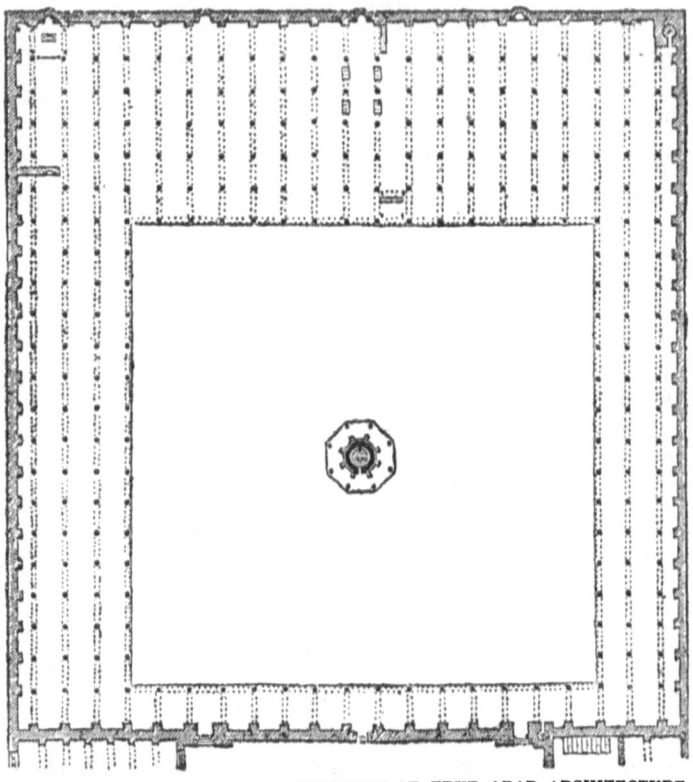

PLAN OF MOSQUE OF AMRU.   SPECIMEN OF TRUE ARAB ARCHITECTURE,
DESERT INFLUENCE PARAMOUNT.

It is in their general plan and arrangement that the merit of these early mosques lies. Every one coming into them is struck by the large simplicity and restfulness of the scene. There are the elements

THE INDEFINITE ARAB ARCH.

ARAB ARCHITECTURE

here of a certain grandeur. The simplicity of Arab character, the fewness of their needs, insured this effect. They asked for little, but they all agreed in asking for the same things. And this economy, combined with this unanimity, has acted on the building almost like an artistic knowledge of effect. It has delivered it from all irrelevancies and redundances; it has kept it perfectly simple and legible; it has given meaning and purpose to every part, and something approaching unity to the whole.

That is the first impression of the mosque. The reader must couple it in his mind with that early ballad poetry of theirs, so direct and genuine and sincere, of which I spoke in an earlier chapter. But when we begin to look into their architecture for a confirming and deepening of the first impression, we find ourselves met by deficiencies much like those which met us in the poetry. Their architecture cannot be called beautiful. It lacks something that is necessary to beauty. It has not depth enough of thought and feeling.

Suppose we were to compare for a moment these arcades with an arcade of Bramante's. What we should immediately feel would be that Bramante was supported by a whole era of civilisation; that he was backed up and nourished by thoughts and feelings which are profound and subtle and complex. This is what gives his work the quality that makes us never tired of looking at it. It is not easily exhausted. It has depth. Bramante, in short, got a great deal out of life that the Arab builder could not possibly get out of life; and so he put a great deal into his work that the Arab could not put in. The mosque pleases up to a certain point. It is very convenient and absolutely honest. It gives the kind of pleasure a thing gives which is obviously well adapted to its purpose, and which, by the way, the works of birds and animals can give equally with the works of men; but it does not go deep enough for beauty. It is too obviously the outcome of a soil intellectually barren.

This becomes apparent directly we get to the detail. It is all bad, and bad in a way that shows us that the simplicity of the whole is due to no correctness of thought or feeling, but to mere convenience. The arches are the weakest of their kind. They are of that unhappy description which does not know its own mind. They are intended to be of the horseshoe pattern, but if you look closely you will perceive many variations. No two are exactly alike. In some the horseshoe is more pronounced than in others. In some, again, it is more pronounced on one side than the other. In few or none is the curve of the arch severely accurate. In each one, looked at carefully, you will read in the mind that made it unsureness of purpose, instability of will. Not one of them but bears witness to that vague, unsettled mental condition in which the Arab lives.

Throughout the rest of the building the same slovenliness everywhere appears. It is composed almost entirely of fragments of classic buildings. The mihrab is of course the place of honour. Its two columns have Byzantine capitals, and its marble panels are worked in Byzantine designs. It is the one bit of detail that tells. Elsewhere all the shafts and all the capitals have been pillaged from Roman ruins. The

ARAB ARCHITECTURE

capitals appear to be of white travertine, and are much chipped and broken. They are all, or almost all, of the usual florid Corinthian or composite order of late Rome.

These capitals and columns are what give the interior its architectural character, and these the Arabs did not

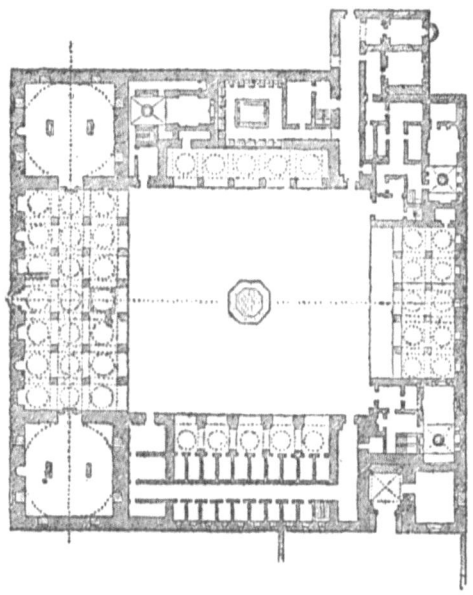

PLAN OF MOSQUE OF SULTAN BARKOOK. TRANSITION MOSQUE, SHOWING DECLINE OF DESERT AND RISE OF CITY INFLUENCE.

make, but collected. All that remained for them to do themselves was to put the fragments together. How did they do this? About as hurriedly and carelessly as it could be done. The capitals are often too large or too small for the shafts they stand on. The shafts are often not of the right length, and are made longer by rude blocks of stone thrust in at the top or bottom. Many of the capitals have been hastily patched up, where broken, with common plaster.

One little feature deserves notice. The imposition of arches on these classic capitals made it necessary to provide them with abaci. These, the only original Arab features here, are of wood. The Arabs could not spare time or trouble to fashion them of stone.

These traits are not in any way peculiar to the Kairwán mosques. They are typical of Arab architecture. On turning over a diary kept in Cairo some years ago, I find similar notes of mosque after mosque. Of the shape of the arches I find the words "indeterminate" or "indefinite" used again and again. Again and again I find myself in doubt as to the actual shape they are meant to assume, and especially I find it difficult to decide whether their tall, weak, egg-shaped summits are meant to have a point at the top or not.

As regards their indefiniteness of shape, I find it noted in my Kairwán diary that the interior arches of the east-end arcades, which form the mosque proper, are round-headed, *except* the central nave, the arches of which, resting on coupled columns, are "slightly pointed." Of the exterior arches of the quadrangle I have the note, "of the usual unmistakable Arab form: tall, flat soffit, slightly pointed, with their weak and indecisive cutting." I lay stress on these notes because they deal with a point commonly ignored. In all the accounts I have seen of the Great Mosque the arches are called simply round or horseshoe. No hint of a variation is suggested. Similarly as regards the Tooloun, El Hakem, and other mosques in Cairo, their arches are always categorised unhesi-

ARAB ARCHITECTURE

tatingly in a certain class, as if they were all alike and all of unmistakable shape. Nay, the illustrations of these mosques and of the Kairwán mosque are, so far as I know, always drawn in such a way as to convey the same, but totally erroneous, impression of perfect uniformity and decision of outline. Re-

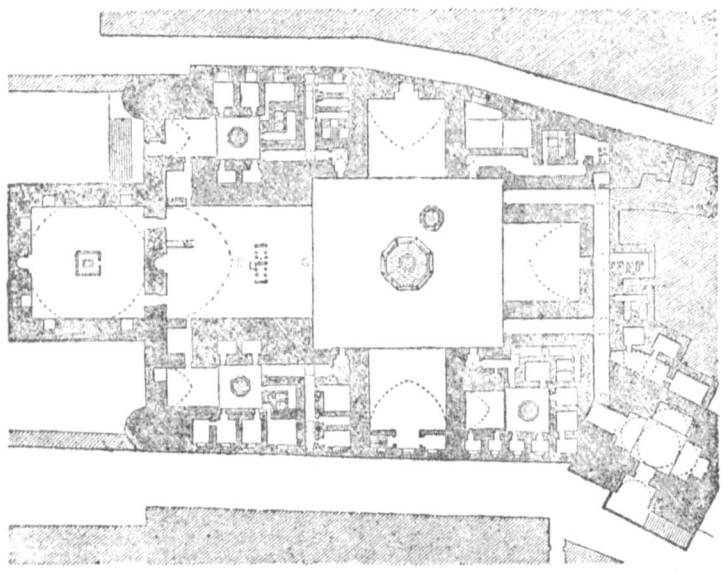

PLAN OF MOSQUE OF SULTAN HASSAN. SPECIMEN OF MOORISH ARCHITECTURE. CITY INFLUENCE PARAMOUNT.

porters have described or copied not what the Arab has done, but what they thought he meant to do.

All this is very characteristic. An Englishman or a Frenchman hates an indefinite line. To draw an arch which is not quite sure itself whether it is round or pointed is to him almost impossible. It is an outrage on his sense of form. He makes up his own mind on the subject first, and then makes up the arch's mind for it afterwards. Unfortunately, in doing so he strips the arch of just exactly what constitutes its particular interest. It is just this indecision and vagueness which makes it so perfect a sample of Arab character. It is in this that its interpretative value lies.

The best way, it seems to me, to bring out this character in Arab architecture is to contrast it for a moment with Gothic. There is enough resemblance to justify the comparison, and a relationship between the two styles has always been felt. Both were the distinctive national styles of the races which, from the East and South, overran the decaying empires of Rome and Constantinople. Both represented an assault by the pointed arch, and all the pointed arch stood for, on the round. Gothic broke up Romanesque just as Arab had, wherever it could reach it, broken up Byzantine five centuries before. The two invading styles were alike in their character of consuming energy, so typical of the races that gave them birth. But there is a difference in the quality of that energy. The Gothic energy not only breaks up Romanesque but goes on to achieve a purpose of its own. It clears the Romanesque idea out of the way to make room for its own ideas; and the architecture it proceeded to develop, so resolute, so uniform in character and feeling, so logically and thoroughly carried out in plan and detail, shows with what virile tenacity and sureness that purpose and those ideas were grasped.

Arab fervour, on the other hand, is not of this quality. It is not fervour in pursuit of a definite object. Its destructive power is great; but its con-

GOTHIC SURENESS OF PURPOSE.

ARAB ARCHITECTURE

structive power is *nil*. The most remarkable thing about it is its intense animosity towards all forms suggesting calmness and repose, such as the plain arch and round vault. The fury with which it attacks these and the eagerness with which it sets to work to twist and distort them give to all its doings a similar character. But if from these negative achievements we turn to look for positive ideas and a constructive purpose, none such is forthcoming. I know of no other architecture of which this can be said. All other styles have a constructive purpose of their own. Egyptian, Roman, Greek, Gothic, Renaissance, each in turn calls up the thought of distinct and clearly-articulated structures. Arab alone, except in its primitive stage, calls up no such thought. All it suggests is complicated designs, eccentric arches, and fantastical decoration. We know it, in short, by detail and not by structure.

And yet it would seem as if the Arabs had, as a race, much the same opportunity as the Goths. The definite work of reviving a languid, stereotyped society and building up a new civilisation, which lay before the northern invaders, seemed to lie before the southern ones too. But if the Arab had the opportunity he had not the gifts of character to take advantage of it. When he had broken up Byzantine society his ideas gave out. He was not able to re-organise it on a permanent basis and evolve a durable civilisation of his own. He exhausted himself in whim and fancy. And just as the Gothic purpose is felt in its thorough and systematic style of architecture, so the Arab lack of purpose is seen in all its whimsical and capricious details. The Arab style is essentially destructive. It can break the

Byzantine round arch, or the smoothness of the Byzantine vault; but when it has done that much it is at a loss. It stops exactly where the whole scheme of Arab civilisation stopped. Just when the world began to expect something worth having, just when the race had cleared the stage for itself, it glided off into the fantastical and the unreal. All its precious astrological and necromantic fancies, with which it turned solid subjects into unrealities, are the very counterpart of its weak and whimsical style of building. They represent the disintegration of fixed forms, but discover no purpose beyond.

I know of nothing more comical than the contrast between the headlong fury with which the Arab cast himself on the Byzantine system of life, the impatience with which he thrust it all aside, the breathless hurry with which he started a system of his own, and then, all of a sudden, when it came to a definition of that system, his pathetic helplessness and failure. From that moment on the movements of this prompt and haughty warrior are the movements of an imbecile or a naughty child. It is scarcely possible to believe that all the splendid, irresistible energy of his campaigns and conquests should have evaporated in forms and ideas so purposeless and vague. That, however, is the Arab way. Set him to pull down, and he is a very Samson. Set him to build, and he is left "weak as is a breaking wave."

Such is Arab character. Ask the dry waves of sand, when they have obliterated the road, the cliff, the oasis, what their own ideas are and what purpose of their own they have in view. None, they will tell you; they have done all they want to do. So it is with the Arab. When he has smashed the existing

ARAB ARCHITECTURE 261

order of things he is at the end of his tether. The weak eccentricity, the absence of the constructive architectural sense, this it is in Arab architecture that gauges the man. His failure is written in his flimsy and fantastic style of building. Directly we contrast it with the style that went on, that had ideas of its own, directly we note, in Gothic, the bold and logical design carried out in detail and main plan, so daringly and resolutely, we feel the difference between a constructive and non-constructive people. Arab and Goth were equal rivals once. Order and chaos fought in their persons for the Roman inheritance. Step by step chaos has yielded to order. We can trace the contest now as a contest between opposing principles. The difference between the volatile Moslem hordes that whirled through South Europe and the virile and stubborn races that carved out the nationalities of the north was that one had purpose and the other hadn't. That is the difference we can read still between Gothic architecture and Arab.

The quality of Arab masonry the reader will have guessed already from what has been said. Most of their mosques are built of bricks with joints as wide as the bricks themselves, and the mortar is of such wretched consistency that it falls out and crumbles, like earth, at a touch. Looking along the face of a wall you see that it is never perfectly flush, but always bulges and gives in places. Most of the mosques in North Africa are, in fact, falling to ruins, though many of them are single-storey buildings, and in that climate the wear and tear of material is reduced to a minimum. To examine, however, the jointing and setting of the masonry is enough to account for this. The wonder rather is that such crazy constructions should have lasted so long. None of the feeling we associate with the remains of great ruins belongs to the ruins of Arab architecture. The idea of shattered strength, of fragments bearing witness to the original power of material and workmanship—columns rising out of green turf, their arches twisted about with ivy, west windows framing nothing but the blue sky, yet each beetling crag of it still imposing and grand in its decay—all this, which makes up the attraction of a northern ruin, is foreign to an Arab one. The Arab building is so constructed that when it begins to go to pieces it crumbles and dissolves into a *débris* of dust and plaster and fragments of brick, of which you can provoke a fresh cataract at any time by a poke of your stick.

If the reader care anything for architecture he will know the significance of this. It would probably be true to say that every one who has built in good masonry has built finely and well. It would certainly be true to say that no one has built finely and well who has not built in good masonry. People who care for form feel above all the need of exactitude. In architecture the significance of every line and contour depends on perfect accuracy; the lines and curves of great architecture being so charged with expression that the slightest indecision or uncertainty is felt and noticed in an instant. On the other hand, it is impossible to avoid this indecision and wavering unless the masonry composing the building be finely and evenly jointed and perfectly firm and accurate. This makes the quality of masonry always the prime test of a good building age. And when we find, as we do throughout all Arab work from beginning to end, that the masonry

ARAB LACK OF PURPOSE.

ARAB ARCHITECTURE 263

employed is of a most wretched and inferior kind, it is a proof positive that the race was lacking in the architectural sense. Such faults as incorrect arches and untrue walls bear the same relation to bad masonry that immoral or criminal actions do to a vicious character; they are the inevitable outward signs of inward corruption. Masonry is the character of architecture, and all possibilities of form and expression depend upon it. It is in this, the very material out of which a definite purpose has to be forged, that the Arab weakness most clearly shows itself.

Of decorative design there is not very much in these early mosques, and here at Kairwán there is less than in the Cairo examples. In those early days the Arab had not learnt to concern himself seriously with the idea of decoration. When, indeed, he had recourse to colour, and panelled his walls with lustrously-glazed tiles, he produced results second only to the Persian. But directly he tries his hand at sculpture his invariable procedure is to honeycomb the surface with small, undecipherable patterns, leaving no margins or background of smooth material to set off the decoration. The work is on so minute a scale that, not being disciplined or controlled by any bold, prominent lines, it is at a few yards totally illegible. The eye cannot see it, and turns from it in weary disgust. Indeed, it does not deserve the name of design at all.

Here in the detail, as in the masonry and main forms of Arab architecture, a definable intellectual purpose, a foreseen effect wrought out by appropriate means, will be sought for in vain. It will be sought for in vain in the architecture because it will be sought for in vain in the man. Again and again I have been struck and arrested by tricks of manner and habits of the Arabs which recalled their characteristic methods in art. I find, for example, this note in my diary on camel-loading in the desert: "Quick, nervous, restless, they introduce strings and knots in all directions. They have a preference for a number of bits tied together to one plain rope. They are full of ineffectual, ingenious contrivances for hitching up this or hanging up that. The load, instead of being held by one or two stout cords passed around it, is balanced by a number tangled together. It is certain to slip before we have been out long. When that happens the Arabs throw themselves upon it in a great state of agitation and zeal. They grapple with the tottering mass, their eager fingers pluck and tear and push. They are possessed with a frenzy of nervous agitation. And when they have finished the nodding load appears covered with a fresh network of string, one bit made fast to another in inextricable confusion, the whole arrangement so lacking in simplicity and strength that a touch will upset it." To this I have added as a parallel case: "The commonest of all Arab designs is that of a pointed leaf with stalk emerging from the point, expanding into a fresh leaf, emerging again from the point of that one, and so continuing, stalk melting into leaf, leaf into stalk, without beginning or end. These threads the Arab takes and winds about and entangles until he has covered all the surface he is dealing with. So far as the design is concerned, that is always the same—an ingenious, weak muddle."

Exactly, in fact, like the camel-loading: "wanting in simplicity or strength." I never see that futile

ARAB ARCHITECTURE 265

leaf and stalk tanglement—I saw it but yesterday on the ceiling of a Great Western Railway carriage—without thinking of the ingenious weak muddle that our drivers wove that morning on the backs of the camels.

Or, again, since we are coming to matters of everyday life, what is it that I feel here in Kairwán, as I walk about the streets or stand in the dim covered bazaar? What is it that gives its special character to this place, and differentiates it so utterly from an English town? It is the lack of order, method, purpose in all I see. Of these streets and houses, or hovels, is there one that knows its own mind, that has succeeded in being the thing it set out to be, or ever, rather, had an idea at all of what it was going to be? Is there one street straight and regular, one building with exact perpendicular walls, with cleancut angles, with a firm and level roof? In all this jumble of tottering walls and broken outlines is there anywhere discoverable a single glimpse of the great architectural sense, the sense of purpose?

But these are outward manifestations. It is to the people you must come at last. Watch, in the streets, the groups that pass or loiter, that now collect and now hurry on. The impression produced is like that of the fluctuating uncertain motion of summer gnats eddying or pausing in the air. Each individual, if you watch his progress, will exhibit in his own movements this general uncertainty. Now he will start running, as though anxious to get to his destination as soon as possible. In a hundred yards he will pull up and dawdle along vacantly singing. Next he will meet a friend and fall into talk with him, the interview being generally of an excitable and gesticulatory as well as affectionate kind. Then off again at top speed, until an old water-carrier coming along, chinking his cups, attracts his attention, and he has a drink and exchanges a certain amount of voluble repartee. Then the thought strikes him of a cigarette. This he rolls and lights and pauses a moment to inhale a few whiffs under the shadow of a mosque porch with other loiterers. This is his progress. This is one of those aimless threads of which the whole crowd is made up. I used to watch the vague, spasmodic movements of these passers-by at first with that sense of discomfort one has when one is watching manœuvres one does not understand. I could feel that here was something, a character or spirit prevailing, different from that which prevailed in Western crowds. But what was it? Then with the consciousness one began to have of the meaning and significance of their wavering arches and weak designs, came the recognition that the crowd itself was but a human expression of qualities of which the architecture was a brick-and-mortar expression. What other kind of crowd, indeed, could walk in such streets or rest under such arcades?

My thoughts flew back to English thoroughfares. I saw the people coming and going, an average steady pace bearing witness to a purpose easily borne in mind. Even on holidays and Sundays I remembered how people who walk for pleasure walk, as it were, with decision. So accustomed are we to have an object, to be going about a definite business, that a purposeful gait has become second nature to us, and even when we have no purpose in view, we walk as if we had one.

Photo., Garrigues, Tunis.

STREET ARCHITECTURE IN KAIRWĀN.

ARAB ARCHITECTURE

And to right and left above these steady walkers I saw the curt, determined lines of Western architecture; each window-frame exactly cut, each pillar and arch and pediment and moulding accurate to a hair's breadth; ugly enough, it may be, but what a grim tenacity of purpose lurks in every stroke and outline. Does not the architecture here, too, reflect the very character and manner of the crowd beneath? is it not as much the architectural expression of the Western temper as these vaguely distorted walls and arches are the expression of the Eastern? Is not the whole contrast, if we like to push the matter, between Western history and Eastern built into these streets and houses?

Has the reader ever chanced to see an Arab crowd in a violent state of excitement? The sight is a little perplexing, and more than a little amusing. I once saw an Algiers crowd which, on the occasion of some anti-Semitic disturbance, conceived it had a mighty grievance. Under such circumstances, the procedure of an English crowd is familiar to us. It commonly collects in immense, disciplined bodies with flags and drums; marches in a quite orderly way through the streets—submitting all the way to the directions of the usual police organisers of the traffic; arrives at Hyde Park; *demonstrates* its numbers and convictions, and marches stolidly home again.

It knows exactly what it wants, and it adopts those quiet means and measures which it thinks are likely to get it what it wants. The Arab crowd, on the contrary, does not know in the least what it wants. It is conscious of nothing but its own fury. Dangerous, should you come in contact with it, it is possessed by an impotence which may seem strange to those who observe only its apparent energy. The truth is it is impotent because it is incapable of forming a *design*, of carrying out a *purpose*.

This clue held, my discomfort in watching the Arabs gave place to a secret enjoyment. I saw in them a part of their surroundings. I recognised in them the living source of those vague and fitful impulses which I had been studying in their arches and tracery. And not that only, but turning back into their past it was impossible not to see the same fatal deficiency everywhere attending them; not to see that their whole civilisation and history is lacking in that quality which comes out so strongly in Western crowds and streets, in the Western arch and wall and face, and walk and manner and character.

It helps one to a comprehension of all this to be in the desert, to feel around one the influences which, the same here as in his native Arabia, have evolved the desert type. Here in the desert, indeed, the whole problem of environment is reduced to its simplest form. The scenery is of one universal character, scarcely diversified at all, showing one or two powerful traits and no more. For centuries untold the Arab tribes have been exposed to these strong and simple influences. For countless generations they have pitched their tents on these wastes of fickle, burning, restless sand, and breathed this stimulating, fiery air, until the characteristics of the desert have so entered into them that in describing one you describe the other. Sometimes at the mid-day halt, when the desert is locked in that grim repose I have spoken of, I have sat and watched it, imbibing the

Arab Decorative Design.

Photo, Garrigues, Tunis.

air and view, until, as happens in some moods, I have felt myself to be almost a part of my surroundings. And then my glance has strayed to the Arabs crowded near: never lolling or dozing; attentive; their dark, piercing eyes glancing over the scene, their fingers restlessly passing and dropping their rows of beads, their mobile features expressing a succession of light and fleeting emotions, and I used to think that, like the nymphs of streams, or fauns of woods, they were the genii of the place, the incarnated spirits of the Sahara.

Emanating from such a source, the Arab, in spite of all his fickleness and irritability, is so much of one piece, all that he has ever done and said and thought is so identical in character, that if you understand him in one respect, you seem to understand him in all. If you understand him as a knotter of camel loads, you understand him as fighter, as builder, as artist, as poet, as philosopher. Only to understand him aright in any particular, it is necessary, perhaps, for once to stand on this shifting desert floor and watch the Bedouin tribes that come and go, and fold their tents, and flit and wander across its surface, and leave no trace of their presence upon it. Such, indeed, has been the Arab progress through the world.

CHAPTER XVIII

THE MOSLEM SPHERE OF INFLUENCE

Arab society, its nebulous and incoherent character—Arab thought, its lack of depth and solidity—Immobility of Arab civilisation—The same true of all Moslem races—The orthodox faith responsible for this—Parallel between Islam and Christianity—Influence of Christianity on Western thought and society—Moslem liberalism anxious to attain the same results—It adopts principles similar to the Christian—The Wahhabi reaction—The Babis—Prospects of Moslem liberalism—Real strength of Islam in the orthodox party—The life of the desert the source of its strength.

HERE at Kairwán our pilgrimage ends; but before finishing I would like to submit to the reader an idea of the effect which the Moslem faith seems to have had on Moslem society.

Two main traits, as I endeavour to estimate what the Arab has been and has done in the world, strike me concerning him. One is the lack of cohesion in Arab society. Groups form, dissolve, and form again. There is no enduring organisation. And, though there is much vague and fluctuating movement, there is no regulated progress. All is loose, eddying, nebulous, and incoherent.

And besides this social peculiarity there is to be

THE MOSLEM SPHERE OF INFLUENCE

found, in the working of the Arab mind and intelligence, in Arab architecture, Arab poetry, Arab philosophy, a perpetual sticking to externals, a want of depth, an apparent inability to penetrate. I think these are the two deepest impressions one gleans from Arab life and thought—a want of coherence in Arab society, a want of depth in the Arab mind.

Both these traits are natural to, and the proper characteristics of, what I have called, because of its delight in personal deeds, the ballad-poetry stage of civilisation. Thought in such an age is without depth because depth of thought means the forgetting and thrusting aside of self. Society in such an age is without cohesion, because the social cement is made of what each individual gives up and surrenders to the common stock; is, in fact, the measure of the self-sacrifice of the units composing society. Consequently, where the rule and ideal of life is that a man gives up nothing, but glories in self-assertion and bending everything to his own will and his own ends, thought is bound to lack depth and society to lack coherence.

All races pass through this phase, but the Arabs have remained in it. And not only have the Arabs remained in it, but all Moslem races have remained in it. The Turks have had in the last four hundred years every opportunity of progressing; yet intellectual barrenness and social instability remain the outstanding traits of their civilisation. Any observer, I think, must be struck by these peculiarities in connection with the Moslem religion, and be led to question the religion itself for the cause. And if he is led to do this, he will only be doing what all liberal-minded and intellectual Moslems are themselves doing. For what the party of progress in all Moslem countries feels is that it is inflexible orthodox Mohammedanism that keeps Moslem thought and Moslem society what it is. And so all effort that has for its aim the consolidation of society and the joining of the Moslem mind in the intellectual work of the age is directed primarily towards modifying the orthodox faith.

If we turn back to the days when we, too, were in our ballad-poetry stage, when we and the Arabs were at one in our view of life, and thence note our divergence—we under our religion, they under theirs—we shall ascertain, perhaps, what it is in Mohammedanism that the Moslem progressives object to. For the truth about the Moslem problem seems to be that Moslem liberalism is bent on getting out of the Moslem religion —and so altering it as to make this possible—what Europe has got out of the European religion.

Taking, then, any, or all, the centuries from the fifth to the twelfth, and comparing European society with Arab, we find that both looked at life with much the same eyes. Both admired the same hardy virtues, delighted in the same enterprises, and gloried in the same achievements. No doubt, in a kind of civilisation, the Saracens were the more advanced; but the attitude of both towards life was essentially the same. It was the aggressive, self-assertive attitude. For us as for them it was the ballad-poetry phase. European thought and European society bear all the marks of that phase. The thought is without depth. The society is without coherence.

Nevertheless, between these two societies, so similar in spirit, there existed one very vital point of difference. The European society possessed a moral doctrine, or

THE MOSLEM SPHERE OF INFLUENCE 273

theory of life, which was not only at variance with, but in direct antagonism to, the prevailing and mundane view of life. Usually, of course, a religion is mainly, like art, the expression of the life of its age. Mohammedanism was, through these centuries, for instance, entirely the expression of Moslem life in that age. But mediæval Christianity was not the expression of European life. It was, on the contrary, utterly opposed to life; so utterly opposed to it that it had to build itself cloistered forts of its own and subsist by the ministrations of men totally divorced from the world. The fact is, it had elected to build on exactly that principle which in that age was least understood. In an age of physical force and a vigorous self-assertion it laid stress exclusively on meekness and self-sacrifice. There is scarcely a quainter contrast in human history, I should think, than the contrast between mediæval life and mediæval religion.

The barons went on pillaging their neighbours and cutting their prisoners' throats. The monks went on preaching the beauty of meekness and self-sacrifice. Times changed by degrees, manners grew less militant, hearts softened. The besieged doctrine crept out of its cloisters and began to mix a little in the world.

At this point the European and the Arab diverge. Up to now, though they had fought like mad, they sympathised with and understood each other. They admired the same things. Their poetry, manners, and chivalry were similar. They borrowed from each other their ideas of what was fine and becoming. But from now on, though they gave up fighting, they never sympathised with or understood each other again.

Slowly Western society and Western thought changed under the influence of the new leaven. Western thought was deepened. The new principle was found to apply not only to the sphere of morals, but to every kind of intellectual and spiritual research. It not only placed man in right relation to God, it placed him in right relation to the universe. When Wordsworth says—

> "Give unto me, made lowly wise,
> The spirit of self-sacrifice,"

he is not thinking of the moral precept in its moral sense. He is thinking how entirely dependent that power of entering into the essence of things, in which all his own joy lies, is on his ability to utterly thrust aside and forget himself. So, in the field of science, Darwin's attitude towards his monkeys and pigeons and earth-worms is precisely of a similar kind. Wherever, in whatever way, the mind of man was applied to the search for truth, this new principle—new at least among the societies of the West, and more directly and powerfully affirmed now than it had ever been previously — became the basis of the inquiry and the condition of its fruitfulness.

But this new teaching was something more than an abstract principle. It was embodied in a great human organisation. It supplied to distracted society the means and idea of union. Amid general chaos and anarchy it stood for a universal social bond, the only one that existed. It may sound daring, in an interval of reaction, to talk of the efficacy of this principle from the social point of view; but let the reader cast his glance back over the course of events in Europe for the last six or eight centuries, and he will see that the

THE MOSLEM SPHERE OF INFLUENCE 275

tendency has been for society to form on an ever-widening and more secure basis. Peace and law and order, however liable to interruption, have become the normal conditions of life, instead of their contraries. In short, what has happened with us since we left the ballad stage of our civilisation behind, is that the mind of man has acquired depth, and society has acquired coherence.

Whether any principle or doctrine would have sufficed to drag the Arab through that phase of civilisation to which nature and breeding seemed to have suited him, may perhaps be doubted. Anyhow the experiment was not tried. Starting level with us in other respects, Arab society, instead of a religion at variance with half-way ideals, and pointing to something more profound, possessed a religion in accord with those ideals and tending to perpetuate them. The consequences have been felt all through Arab history and life. The want of feeling, the want of depth, in the Arab religion has become the characteristic of the Arab mind and of everything the Arab mind produces. Moreover, no great universal social organism has instilled the idea of a possible union into the fluctuating Arab life. Consequently the old outward and external point of view, the old social incoherence, which we and they shared in common in mediæval days, have remained to the present time the characteristics of Arab thought and Arab society.

Or rather, they remain the characteristics of Moslem thought and Moslem society. The anarchy that possesses Moslem society is generally the most remarkable thing about it, and in these days it is, too, the most practically important thing about it. That Moslem races cannot provide anything of value in the domains of thought, literature, and art, is a matter which chiefly concerns themselves. But that society with them means chaos is a matter which is bound more and more to concern other people as well. I have pointed out how, as social coherence and the ideas of law and order spread through the West, the Arab sphere of influence dwindled and diminished. It is now practically extinct. But the Moslem problem does not end with the Arab. All its elements appear in the Turkish Empire. More virile and stubborn than the Arab, the Turk displays the same well-known Moslem traits; the same sterility of mind, the same reliance on physical force, the same indifference to the idea of social order and stable government. What is intolerable to the sense of Europe in Constantinople to-day is just what was intolerable in Algiers three-quarters of a century ago. Though we have shifted the ground of difference from religion to politics, the political difference is only the outcome of the religious difference. When we say that Turkish or Arab ideas of law and order, Turkish or Arab ideas of government, are incompatible with European ideas, we really mean that a state of society which is the outcome of Mohammedanism is incompatible with a state of society which is the outcome of Christianity. We do not call our quarrel a quarrel of religions, but it is so all the same. In the old days the crescent and the cross contended directly. Now they contend in their effects. Their social systems contend, their politics contend; but the real division lies beneath them. It lies in the fact that the Western religion has given to the Western people an ideal which has profoundly modified the old outward conception of

THE MOSLEM SPHERE OF INFLUENCE

life, an ideal which is tending to the ordering and consolidating of society on an immense scale, and which has impregnated every action of the Western mind with a certain quality of inwardness and depth. While, on the other hand, Mohammedanism not having such an ideal to propose, no such change has taken place in Moslem society or in Moslem ideas.

Unless we realise the contrast in these results we shall scarcely comprehend the questions that agitate the Moslem world to-day. For the liberal and progressive movement in Islam is partly a religious and partly a political and social movement. And those who would deepen the religion, and those who would turn it into a more perfect civilising instrument, work in unison.

The religious reformers object to the faith because it is lacking in depth and emotion, and the whole course of action of the great Shiite heresy is the history of an endeavour to supply this want by introducing the idea of self-abnegation and self-surrender into the faith. The social and political reformers object to it because it is in its nature isolating and anti-social. Their quarrel with it is not that it fails to put a man into right relation with God, but that it fails to put him into right relation with his neighbour. They profoundly dissent from the effects that orthodox Mohammedanism has produced in the way of civilisation. The object of their endeavours is to bring the Moslem mind into touch with the European, to animate Moslem society with the spirit of progress, to give it common aims and aspirations, and make it capable of collective and coherent action. But these two parties, the party that wants to make the faith a more satisfying religion and the party that wants to make it a better civilising instrument, are really one party. They are fronted by the same adversary, and similar measures of reform suit both.

There have been during the last couple of centuries two opposing impulses in Islam which perfectly illustrate the objects of the liberal movement and the nature and power of the force that is opposed to it. The reform inaugurated by Abd-el-Wahhab, about the middle of the eighteenth century, was puritan and reactionary in character. A return to the narrowest and strictest interpretation of the Koran, the fiercest intolerance, and a hatred of all foreigners were the salient traits of the movement. Needless to say such an impulse was desert-born. It was instinct with the desert temperament and teaching and the desert fanaticism, and its success among the Arabs of Arabia was proportionately great. It has been a movement, the strongest of modern times, towards the resuscitation of the vigour and influence of orthodox Mohammedanism, and it illustrates in its own character the elements on which orthodox Mohammedanism relies. This spirit it is which is so inveterately opposed to liberalism in Islam.

The second impulse, the impulse on the liberal side, springs, as it is also needless to say, from Persia. The pretension of Seyed Mohammed Ali to be the Bab, or Gate, or "intermediary," was in effect an attempt to supply the thing needed in Mohammedanism, both socially and religiously. It was an attempt to humanise and vitalise the faith and to endow it with an authoritative, recognised presence and voice, such as it must possess if it is to form a rallying point for social organisation. Consequently when the Bab declared himself, social and religious reformers alike saw in him their opportunity, and he was backed up not only by

THE MOSLEM SPHERE OF INFLUENCE 279

the spiritually-minded, by mystics, enthusiasts, and visionaries, but also by men of affairs, men of intellect, sagacity, and learning. A liberalism of ideas became the characteristic of the new sect. It was distinguished by its cheerfulness, hospitality, and charity. In nothing was its enlightenment more shown than in its treatment of women. The old Eastern degradations and disabilities were abolished. Polygamy, concubinage, the use of the veil, were disallowed or discouraged. The equality of the sexes was recognised. And all this reform, all this liberalism, all this spirit of progress gathers round the person of an individual who aspires to play much the same part towards Mohammedanism that Christ played towards Judaism.

This, it seems to me, is the curious and interesting feature about Moslem reform. The whole history of Shíism, with its saints and martyrs and Christs, its insistence on charity, meekness, long-suffering, is the history of an endeavour to introduce into the Moslem faith ideas with which Christianity has long since made the West perfectly familiar. But the Moslem movement is just as much social and political as religious. The people who are concerned about civilisation and progress are as anxious to adopt these ideas as the people who are concerned about religion. The Persian liberal is as ready to believe in a Christ as the Persian saint—not that he wants his help in getting to heaven, but that he wants his help in attaining his objects on earth. The want of depth in Moslem thought, the want of cohesion in Moslem society, are instinctively identified by the party of progress with the influence of the old orthodox faith; and this party, whose aim it is to join in modern civilisation and modern thought, finds itself perpetually fumbling and feeling after that very principle which made the difference between European and Arab society in the mediæval ages.

What are the prospects of Moslem liberalism? Not, so far as I can make out, very brilliant. The strength and vigour of Mohammedanism are in the orthodox party. As the religion of the half-way stage of civilisation, orthodox Mohammedanism has a part to play in human affairs. Mr. Wilfrid Blunt tells us that he does not see in its "territorial losses a sign of Islam's ruin as a moral and intellectual force in the world." He looks to the time when the Caliphate shall be once more established at Mecca. "It is to Arabia that Mussulmans must in the future look for a centre of their religious system." Centred in Arabia, their religious influence is to extend through the low latitudes, and in the decay of Buddhism it will be Mohammedanism, not Christianity, that will be the form under which God will eventually be worshipped in the tropics.

In Burmah, in the Malay Archipelago, in India, China, and Tartary, and all through Central Africa, the rapid advance of Islam is, year by year, lending great colour to these prophecies of Mr. Blunt, made three-and-twenty years ago. On the other hand, Mr. Blunt recognises that the days of Islam in Europe are numbered. Throughout the Balkan Peninsula and the east of Europe generally it is steadily on the decline. The Turks themselves are profoundly conscious that the period of their rule at Constantinople is limited, and "ancient prophecy and modern superstition alike point to a return of the crescent into Asia."

Such a move will carry Islam into its right sphere of operations. It can teach self-respect. There is in its

THE MOSLEM SPHERE OF INFLUENCE

simplicity a certain nobleness. Among the tribes of the Sudan, among Burmese and Malays, its influence is salutary. If we divide human progress into the three phases of self-indulgence, self-respect, and self-denial, it is in the central one of the three that orthodox Mohammedanism holds sway. Hence over the races still in the lower phase it exerts an influence for good, and Mr. Blunt is perhaps right when he says that these will turn more and more to the Moslem faith. Only where the higher principle reigns does Mohammedanism find itself powerless and stop short as at a word of command. With Western thought and Western civilisation it is out of touch, and its hold upon life is conditional upon life stopping short of these.

It is, so it seems to me, because the desert life naturally stops short of these that the desert is the true stronghold of the faith and Mecca its central shrine. Orthodox Mohammedanism, reeking as it does of the desert, energetic and militant, yet failing in just the qualities which give depth to thought and coherence to society, is, after all, the best clue to the Arab's character and history. It explains both his successes and failures. It explains the fury of his attack, the rapidity of his conquests, and his success in destroying and consuming all that is rotten, effete, and worn out in the world. It explains the lack of definite purpose in all his undertakings, and his failure to build up anything durable and solid of his own. It explains why in the twilight of the middle ages he was so prominent and terrible a figure, and why to-day he is back in the desert once more.

. . . .

But yet, I think to myself, as the image of the desert

itself rises before my mind's eye, who can set bounds to such a force as this or foretell its operations? Idle and empty the sand sleeps in the sun. It has looked so always, yet how deceptive has that vacancy and calm been often proved to be! The memory recurs to me of Wady Halfa, in those days when Wady Halfa and its little outpost Sarras were frontier stations, and when the safety of all Egypt was in the hands of a dozen or two of English boys and their Sudanese troops. North of them the Egyptian fellaheen sowed their crops and watered their land in peace. South of them the dervishes raged at large, threatening the wild onslaught that might come at any moment. Later, travelling in these confines of the Sahara, I have found the same thing; only here it is young Frenchmen who are drilling and organising their black troops and leading them out to fight and chase Arab marauders. They, here, are Europe's guardsmen, the representatives of her creed of law and order, and to north of them lie the secure Algerian vineyards and olive groves, and to south the unrest and chaos of the desert.

And when I struck the hills at Sbeitla, the hills that overlook the great Saharan plain, and came on one of Rome's ancient settlements with the walls and columns of its temples erect among the surrounding desolation, I recognised on the testimony of every fitted block that Europe when she was here before was on the same business that she is on to-day. Law and order marched under the eagles, as they do under our flag and France's.

For the conflict between Europe and the desert is not a conflict of nations or races, but a conflict of

THE MOSLEM SPHERE OF INFLUENCE 283

ideas. It has passed through many phases and been conducted by many hands, but it is always the same conflict. The centurion who watched from these walls of Sbeitla (I think I see the figure of the man and the set face fronting south) and the subalterns who guard their mud forts by the desert's edge are, in this quarrel, not Roman, or French, or English, but fellow-soldiers in one long campaign which is not ended yet.

Looking back at the incidents of that campaign, one would almost say that, in some blind way, the desert knew when its opportunity had come. When, twelve centuries ago, the cataclysm burst over the West which the West was so ill-prepared to face, it was found that the Arab had timed his effort to the hour. The moment of dark twilight which divided, in Europe, the classical from the Christian civilisations was, as I have said, the greatest opportunity the child of the desert ever had. During Rome's long rule he had remained quiescent. The walls and fortresses, garrisoned with the order and discipline of the Roman government, advanced to the very edge of the desert and overlooked him in his sanctuary. In the presence of that terribly perfect disciplinary system the poor Arab shrank, as you may say, to his smallest stature. Those were evil days for him. He could neither endure nor resist the tyranny of the great imperial machine, and so he buried himself in the heart of his sands, the one place sacred to lawlessness in the prevailing dominion of law, and bided his time.

It came. The great imperial machine began to creak, and the whisper that something was wrong with it went through the desert. Gradually the feeling that a great moment was at hand grew. The wandering Bedouin tribes scented the adventure which was to unite their hitherto distracted energies, and during the last two or three centuries of that long waiting every means was put in practice to prepare for the coming exploit. The scattered clans drew into a single people. A common language penetrated the peninsula. Never had the spirit of the race been so high as at this moment when the noble Arab minstrelsy struck its most ringing notes, calling to high adventures and acts of daring. In that instant, just as it crouched for its spring, the desert breed, for the first time in history, was a nation. All ignorant of the uses it was to be put to, it resembled some infernal machine or bomb of unprecedented power gradually maturing in mid-desert. And while it grew in deadliness and power its rival, the great imperial machine, wobbled and rocked more and more, until finally it came to a standstill altogether. I have always thought that this moment, the moment of Western relaxation and prostration on the one side, and of the fierce eyes gathering and glaring out of the desert on the other, was one of the most dramatic in all history. There was but one thing wanting to the Arabs, an inspiration and war-cry to hurl them forward with a single impetus. That, as we know, was supplied. In the year 622 a certain Mohammed, the orphan son of Abdallah, a native of Mecca, touched with his match the fuse of the desert bomb, and in five minutes (roughly speaking) the Arabs, who had never hitherto shown their noses outside the desert, were everywhere.

Now pass over eight hundred and seventy years and come down to New Year's Day of the year 1492. It

THE MOSLEM SPHERE OF INFLUENCE 285

is the day of the fall of Granada, and the final extinction of the Arab power in Europe. Granada had always been loved by the Moors. It was by nature more beautiful, in its glowing, shady gardens and views of the encircling hills, than most cities, and no pains had been spared to beautify it architecturally. Its loveliness is still a tradition among the Moors of North Africa, and they still lament, in their wistful and melancholy poetry, the loss of the earthly paradise in which they once sojourned. I am told, here in Kairwán, that in certain families there are still preserved the old keys of those castles in Spain of theirs the memory of which yet haunts their imaginations. It was sore to go, and to his last stronghold the Arab clung with desperate tenacity. But the end was inevitable. The Moorish expulsion was no result of one man's policy nor of any campaign or series of campaigns. A royal marriage might promote the union of Spain and the consequent stability of rule might generate law and order and strengthen the state for its final struggle with the Moors. But these tendencies were not peculiar to Spain or the rulers of Spain. All Europe was building upon them its development and civilisation. From the moment that the northern barbarians had cleared the ground for themselves and settled down in the countries of their choice they had begun to organise themselves, to evolve order out of chaos, and to lay down the foundation of a disciplined and progressive society. This was the process that was fatal to the Arab. It signified the reconstruction in Europe of a social system, differing of course from the Roman in many ways, yet similar to it in its intellectual qualities of organisation and cohesion. It tended therefore to reproduce just those conditions which, in the classic age, had hemmed the Arab in upon the desert; and step by step, as those conditions were once more evolved, the Arab once more fell back upon the wilderness he had emerged from, until finally, in 1609, just three hundred years ago, the last of the race were spurned from Spanish shores and crossed the Mediterranean to reinforce the pirate fleets of Algiers.

And then there came a day at last, but eighty years ago, when the Arab's visit to Europe was returned. The French, representatives of law and order, took Algiers, promising to evacuate it shortly. We promised the same thing when we occupied Egypt. But the idea we represented was too strong for both of us. The state of chaos which rendered the introduction of law necessary required not only its continued presence but its indefinite advance. The French were drawn on to annex Algeria and Tunisia and encroach upon the desert. The English were drawn on up the Nile to the conquest of the Sudan. Thus after long delay the Arabs have once more been driven in upon their own breeding-ground.

Such have been the fluctuations, but what do they portend? Why do Europe and the desert act like a seesaw, the decline of one registered in the rise of the other? Why, whenever Europe waxes and grows strong, does the Arab, in like degree, shrivel up and collapse? And why, when Europe collapses, does the Arab dilate and become a figure of terror?

The answer is scattered through these pages, and I will not recapitulate old arguments. If I have made the reader in any way conscious of the desert he will

THE MOSLEM SPHERE OF INFLUENCE

be aware of it as an environment dedicated to the development of individualism. He will feel that in all it gives as well as in all it withholds, in all the tests and trials of its dangerous, lonely, wandering life, no less than in the absence in it of all the opportunities that draw men together into settled communities and teach them to coalesce and depend on each other, the desert is the great tutor of solitary manhood and self-dependence. Not less certain is it that what Europe stands for, and has always stood for, is the collective principle, the instinct for combination, and the power of a society not only united in the bonds of law and order at the present moment, but united by a common sequence of ideas with the generations which have preceded and are to follow the present one. As a school for individual manhood of the purely virile type, no school equals the desert, nor have I ever met a man whom, for dignity, courtesy, self-control, and the qualities generally which we associate with the word "gentleman," I could place on a level with the Arab. Yet the strength of the finest individual type is as nothing to the strength which springs from cohesion and combination. The Arab is formidable only to two kinds of races—to those which have not reached or have lost the power of collective action. Savages and decadent civilisations are his natural prey. The empire he dismembered had lost its faith in the ideals which work for unity and was already in a state of social disintegration when he fell upon it. And as the loss of social cohesion let him in, so the recovery of it drove him out. Every step in Europe's progress has been scored in Arab losses.

They stand pitted against each other, these two, like two boxers sparring for an opening; yet it seems that at present we can afford to despise an ancient enemy. It is low tide with the Arab. He is back in the sand again. The moment is come—

> "When that which drew from out the boundless deep
> Turns again home."

I stood, at Sbeitla, by an old high-water mark. The tide of Western civilisation had been there long ago, but had ebbed since then. Now it was here again, and I watched it flooding in and lapping round the same old stones and pouring over and beyond. When will it, or will it ever, turn? "Esto perpetua!" exclaims Mr. Belloc as he turns his face to Europe from Algerian wanderings: let the European system endure for ever. So be it; yet the Arab has a terrible ally. He is backed by the desert. So long as the desert remains the desert it will continue to breed men of the Arab type. If the time should come when European civilisation declines, when its cohesion relaxes and society tends to disintegrate, then, it is likely enough, there will be found specimens of desert manhood ready to take an old occasion by the hand. A thousand years are but as yesterday in desert chronology. Who can tell but that a thousand years hence those old Kairwán keys may be fitted to Spanish locks again?

Appendix

NOTE A.—ARAB CIVILISATION (p. 9).

DR. T. I. DE BOER, of the University of Groningen, has written lately a work on the "History of Philosophy in Islam," which has been translated into English, and from which I will quote a few sentences. It gives such an analysis of the Arab mind as accurately bears out the impressions one receives from their art and poetry, their towns, their history, and their life. The sources of Arab philosophy, according to Dr. de Boer, were Greece, Persia, and India. Of these the last two represented speculative subtlety and the first order. "Oriental wisdom, astrology, and cosmology delivered over to Muslim thinkers materials of many kinds, but the Form—the formative principle—came to them from the Greeks. In every case where it is not mere enumeration or chance concatenation that is taken in hand, but where an attempt is made to arrange the manifold according to positive or logical points of view, we may conclude with all probability that Greek influences have been at work." The idea of Form as not of Oriental origin, and not inherent in the Arab mind and character, is the impression which is most strongly borne out by Arab architecture.

I gather from Dr. de Boer that in Arab thought generally it was Oriental subtlety rather than Greek form which played the leading part. Arab philosophy has, he tells us, "no important advances in thought to register." Of their beautiful caligraphy, he says that it is "more decorative in its nature than constructive, like Arabic art in general." And he adds, "In the very characters of the Arabic speech we may still see the subtlety of the intelligence which formed them, although at the same time we may see a lack of energy which is observable in the entire development of Arab culture."

Of the verses of a celebrated poet of the tenth century, Mutanabbi, we have the remark, "frightfully tedious in their contents, although epigrammatic in their form." And of the philosophic poet, Abn-l-Ala-al-Maarri, we hear that "he is almost entirely wanting in the gift of combination. He can analyse, but he does not hit upon any synthesis, and his learning bears no fruit." Of the science of astronomy there is much the same tale to tell. "According to the different conceptions entertained of the relation which subsisted between the heavenly bodies and sublunary things, either a rational astronomy was developed or a fantastic astrology." But "only a few kept entirely free from astrological delusions." Again, "in the domain of natural science Muslim learned men collected a rich body of material; but hardly in any case did they succeed in really treating it scientifically. . . . To establish the wisdom of God and the operation of Nature . . . alchemistic experiments were instituted, the magical virtues of talismans tested, the effects of music upon the emotions of men and animals investigated, and observations made on physiognomy, while attempts were also set on foot to explain the wonders of the life of sleep, and of dreams, as well as those of soothsaying and prophecy."

Medicine was a science which much occupied the Arabs, but in their practice of this subject, too, we find the same tendency to the vague and conjectural. "The old-fashioned doctor was disposed to be satisfied with time-honoured magical formulæ, and other empirical expedients; but modern society in the ninth century required philosophical knowledge in the physician. He had to know the 'natures' of foods, stimulants or luxuries, and medicaments, the humours of the body, and in every case the influence of the stars. The physician

APPENDIX 291

was brother to the astrologer. . . . He had to attend the lectures of the alchemist," and so on.

In short, the study of the Arab mind and processes of thought which Dr. de Boer has elaborated in his book confirm in every way the impression one receives from observing Arab life and art. Fancifulness and lack of common sense attend him. He was destitute of the constructive instinct, and when he had cleared the ground for himself in South Europe he was not able to avail himself of his opportunity. The prevailing tendency to exaggerate his performances arises, I suppose, partly from a certain outward show of luxury and splendour which his civilisation bore—though the materials and even architects of it were mainly imported from the East—partly from the romantic glamour that colours and hides everything Arab, but chiefly, no doubt, from the fact that he had the advantage of exercising his talents at a time when the rest of the world was sunk in semi-barbarism. In the darkness that separates ancient civilisation from modern the brilliance of the Arab is salient. Like the glowworm, he—

> "Shows by night a feeble beam,
> Which disappears by day."

It is sometimes said that this very fact that the Arabs at a given period were "more advanced" than other people is a sufficient claim to admiration. Even if their civilisation was not a very first-rate affair, no other race for half a dozen centuries could show as good a one. But the point is that during these centuries no other race had yet produced the civilisation proper to it at all. The fruit-time of the other races was to come; but these centuries were the fruit-time of the Arab. His harvest was over, he was decadent all round, before he was driven out of Europe. By this civilisation the constructive power of the race must be judged. We do not say of Greek civilisation that it was great *because* it excelled that of the Phrygians, nor of Roman civilisation that it was great *because* it was in advance of that of the Huns. We say of Greek and Roman civilisation that they were great because they have bequeathed what is of permanent value to the mind of man. Arab philosophy, though most of what passes as Arab philosophy appears to have been Syrian or Persian, may have influenced mediæval scholasticism, but can we say that Arab thought and literature has bequeathed anything of permanent value to mankind?

NOTE B.—OLD AND NEW FRENCH COLONISING (p. 71).

It is the fashion to speak of the new French colonising as a *renaissance*. The difference, however, between the old and new methods of colonising seems to be more remarkable than any resemblances. There appeared a book a year or two ago by Sir Gilbert Parker and Mr. Bryan called "Old Quebec" which gave an admirable sketch of the old system as it was applied to Canada. That system consisted simply in the transplantation to the new land of a section of French society as it existed at that time in the mother country. A complete little feudal system was established on the banks of the St. Lawrence.

"The Canadian seigneurs held their land of the king, and the *habitants*, or cultivators of the soil, held theirs of the seigneurs upon the performance of specific duties and the payment of *cens et rente*. On the St. Martin's Day, when the censitaires commonly liquidated the obligations of their tenure, the seigneurie presented an animated scene. Here were gathered all the tenants, bearing wheat, eggs, and live capons, to pay for their long, narrow farms at a rate ranging from four to sixteen francs."

Nor did his rent complete the tenant's obligations. "Throughout the year he must grind his grain at the seigneur's mill, paying one bushel in every fourteen for the service, bake his bread at the seigneur's oven, work for him one or two days in the year, and forfeit one fish in every eleven to the lord of the manor."

APPENDIX

Founded as a missionary trading post, Quebec had always been noted for a certain docility of piety. She had been brought up under priestly control. Her early governors— Champlain, D'Ailleboust, Montmagny—were military monks. The Jesuits lent their powerful influence to foster the prevailing spirit of submission, and obtained, by a judicious alternation of persuasion and penance, a remarkable hold over the community. Absence from church was punishable by law, as also was absence from confession. The calendar was filled with special days for prayer and purification. Priests, monks, and nuns crowded the city in numbers disproportionate to the lay population. The Conseil Supérieur took careful note of the least religious laxity, and the pillory, the stocks, and a certain "wooden horse with a sharp spine," were the ready instruments of correction.

Such a glance sufficiently indicates the spirit of the French colonising of that day. The life was not unhappy nor unbeautiful. Feudalism lost much of its harshness in transplantation. The Canadian peasant, dreaming out his peaceful existence in the shadow of the châteaux and the church, supervised with affectionate assiduity by the seigneur and the priest, enjoyed a lot which to many people, who love the backward rather than the forward glance, still seems the happiest possible. But to colonisation, which is essentially a forward-looking business, such a lot bears no sort of application. The life of the French settlement, for all its beauties and amenities, was a stereotyped and outworn life, a life incapable of adapting itself to new conditions and a new country. Some adventurous spirits there were who rebelled against it, and accepted outlawry as the consequence. These *coureurs de bois*, as they were called, whom the excessive lawfulness of the settlement drove to the utter lawlessness of the backwoods, are a singular testimony to the irksome influence of formalism amid surroundings which called, above all, for a flexible adaptability. The attitude of the ruling powers towards them is sufficiently shown by the edict which provides that "any person going into the woods without a licence should be whipped and branded for the first offence, and sent for life to the galleys for the second, while a third offence was punishable by death."

Compared with the British Colonies, living their own lives and grappling with Nature on equal terms, the French were like branches of an ancient tree cut off and thrust into the ground as compared with handfuls of seed scattered over the soil. They lacked the vitality which is not to be separated from the idea of liberty. The opinion, which still in many quarters lingers, that the French are "no colonists," was derived from these past experiences. It was a legitimate conclusion at the time. But the conditions of their colonising to-day are wholly different. The decaying bulwarks of feudalism no longer stand between the colonist and the colony. And the consequence, in the case of North Africa, is a remarkable quickening of public interest in colonial life. Settlers, possessing the soil they cultivate, overspread the land; industries, public works, improvements —the draining of swamps, the irrigation of deserts, the engineering of railways and roads—are pushed forward with vigour and intelligence. More than twenty years ago it was remarked by one of Algeria's acutest historians, Maurice Wahl, that the Algerian colonists soon became distinguished from their countrymen at home by a certain audacity of character and mind, and a readiness to adopt advanced methods and new ideas, and to apply the latest discoveries in science to the uses of agriculture and industry. This is, of course, the true colonial temper, and the development of it by the French under present conditions suggests that our ancient competition with them should be regarded not so much as a competition between Frenchmen and Englishmen as between Feudalism and Freedom. The English settlers, in the act of emigration, had escaped from a system which the French failed to escape from. They had shaken off fetters which their rivals carried with them. It was this, perhaps, rather than any racial disqualification,

APPENDIX 295

which accounts for the French failure and our success. At present these hindrances no longer exist, and France as a Republic may achieve—and is, in fact, rapidly achieving—successes in colonisation which to France as a despotism were out of the question.

Note C.—Arab Rule (p. 113).

In Sir Charles Eliot's book on the East Africa Protectorate there will be found an account of the Arab occupation of Zanzibar and of Arab rule in the interior, which is in all essentials an exact replica of the history of Algiers. Slavery is the Arab vice. It is much more than an ordinary social evil resulting from conditions that pass. It is a profound racial characteristic. The Arab takes to slavery as a Chinaman to opium. The tracking down of his less strong and courageous quarry, the panic created by his appearance, the flight, the pursuit, the capture, the ruin left behind, are rapture to him. It is the one form of industry the race has developed in the course of its rule. "It is," says Sir Charles Eliot, "as slave-owners and slave-traders only that the Arabs have cut a figure in East Africa." They have introduced, he tells us, nothing; they have built nothing. Their long ascendancy is, in short, memorable only for its attempt to pull to pieces such poor vestiges of social order as they could lay hands on.

Another witness to the inability of the Arabs to establish settled government is a French officer, M. de Champeaux, who writes from personal observation of the Central Saharan oases. The leading native elements of these strongholds, which so long defied the French advance, are the Arab and Berber, and the contrast between their instinct for organisation is very noticeable. "Dans les oasis soumises à l'influence arabe il n'existait aucun chef, aucune assemblée permanente pour commander. Dans les circonstances graves les gens le plus notables, les Kebar, se réunisaient pour délibérer sur la conduite à tenir, le parti à prendre et sur les moyens d'action. En temps ordinaire, l'autorité d'un personnage marquant se faisait seule sentir, mais non directement." On the other hand, "Chez les Berbères, au contraire, l'autorité dirigeante n'était pas temporaire. Elle subsistait continuellement dans la djemâa, ou réunion, des hommes importantes de la cité. Dans les djemâas, composées d'individus les plus nobles et les plus influents tant par leur naissance et leurs réputation maraboutique que par leur instruction et leurs richesses, il y avait égalité complète ; et le chef de la djemâa, lorsqu'il en existait un, n'avait aucune prépondérance sur les autres membres."

At the same time the mere personal ascendancy of the Arab has always declared itself, and no native-organised society has been able to resist it. Palgrave speaks of their marked predominance "over whomever they came in contact with among their Asiatic or African neighbours, a superiority admitted by these last as a matter of course and an acknowledged right." He adds that he "would unhesitatingly affirm Arabs to be the English of the Oriental world"; his reason being that they are so vastly superior to their neighbours.

Both the region of which Sir Charles Eliot writes and the group of oases of which de Champeaux writes are instances in which the Arabs have been for many generations left free to work out their own system of social order and government. The results seem to have been quite in conformity with their more ambitious attempts on the Mediterranean coasts.

Note D.—Oriental Drapery (p. 155).

Again and again I find myself struck, while watching Arabs, with what is, I suppose, a lost sense in art with us—I mean the extraordinary significance and beauty of *fold* as interpreting life and movement. Drapery, in its free, natural state, so indicates every changing attitude and motion of the body, so conforms itself to every mood, so instantly expresses the vivacity, dignity, repose, or dejection of the figure it obeys, that it may almost be said to be imbued with something of a human character, and actually to itself share in the emotions it depicts.

Why is it that the crowds of Kaffirs I have often seen huddled under the lee of a compound in the cold grey of a veld morning are so much more vividly present to my memory than any similar European crowd? Why can I recall them, yet cannot recall the groups and figures of English workmen whom I knew much better? Because the Kaffirs' garments made them strike the eye like pictures. Their straight-hanging blankets, drawn over the head and drooping to the legs, were charged with all the feeling of the cowering, forlorn bodies underneath. I can see them now, those still effigies, so mutely suggestive of patience and cold.

It is noticeable that only the human body is able to give this interest to drapery. A cloak flung upon a chair may arrange itself in much the same folds as on a kneeling or stooping figure. But these folds only indicate the form of the chair, a matter so comparatively uninteresting that they attract little attention, and, having no meaning, have little or no beauty; that is to say, little or no beauty apart from colour and the variations of colour wrought by gradations of light and shade. This kind of beauty they have, just as the straight folds of a curtain have it, which interpret no form at all. But the real significance of drapery is an interpretative or borrowed quality; a quality given to it by the form concealed beneath. And it is only the human form which possesses sufficient interest to be able to infuse this quality into drapery in any marked degree.

It is evident how this condition handicaps modern art. You can only put into art what you can get out of life, and this sense of the significance of drapery it is impossible to get out of modern life, because free drapery does not exist in modern life.

Consequently our sense in this direction remains uncultivated, and probably we do not know our own loss. Watching Arabs riding or walking in front of me, or crouched within the doorways of their shops, or loitering and strolling about in groups in market-place or bazaar, has sometimes suggested to me a little of what that loss must be. If once you become aware of the interpretative function of drapery, and begin to look at it with a view to finding out what it has to say, there is literally no end to the expressiveness it will develop. The personality of the wearer will seem to overflow into it. It will come towards you with graciousness and a large and liberal swing, or shrink into the narrow folds of coldness and suspicion, or cower timidly in some corner, quite nerveless and illegible. There is nothing it cannot do or be. It acts the light impetuosity and frolic fun of the children that come scampering up to look at the strangers. It celebrates the noble dignity of the sheyk you visit in his tent. It explains with irresistible pathos the misery and dejection of the old beggar at the gate. I believe the fascination of an Oriental crowd, and particularly the fact that you never tire of it or seem to exhaust its interest, is due mainly to its wearing free drapery.

NOTE E.—ORIENTAL COLOUR (p. 161).

The note of Oriental colour is unmistakable. It consists in two characteristics. First, the colour is the perfect colour, deep and true, not running to shades and half-tones. Secondly, it is not used to define the forms and shapes of things, but is disposed and controlled more by light and shade than by the dimensions of objects. The result of the combination of these two characteristics is that deep and suffused glow which one notices in the work of the great

APPENDIX 299

colourists, and which so easily distinguishes their work from the work of those who use colour to define objects.

The East itself, however, does not supply in art any adequate expression of its own sense for colour. It has not, perhaps, the character, the self-discipline, and self-control which are as necessary as inspiration to a great creative effort. Its sense for colour does not normally get beyond those instances of everyday life which we were just now noticing at Tuggurt. In everyday life, however, its presence is quite unmistakable. It is a popular possession, a popular instinct. Every gipsy that travels westward carries with him, in dress and ornament, marks of this love of colour, which at once to Western eyes proclaim his Eastern origin. And we know that this sense is so profound and innate that even after generations of civilised life, and when, perhaps, the descendants of these aliens have become members of ordinary society, not to be distinguished from their neighbours save by an extra darkness of eye or hair, their craving for colour and, as it were, understanding of colour will still show itself, and will, moreover, invariably take the same turn, a turn, that is, towards the swarthy tints which suggest sunlight, such as orange and crimson and rich brown. While a drop of Oriental blood remains in the race this instinct will manifest itself, bearing witness in an extraordinary way to the depth and permanence of the Eastern sense for colour.

Tracked to its source, the sentiment that underlies Oriental colour, the depth, richness, emotion of it, seems to be the same that belongs to Oriental scenery. In tropical jungle vegetation there is an influence at work different to the influence felt in European scenery. All the moods of Eastern nature are sensuous. The inextricable richness of the vegetation, the tangle of creepers, the gorgeous blossoms, the occasional heavy, almost sickly, scent of lily or lotus, the moisture of the air, the fireflies wheeling in the dusky shadows—these and countless others are features which may be divided in enumeration but are not divided in the profound sensuous impression they produce. And running through all this medley, as its main element, is the gorgeousness of the colouring, a colouring which always keeps a certain glow of warmth and passion in it, and is of the kind for which Eastern races in their own dress and adornment always show so instinctive a predilection.

The only really adequate expression in art to which this sensuousness felt in tropical scenery and tropical colouring has ever lent itself is the Byzantine style of architecture. By Byzantine I do not, of course, mean the so-called Byzantine of Santa Sophia, which is a study of curves strictly structural and intellectual in character, a kind of glorified Roman *thermæ*, impregnated with classic influence, and not sensuous at all. The style of Santa Sophia, if we take Eastern colouring to be the motive aimed at, was a failure; and that the Greeks themselves knew it to be a failure is shown by the fact that they never repeated it. By Byzantine I mean the style as the Byzantines eventually worked it out, the style of plastic gold mosaic, worked into rounded apses and ponderous low domes, obscured by dark shadows and shot with the crimson and azure of the figures portrayed. Of this St. Mark's is the central example. I wish I could place the reader, for a moment, first among the influences of a tropical night, with all its suggestions of veiled magnificence, its richness of gloom, its underglow of tawny colour; and from that scene, while its appeal was fresh on him, transport him suddenly into the interior of St. Mark's. If he did not, here in the basilica, recognise the same character and influence which he felt but now in the tropical jungle, I would agree to forfeit the conviction I hold that every genuine manifestation of art is the expression of perceptions common to human nature.

Once, however, we distinguish the character of Oriental colouring, and realise its central expression in Byzantine art, it is impossible not to perceive that its effect may be

APPENDIX

traced further, and that in St. Mark's itself we have the source of a deep and spreading influence. St. Mark's not only voices the Orientalism of Venice, its control over the subsequent art of the Republic is unquestionable. Venetian colour, as developed in Venetian painting, reeks of St. Mark's. It has the same richness and glow. It suffuses and melts away forms in the same way. It is governed by its own laws and limitations only, that is, by light and shade, not by the dimensions of objects. And these traits are of the East. The source she sucked her strength from comes out in the matured art of Venice. The dark splendour on the canvases of Titian and Tintoret was never of Western origin. It is its own end, it is not used to define. It is sensuous, not intellectual, and may be tracked back through the St. Mark's mosaics deep into the sources of Eastern life and character.

How far the influence has since extended who shall say? But when the reader comes upon any salient and unmistakable example of it, such an example as the painting of Reynolds or Rubens affords, let him remember that the East has spoken through Venice, and ask if these masters have not learnt in Venice the secret of that glow. The subject opens too wide a prospect to be here continued; only in dealing with such common scenes of Oriental life as we have been meeting with at Tuggurt, and may meet with elsewhere, I would wish to link them to the main ideas to which they belong and which lend them significance. They are the little wayside, usual expressions of that sensuous and emotional character which belongs to the East, which differentiates it from the intellectual West, of which St. Mark's at Venice may be taken as the central artistic embodiment, and which, through St. Mark's, has illumined Western art with many a fitful and struggling ray.

NOTE F.—CHARACTER OF SHÍISM (p. 224).

The greatest of authorities on Persian religion and philosophy, according to Professor Browne, who speaks of his work, "Les Religions et les Philosophies dans l'Asie Centrale," as "a classic unsurpassed, and indeed unapproached in the subject whereof it treats," is that very Count Gobineau from whom Matthew Arnold has taken his description of the subject-matter of the plays. Count Gobineau treats the Shíite heresy very largely as a national movement. The old Parsî religion, he thinks, which fell with the national independence of Persia before the Arab invasion, became identified with a sentiment of patriotism. The sanctification of Ali and the denial of the legitimacy of the first three Caliphs was a device more political than religious. It aimed at undermining the authority of the reigning house. The temporal and spiritual powers being united in the persons of the Caliphs, to aim at one was to strike the other. To deny the claim of the reigning Caliphs to the apostolic succession was to deny their right to rule and govern. In short, the Shíites were cloaking an act of political treason under the guise of religious reformation. Still, I suppose Count Gobineau would not have us ignore the religious significance of the movement. A host of questions at once arise if we do so. How is it that the Shíite doctrine has so long outlasted its political significance? It is as vital to-day as ever it was; it excites the fury of the Sunnite faction in as high a degree as ever it did. The Persian pilgrims are liable still, as Burton relates, to every kind of insult and outrage from their Sunnite rivals, on account of this belief of theirs. Yet the temporal power of Islam has long disappeared from Persia, and there can, therefore, be no longer a direct political meaning or threat attachable to the doctrine. What makes it last, then, if not its religious meaning?

Again, if Shíism is primarily political, how is it to be

accounted for that all the innovations it has sanctioned—Sufism, Gnosticism, Mysticism, Babism—are all similar in their religious and philosophical character, are all obviously directed to a similar religious purpose? The activity of Shíism is evidently to-day a religious and philosophical activity, not a political activity, though it may have reinforced itself at the beginning with a political motive.

Moreover, the Indian people and the Persians are in character and temperament much alike. Both showed the same desire, under Mohammedanism, to revive the ancient forms of a pantheistic religion. In the case of the Indians there is, I believe, no question of politics as a motive. They had no political end to gain. Their motive was pure discontent with the cold aloofness of the Moslem creed. Why should not such a motive equally explain the attitude of the Persians?

Sufism, Count Gobineau is inclined to regard as a kind of disease of the Oriental intellect resulting from an almost abnormal subtlety and activity of mind constantly working upon the incomprehensible. Still there are some sentences in Count Gobineau's own description which seem to point to the want that the new teaching was intended to meet. Thus he speaks of it as "a passive attitude of the soul which surrounds with a halo of inert sentimentalism all imaginable conceptions of God, man, and the world." And again he calls it, "a general disposition to make everything pass like a spectacle before the interior man." The philosophy of Sufism is that "the sensible man should shut himself up in himself. It is in his own heart only that he can find joy, security, pardon for faults, tender indulgence, and finally God."

Now, granting all the abuses that this system of thought led to, and the sanction for every kind of self-indulgence that it involved, there is still this about it, that it has depth, that it is an interior development, and is, in that respect, in marked contrast with the Mohammedan religion. Looked at close, one may see in Shíism at one time a patriotic, at another a quietest movement; but looked at in connection with Mohammedanism, one sees in it a protest against a deficiency in the Arab religion, and an attempt to make that deficiency good. The real aims of the Shíite sect are best set forth in the Encyclopædia compiled by an association of philosophers in Basra in the second half of the tenth century. Political considerations were not wanting, but discontent with the Moslem limitations was the ruling principle. "There is found in their Encyclopædia," says Professor de Boer, "an eclectic Gnosticism built on a foundation of natural science, and provided with a political background. . . . The whole representation is that of the doctrine of a persecuted sect, with the political features peeping out here and there. We see also something of suffering and struggle—something of the oppressions to which the men of this Encyclopædia, or their predecessors, were exposed, and something of the hopes they cherished and the patience they preached. They seek in their spiritualistic philosophy consolation and redemption." The influence against which they had to contend is marked by themselves. "Our Prophet, Mohammed," they said, "was sent to an uncivilised people, composed of dwellers in the desert, who possessed a proper conception neither of the beauty of this world, nor of the spiritual character of the world beyond. The crude expressions of the Koran, which are adapted to the understanding of that people, must be understood in a spiritual sense by those who are more cultured."

From this point of view of the general tendency of Persian innovation it seems to me that Matthew Arnold's remarks still have great value. He does not, it is true, allow much for racial differences. He does not distinguish the immobility of Arab civilisation and the anti-social life of the desert, which have so much to do with the maintenance of Mohammedan orthodoxy. But he brings out with great clearness what, after all, is the very crux of the matter—the lack of feeling in the Moslem religion, and the need for supplying it.

www.ingramcontent.com/pod-product-compliance
Lightning Source LLC
Chambersburg PA
CBHW021817300426
44114CB00009BA/216